THE CLASSICS
OF WESTERN
SPIRITUALITY

THE CLASSICS OF WESTERN SPIRITUALITY
A Library of the Great Spiritual Masters

Vincent de Paul and Louise de Marillac
RULES, CONFERENCES, AND WRITINGS

EDITED BY
FRANCES RYAN, D.C. AND JOHN E. RYBOLT, C.M.

INTRODUCED BY
HUGH F. O'DONNELL, C.M., FRANCES RYAN, D.C.,
LOUISE SULLIVAN, D.C., VIE THORGREN AND
EDWARD R. UDOVIC, C.M.

PREFACE BY
AMIN A. DE TARRAZI

PAULIST PRESS
NEW YORK • MAHWAH

Cover Art: Collaboration—so much a part of Vincent and Louise's relationship and so much a part of this text—was also a prominent factor in the development of this cover illustration. The original pen-and-ink portraits of Vincent de Paul and Louise de Marillac upon which this color-enhanced, computer-generated image is based are the work of DAVIE E. SMITH, JR., a leading illustrator, portrait artist and graphic designer from the Washington, D.C. area. Smith's work has long been influenced by heroes—from Dr. Martin Luther King, Jr., to St. Elizabeth Ann Seton. It is the admiration for the excellence of such portraits that led the Vincentian Studies Institute to a long-time working collaboration with the artist, during which time these portraits of the two Vincentian founders were commissioned. Smith is a member of the Art Directors Club of Metropolitan Washington and the American Institute of Graphic Arts. The composition of the cover illustration was influenced by the work of SR. ELLEN M. LaCAPRIA, D.C., a Daughter of Charity who works as an art therapist in the Washington, D.C. area.

Copyright © 1995 by Vincentian Studies Institute

Library of Congress Cataloging-in-Publication Data

Vincent de Paul, Saint, 1581–1660.
  [Selections. 1995]
  Vincent de Paul and Louise de Marillac : rules, conferences, and
    writings / edited by Frances Ryan and John E. Rybolt.
      p. cm. — (The Classics of Western spirituality)
    Includes bibliographical references and index.
    ISBN 0-8091-0471-7 (alk. paper). — ISBN 0-8091-3564-7 (pbk. :
  alk. paper)
    1. Spiritual life—Catholic Church. 2. Church work with the poor—
  Catholic Church. 3. Vincentians—Spiritual life. 4. Daughters of
  Charity of St. Paul—Spiritual life. 5. Vincentians—Rules.
  6. Daughters of Charity of St. Paul—Rules. 7. Catholic Church—
  Doctrines. 8. Vincent de Paul, Saint, 1581–1660. 9. Louise de
  Marillac, Saint, 1591–1660. I. Ryan, Frances, 1937–   .
  II. Rybolt, John E. III. Louise de Marillac, Saint, 1591–1660.
  IV. Title. V. Series.
  BX2350.V52525 1995
  255'.77—dc20   95-3447
                                                CIP

Published by Paulist Press
997 Macarthur Boulevard
Mahwah, New Jersey 07430

Printed and bound in the
United States of America

Contents

CONTENTS

DEDICATION

This book is dedicated to the memory of the Vincentian Studies Institute members who lived and died in faithful commitment to the way of Vincent de Paul and Louise de Marillac in service to the poor. These members were: Father William C. Eigel, C.M., Father Frederick J. Easterly, C.M., Sister Jacqueline Kilar, D.C., Father James R. King, C.M., Sister Hilda McGinnis, D.C., and Sister Mary Basil Roarke, D.C.

Co-Editor of this Volume
Author, in Collaboration, of the Introduction
FRANCES RYAN, D.C., is a member of the East Central province
of the Daughters of Charity. She received her bachelor's degree in
English and Secondary Education from Marillac College, Saint
Louis, a Master's in Social Work from Saint Louis University, and
her doctorate in counseling psychology from Loyola University of
Chicago. She has written and lectured in her field. Current publica-
tions include "The 1990's Loss Process and Vulnerable Personali-
ties," a chapter in *Personal Care in an Impersonal World;* "Reaching
the Child's Perception of Death," a chapter co-authored with Nan
Giblin, Ph.D. A member of the Vincentian Studies Institute, she
published "Sister Rosalie Rendu, D.C. (1796–1856)," *Vincentian
Heritage* 10:2 (1989), and edited, with John E. Rybolt, C.M., "The
Daughters of Charity in the Spanish-American War," *Vincentian
Heritage* 8:2 (1987). At present, she is an associate professor and
program chair of the Master's in Human Services and Counseling,
School of Education, De Paul University.

Co-Editor of this Volume
JOHN E. RYBOLT, C.M., was ordained to the priesthood in
1967. He began graduate studies in scripture and earned a Master
of Arts from Harvard University, a Licentiate in Sacred Theology
from the Catholic University of America, a Licentiate in Sacred
Scripture from the Pontifical Biblical Institute, Rome, and a doctorate in biblical studies from Saint Louis University. He has
taught in various seminaries conducted by the Vincentian community, and in May 1993 completed his term as rector of Saint
Thomas Theological Seminary, Denver. He has edited and written
extensively in the area of Saint Vincent de Paul and the American
Vincentians, including editing *The Life of the Venerable Servant of
God Vincent de Paul*, written by Louis Abelly, and serving as editor
in chief of *The American Vincentians: A Popular History of the Congregation of the Mission in the United States*. Presently, he is the director
of the Centre International de Formation: Saint Vincent de Paul,
in Paris.

Authors of the Introduction
HUGH F. O'DONNELL, C.M., joined the Congregation of the
Mission in 1952. He was ordained to the priesthood in 1961. In

addition to degrees in library science and Latin from De Paul University, he holds a doctorate in theology from the University of Fribourg, Switzerland. After teaching at Vincentian-directed seminaries in Saint Louis and Denver, he was elected provincial superior of the Midwest Province in 1978, and held that post until 1987. He served on faculty of Saint Thomas Theological Seminary, Denver, until his appointment in 1993 as provincial superior of the province of China, with headquarters in Taiwan. He has written and lectured widely on Saint Vincent de Paul. Recent publications include *Praying in Saint Vincent's Spirit* (1990), which he authored and *Vincent de Paul and Charity*, by André Dodin, C.M. (1993), which he edited.

LOUISE SULLIVAN, D.C., is a member of the Northeast Province of the Daughters of Charity. A professor of foreign languages at Niagara University, and chair of the department, she received her Bachelor of Science degree in elementary education and foreign languages from Saint Joseph College, Emmitsburg, Maryland. She received a Master of Arts degree in French language and literature from the Catholic University of America, and her doctorate in French and comparative literature from Université de Paris IV: Sorbonne. She is the author of several articles and books about Saint Louise de Marillac and the Daughters of Charity, including *Spiritual Writings of Louise de Marillac, Correspondence and Thoughts* (1991).

VIE THORGREN has a Bachelor of Science degree in Education from Indiana University, a Master of Arts in Psychology from the University of West Florida, and a Doctor of Ministry degree in Spiritual Direction from the Graduate Theological Foundation, Donaldson, Indiana. She has had more than twenty years professional ministry experience with youth and adults on the parish and diocesan levels. At present she is the Director of Spiritual Formation at the Vincentian Institute of Pastoral Studies, Saint Thomas Theological Seminary, Denver. Married and the mother of two children, she finds time to lecture and write about Louise de Marillac, Mother Seton, and others prominent in the Vincentian heritage. Recent publications include "God Is My God: The Generative Integrity of Louise de Marillac," *Vincentian Heritage* 12:2 (1991).

EDWARD R. UDOVIC, C.M., a member of the Midwest Province of the Congregation of the Mission, received a Bachelor of Arts degree in history from De Paul University, a Master of Divinity degree from De Andreis Institute of Theology, and a Master of Arts in history from Saint Louis University. He is presently a doctoral candidate in church history from the Catholic University of America. Among his publications are "What about the Poor? Nineteenth-Century Paris and the Revival of Vincentian Charity," given at the Vincentian Heritage Symposium, De Paul University, and published in *Vincentian Heritage* 14:1 (1993). He is a contributor to *The American Vincentians: A Popular History of the Congregation of the Mission in the United States* (1988). He serves as academic dean of Saint Thomas Theological Seminary, Denver. He is the presiding officer of the Vincentian Studies Institute of the United States.

Author of the Preface

AMIN A. DE TARRAZI is International President Emeritus of the Society of Saint Vincent de Paul, with headquarters in Paris. A native of France, he took university degrees in political science, law, and English. He joined the Society of Saint Vincent de Paul in 1948, and exercised numerous responsibilities. In particular he was the president of the National Council of France (1967–1980) and president of the International Council General (1981–1993). In addition, he was a member of the pontifical council "Cor Unum" (1984–1989), appointed by Pope John Paul II, and of many other organizations in charitable, social, and cultural fields. He has written and lectured widely on Vincentian topics.

Foreword

Vincent de Paul and Louise de Marillac left an indelible impression on the Church in France in the seventeenth century. Those who look to them for guidance on their individual spiritual path have found in their lives and teaching a particular nourishment for the journey. The purpose of this volume is to present the main lines of the spiritual teaching of these two founders. Their spiritual way has special relevance today since it is centered on Jesus for the poor. It emphasizes collaborative practical action rooted in contemplation.

The introduction to this volume locates Vincent and Louise within the framework of the spirituality of seventeenth-century France. The introduction continues by presenting briefly the legacy of those two saints in the work of Saint Elizabeth Ann Seton, Sister Rosalie Rendu, D.C., and Venerable Frederick Ozanam.

Following this introduction come the original rules of the two communities, commentaries on those rules, and a selection of letters and other writings from both the founders. The rules for the Congregation of the Mission and the Daughters of Charity of Saint Vincent de Paul breathe the spirit of the founders. The rules of the Daughters of Charity, in particular, have guided the development of numerous other congregations who either adopted or adapted that rule for different circumstances. In both cases, early (unofficial) versions of the rules have been compared with the official rules to show more fully the original inspiration behind them.

Fortunately for future generations, Saint Vincent de Paul left commentaries on the two rules. These took the shape of conferences given to the members of the two communities on their respective rules. Monsieur Vincent alternated between formal, even theological, presentations and informal practical discussions. The conferences chosen for this publication are those that appear most illustrative of his intent.

A large number of letters written by Vincent de Paul have

survived the centuries. As with the conferences, those selected here demonstrate both his spiritual way and his daily concerns.

Although we do not have texts of conferences given by Louise de Marillac, we do have a significant number of important letters and documents from her pen. Those writings presented in this volume have been organized thematically.

The editors wish to thank the members of the Vincentian Studies Institute, which is sponsored jointly by the provincial superiors of the Daughters of Charity and the Vincentian priests and brothers in the United States. The members of the institute have collaborated in selecting texts, writing commentaries, and evaluating one another's work.

We especially want to thank Father Joseph Hubbert, C.M., for selecting, introducing, and annotating the conferences of Vincent de Paul to the members of the Congregation of the Mission. Sister Betty Ann McNeil, D.C., contributed to the project by selecting, editing and reviewing the texts of the writings of Louise de Marillac. Sisters Martha Beaudoin, D.C., Audrey Gibson, D.C., and Kieran Kneaves, D.C., helped to select and introduce the works of Louise de Marillac as well as the conferences of Vincent de Paul to the Daughters of Charity. Vincentian Fathers John Sledziona, James Smith, Warren Dicharry, and Stafford Poole reviewed the text, and gave encouragement and support throughout the project. Warm thanks, too, are owed to Dr. Victoria McCabe, our literary editor, for her willing interest in unifying and clarifying the text.

The editors are also grateful to Mr. Amin A. de Tarrazi, International President Emeritus of the Society of Saint Vincent de Paul for his discerning preface. Under his careful guidance, the society has grown throughout the world, and continues to live out the Gospel as mediated by Vincent de Paul and Frederick Ozanam.

Preface

*A*s a humble member of the Society of Saint Vincent de Paul, a junior branch of the Vincentian spiritual family, I feel rather unworthy to sign the preface to this book dedicated to the writings of those who have been the illustrious inspirers of the great Vincentian movement of charity, witnessing Christ's love for the poor and the humble throughout the world.

Saint Vincent de Paul and Saint Louise de Marillac can be portrayed only with difficulty, and no commentary can entirely explain their message. Only by encountering them in their writings, their acts, and their achievements will we achieve insight into the true dimension of their spirituality, their intelligence, their prophetic character and their generosity. Meditation on their writings helps us to perceive the true meaning and depth of their outstanding example. One may therefore rejoice over any initiative such as this volume, which aims at revealing the outstanding figures of Vincent de Paul and Louise de Marillac.

My own meditation on them leads me to present the following few points.

SPIRITUALITY AND ACTION

We arrive at the very heart of their wise and well-balanced testimony when we read "So also faith of itself, if it does not have works, is dead" (Jas 2:17). Inversely, works achieved without the support of faith are cut off from the spirit that is the seal of Providence, beyond all human contingencies.

Vincent de Paul and Louise de Marillac were both fully aware that, had they not lived in close relationship with God, their actions would have had limited significance. It is, after all, only with the Lord's grace that we may love and serve the most deprived. In the Vincentian vocation, prayer and commitment are thus inseparable.

Humility and Audacity

In a time such as ours, when obsession for fame, greed for power and wealth, and the temptation of success motivate so many human beings, one is all the more impressed by Vincent de Paul's and Louise de Marillac's humility amid their exceptional achievements. It is remarkable, too, that their modesty did not alter their audacity in fulfilling their common mission.

Charity and Justice

When Monsieur Vincent states that there is no true charity unless it is accompanied by justice, he suggests that, far from being contradictory, these two virtues complement each other perfectly. Indeed, they enrich each other. What form of justice can be considered authentic without being inspired by love? What form of charity deserves this name if it does not aim at establishing the reign of justice?

Charity, we must admit, often opens the way to justice. Charity humanizes justice. Charity prolongs the effects of justice in the details of an individual life; charity fills its gaps. Justice, on the other hand, amplifies the imaginative works of charity. Justice spreads the benefits of charity. Justice makes compulsory what was optional by giving charity the authority of law. In other words, individual service in favor of the most deprived does not dispense us from working to change social structures.

Simplicity and Delicacy

The two founders spoke and acted with great simplicity, despite their learning and theological acumen. Inspired by divine wisdom and common sense, Vincent de Paul and Louise de Marillac scaled the peaks of delicacy to guide our behavior toward our sisters and brothers in distress. It is, in fact, only in a spirit of poverty, with a genuine heart and in an attitude of deep respect for their dignity, that we may truly encounter the poor.

PREFACE

Present and Future

From the writings of Saints Vincent and Louise, we draw simultaneously a teaching for our own time and inspiration for the future. Their stalwart common sense guides us in today's struggles for charity and justice, and their prophetic intuition prepares us for future charitable tasks.

As we become familiar with their thoughts, we discover the perfect harmony that existed between them in their teaching, their personal witness, and their work. Such unity is most difficult to achieve. Reading Vincent de Paul and Louise de Marillac we acquire progressively the feeling that balance among the various components of our personality is not mere utopia, but that, with the grace of God and the strength of our own effort, we, too, may succeed as they did.

It is always with wonder and joy that one penetrates the world of love and peace of our two Vincentian models who continue to live through their spiritual heritage: the Congregation of the Mission, the Company of the Daughters of Charity, the International Association of the Charities of Saint Vincent de Paul, the Society of Saint Vincent de Paul, and the many other congregations or institutions claiming the patronage of Saint Vincent and Saint Louise.

As a disciple of Frederick Ozanam, who had a great devotion to Saint Vincent, I wish to conclude this preface with a quotation from one of his letters. Writing from Lyons on 17 May 1833, Ozanam addressed his friend François Lallier, one of the founders of the first "Conference of Charity":

> We are now reading, in place of the *Imitation*, the *Life of Saint Vincent de Paul*, so as to better imbue ourselves with his examples and traditions. A patron saint is really no more a trite emblem for a society than a Saint Denis or a Saint Nicholas for a cabaret. He is not even an honorable name for preserving a good appearance in the religious world; he is the model one must strive to imitate, as he himself imitated the model of Jesus Christ. He is a life to be carried on, a heart in which one's own heart is enkindled, an intelligence from which light should be sought; he is a model on earth and a protector in heaven.

Editors' Note

*T*he writings of Saint Vincent de Paul are cited from the edition
of Coste, and are abbreviated as follows. Coste, *CED* followed
by volume number and page, for the French edition: *Saint Vincent de
Paul, Correspondence, Entretiens, Documents;* and Coste, *CCD* followed
by volume number and page, for the English edition: *Saint Vincent
de Paul, Correspondence, Conferences, Documents.*

The writings of Louise de Marillac are cited from the one-
volume English edition of *Écrits spirituels* translated by Sister Louise
Sullivan, D.C. (1991). It is referred to as *Spiritual Writings,* followed
by the identification letter and number of the French document and
page references. The French text employs "L" for letters, "A" for
diverse thoughts and regulations, "S" for supplementary materials,
classified later, and "M" for copies made by Marguerite Chétif.

INTRODUCTION

Seventeenth-Century France

EDWARD R. UDOVIC, C.M.

O n 25 July 1593, Henry IV knelt before the archbishop of Bourges on the stone steps of the great abbey church of Saint Denis north of Paris to renounce his Protestant faith and be reconciled to the Catholic Church.[1] He is reputed to have explained his opportune conversion by dryly observing that, after all, "Paris is well worth a mass!"[2] Whether Henry uttered this supremely cynical phrase or not, it does accurately reflect his realization that, after more than thirty years of religious and civil warfare, France was destined to remain a Catholic kingdom requiring a Catholic king. Therefore, if the first of the Bourbons were to succeed the last of the Valois and reign as the undisputed king of France, he would have to be a Catholic king. This was a price Henry of Navarre proved more than willing to pay.

THE GRAND DESIGN OF HENRY IV

King Kenry IV had a comprehensive plan for the future of France, and for the future of its Bourbon monarchy.[3] This design involved a foreign policy dedicated to maintaining an avowedly "politique" and unrelentingly hostile alliance of Catholic France with Protestant Germany and Protestant England against the Hapsburg rulers of Catholic Austria and Catholic Spain.[4] This policy eventually included expanding and securing the borders of France, destroying the threat of Hapsburg power, and making France the predominant force in the balance of power in continental Europe.[5]

Henry's domestic policies aimed at developing an effective royal absolutism that would make him and his successors the undisputed masters over all the disparate regions and peoples of France; over a nobility jealous of its own traditional rights, privileges, and power; over the party of the *"dévots,"* which strenuously opposed many royal policies; over the various local *parlements* and other traditional judicial institutions; over the hierarchy and institutions of the Catholic Church; and over the troublesome Protestant minority.

Henry correctly understood that the French dominance he envisioned in Europe depended directly on the strength of the personal absolutism of the French king within a strong, united, and prosperous kingdom. Bourbon precapitalistic economic and fiscal policies also aimed at providing the crown with the necessary national wealth to create the vast sums needed to finance these grand absolutist plans.[6]

These policies of Henry IV became the consistent policies of his Bourbon successors. Through the first half of the seventeenth century, Cardinals Richelieu and Mazarin tenaciously pursued and successively implemented them. This happened only amid fierce opposition and monumental costs to the kingdom and its people, especially the poor. By the time of Henry's grandson, Louis XIV (the Sun King), who reigned from 1643 to 1715, the absolutist dreams of the first of the Bourbons were realized.

The Grand Design of Catholic Reform in France

If France were destined to remain a Catholic kingdom, and if it were to become the powerful kingdom envisioned by the Bourbons, an integral part of its underlying unity and strength would have to come from its Catholicism. However, at the dawn of the seventeenth century, despite the Church's official status, its great wealth and power, its remaining at least the nominal religion of most of the French people, and the readiness and the early efforts of elite groups of clergy and laity to pursue its renewal and reform, the Catholic Church in France as a national and spiritual institution was anything but strong.[7] The structural weaknesses and moral abuses that had long plagued the French Church were, moreover, the inevitable results of a long-term spiritual decline. They could be reversed only by a corresponding long-term spiritual renewal.

Although the Holy See had promulgated the decrees of the

reforming Council of Trent in 1564, they had never been "received" officially into France as required by the terms of its 1516 concordat with the papacy. Legally they remained a dead letter in the kingdom until 1615.[8] Yet elsewhere in what remained of Catholic Europe, in the Catholic areas of Germany, in Italy, and in Spain, the doctrinal clarifications, moral reformation, and spiritual renewal of the Roman Catholic Church as legislated and inspired by the decrees and dynamic spirit of the Council of Trent had already progressed substantially. The time was therefore overdue for this Tridentine renewal and reform to spread to the Church in France.

Because of the political and moral weaknesses of the papacy after the scandalous period of the Great Western Schism, the Catholic churches of Spain, Portugal, the Holy Roman Empire, and France had come to enjoy a high degree of national independence and self-determination relative to the direct administrative authority of the Holy See. These nations justified their independence by a highly developed and sophisticated theological rationale aimed directly at what they considered the exaggerated ultramontane theological ideas of papal supremacy in the Church.[9]

When the time came, an essential prerequisite for the Tridentine reformation and renewal of the Catholic Church in France was that the Holy See would have to respect the sacrosanct "liberties," privileges, traditions, and ecclesiologies of the Gallican Church.[10] In France, the crown, the hierarchy, the *parlements*, the magistrates, the theologians of the Sorbonne, and even the faithful operated out of a variety of Gallican ecclesiological perspectives. All these ecclesiologies, to a greater or lesser extent, accorded the Roman pontiff a primacy of honor and acknowledged the necessity of doctrinal and moral unity between the French Church and Rome. However, these ecclesiologies all placed these requisite ultramontane acknowledgements firmly within the context of the traditions of Gallican ecclesial independence.[11]

The seventeenth-century renewal and reform of the French Church would therefore rise and fall not primarily because of direct papal leadership or Tridentine authority but on when, whether, and how the institutions of Church and state in France, not to mention the faithful themselves, would develop the desire, the will, and the spirit to adopt the agenda of the Roman Tridentine reform movement and make it uniquely their own.[12]

THE SPIRITUALITIES OF THE FRENCH REFORM

In the midst of the political, social, economic, and religious background described above, this period of the late sixteenth and early seventeenth century in France witnessed a providential flowering of one of the most remarkable periods of mystical vitality and spiritual creativity in the long history of the Universal Church.

Beginning in Paris, among a so-called *milieu dévot* of what was at first a small group of bishops, priests, nobility, religious, and laity, the formative influences of many old and new Catholic spiritual traditions came to bear on a constellation of personalities extraordinarily well prepared and providentially predisposed to receive, integrate, and act on them.

One of these influences was Christian humanism. It concerned itself with the importance of the living testimony of Scripture, and the teachings of the Church fathers. A second influence can be traced to the writings of a spiritual tradition originating in the low countries and northern Germany, commonly known as the "Devotio moderna." A third influence was the more contemporary "Mediterranean spiritualities" coming from the Catholic renewals in Spain and Italy. These spiritualities were largely identified with newly established congregations, such as the Society of Jesus, or those of the older reformed religious orders, such as the Franciscans and the Carmelites. Another important influence was the optimistic "devout humanism" of the Jesuits, and such saints as Philip Neri. Yet another influence is the specifically Tridentine and ultramontane spirituality promoted by the papacy.[13]

The confluence of these various spiritual influences in the luminous souls of Pierre Cotton, Barbe Acarie, Benet of Canfield, Francis de Sales, Pierre de Bérulle, Saint-Cyran, Angélique Arnauld, Jean Jacques Olier, Charles de Condren, Jean Eudes, Jane Frances de Chantal, Vincent de Paul, Louise de Marillac, and many others not unexpectedly resulted in their developing a charismatic variety of distinctive new spiritual insights, emphases, and perspectives.[14]

Some of these emergent spiritualities were closely related and complementary, but some were obviously not. For example, some, pessimistic about the theological issues of predestination, grace, and human nature, would soon develop into Jansenists. Others, more

4

optimistic, bitterly opposed Jansenist teachings. They would develop in other, more orthodox directions.

All these new spiritualities shared some crucial common characteristics. Each, for example, described a specific charismatic insight into the ways in which a human person was defined in relationship to God. This meant that each also embodied a specific charismatic insight about how this same person should live and act in the world created and redeemed by that God in order to relate to God consistently and authentically. Each of these spiritualities, therefore, was also "an energizing vision, a driving force . . . channeled in a particular (self-transcendent) direction" toward fulfilling a providentially revealed mission in the kingdom of God.[15] For each of these spiritualities the "kingdom" that was the focus of their attention and all their activities was the "kingdom of heaven," above all as it was temporally incarnated around them in their own "kingdom" of seventeenth-century France.

A MISSIONARY SPIRIT

The common vision of these spiritualities, as they were lived out concretely in the lives of the men and women who embraced them, focused on nothing less than the mission of the spiritual reconquest of all of France. A spiritually renewed Tridentine-Gallican Catholicism, would, it was believed, be irresistible. Facing overwhelming obstacles, these men and women knew that this spiritual reconquest would take place only over many years. They acknowledged that their crusade would have to be waged, and won or lost, battle by battle, bishop by bishop, diocese by diocese, priest by priest, parish by parish, religious order by religious order, even house by house, street by street, and person by person.

The traditional call for reform in the Church, even before the Reformation era, had always been for a thorough reform "in its head, and in its members." This type of reform program presumed a "trickle-down" hierarchical ecclesiology that reflected the ecclesiology of the Council of Trent.[16] For the Church to be reformed from the top down, the hierarchical role of bishops and priests in carrying out the Tridentine renewal was paramount. An axiom the

Tridentine reformers would accept fully was that a diocese is only as holy as its bishop, and a parish is only as holy as its priest.

In seventeenth-century France the crown appointed all the bishops of the kingdom. As a result, if France were to have bishops personally committed to reform and renewal, the crown would have to appoint them.[17] Traditionally, however, the primary considerations governing the king's choice of bishops had scandalously little to do with the holiness, faith, or pastoral abilities of the candidate, and much more to do with purely political, economic, and social considerations.[18]

Because of this, the crown needed to be convinced first of the absolute necessity of Church reform, and, second, of the necessity of appointing worthy candidates for the episcopacy. These priests should be spiritually worthy and qualified for the episcopacy, and dedicated to the cause of Church reform. Bringing this about would be helped in turn by ensuring that the priests considered for appointment as bishops had already been given thorough spiritual training and pastoral formation. According to the clerical Tridentine reform ecclesiology, which was fully received and even highlighted in France, the foundation of the hierarchical reform of the French Church would be the renewal of its bishops and priests.[19]

For priests to fulfill worthily and effectively the pastoral mission divinely assigned to them by virtue of their ordination, the Church would need effective means to ensure that candidates for ordination had at least minimal qualifications.[20] To this end the Council of Trent ordered the establishment of seminaries.[21] At the beginning of the seventeenth century, however, few of these seminaries had been founded in France. Consequently, those who presented themselves for ordination received little or no formal pastoral preparation or screening.[22]

This lack of preparation for priests had predictable and disastrous results. Most of the parish clergy were undereducated and unmotivated, liturgically and sacramentally ignorant, spiritually unprepared and morally deficient to perform their pastoral duties worthily.[23] What these parish priests themselves lacked they could not be expected to give to their parishioners. Therefore, it is not hard to understand why large areas of the French countryside had either converted quickly and firmly to Protestantism, or were so spiritually abandoned that they were considered to be virtually dechristianized.

One of the primary national objectives of the forces of spiritual renewal and reform was to bring about the conversion of the French Protestants. One strategy of this mission against heresy was to re-evangelize the Protestant regions of France.[24] The Catholic reformers believed that, if Church doctrine were presented in these areas in all its purity by zealous, holy, and skilled missionaries, the sheer force of the truth could not help but convert Protestants. The Jesuits and Capuchins excelled at this particular type of aggressive missionary effort. Francis de Sales, by contrast, favored a more irenic and charitable missionary approach. Over the years, despite grand expectations and great efforts, this full scale anti-Protestant mission of the Catholic reform resulted in only a small number of conversions. Solving the "problem" of Protestantism would therefore devolve upon the state.[25]

This mission extended also to spiritually abandoned Catholics. The sad spiritual plight of the almost dechristianized rural masses weighed heavily on the conscience of the forces of the Catholic renewal in France. The thought of thousands of men, women, and children dying each year steeped in moral vice, spiritual ignorance, or libertinage, with no hope for their eternal salvation, was more than the spiritually minded could bear. Out of their sense of personal responsibility came the development of a widespread missionary effort to re-evangelize these areas, parish by parish if necessary, to bring the peasants back to the practices of their faith, and then to keep them there at all costs.[26]

As Jean Delemeau has observed, this essentially Tridentine mission had for its ultimate end the task of "completely reshaping the faithful" through the inculturation of Tridentine spiritual and moral reform values in their lives.[27] The means to accomplish this in each parish would be preaching, catechesis, the encouragement of eucharistic and marian devotions, the extirpation of traditional superstitious practices, and a rigoristic code of personal and public morality enforced through the sacrament of penance and the requirement of fulfilling the parochial Easter duty.[28]

It became apparent to those who undertook these country missions that even the most successful burst of intensive missionary activity in these parishes would have few lasting results in the lives of the parishioners if their own parish priests did not continue their pastoral work. The quality of the rural secular clergy was uniformly low. This condition, too, affirmed the desperate need for both the short-term and long-term renewal and improvement of the parochial clergy to make them equal to fulfilling the demands of their parochial ministry as envisioned by Trent.

THE MISSION: REFORM, RENEWAL
REINVENTION OF THE RELIGIOUS LIFE

The map of Paris, indeed the map of all of France, was covered with an astounding number of monasteries, abbeys, priories, and convents, for men and women belonging to the old monastic orders. The general and accurate perception of the times was that these groups had fallen away from the observance of their primitive rules and greatly needed reform.[29] An official nationwide effort for their reform was undertaken under both royal and papal authority. This effort met great opposition from vested interests and met with predictably mixed and inconclusive results.[30]

The renewal of the mendicant orders in France proved much more successful since they were not burdened with laboring under the morally and spiritually draining system of commendatory benefices.[31] In addition, their international character put them in touch with the trend elsewhere in Europe for these orders to return to their primitive observances. Many of these groups also spawned reformed branches—such as that of the Capuchins within the Franciscan tradition—that were highly effective in the pastoral works they undertook in support of the Gallican-Tridentine renewal. The Jesuits, who returned to France in 1603 after the first of their many expulsions from the country, also provided signal contributions to the renewal of the Church in France through their theological, missionary, and educational activities.

The distinctive spiritualities developed by some of the greatest figures of the *milieu dévot* led them to the corresponding development of new and distinctive forms of religious life and mission for men and women. These spiritualities would be incarnated in a variety of new communities dedicated to particular aspects of the great mission of reform and renewal in France.

Included among this group were several new congregations of men. Not considered religious in the canonical sense, they formed

8

apostolic communities to fulfill together a particular mission. Communities such as the Oratorians, the Sulpicians, the Eudists, and of course the Lazarists (as the members of the Congregation of the Mission were known)[32] were characterized principally by their spiritual focus on the priesthood rather than on solemn vows. These communities also valued their secular identity, which placed them immediately in the service of the needs of the local Church under the direction of the bishops. Finally, the apostolic missions of these communities focused on creatively and flexibly meeting the contemporary evangelistic needs of the faithful, and the formation of the clergy.[33]

The greatest obstacle to a corresponding and needed development of new forms of religious life, ministry, and service for women in the Church of this era was the Church's ambiguous attitudes toward women.[34] These attitudes were enshrined in the universal requirement of the cloister, which the Council of Trent had solemnly confirmed.[35]

The Church found it difficult to imagine any vocational options for women other than the controlled cloister of religious life or the controlled "cloister" of marriage. While the reform of the older monastic orders of women depended in part on the requirement of a strict observance of the cloister, the foundation of new forms of community life and apostolic service for women of all social classes depended on the development of new attitudes, options, structures, and values. These developments proved much more difficult to create for women in this era than for men.

Even given these restrictions, the new spiritualities found ways of translating their spirit into dynamic new foundations of orders of cloistered women in France. In their own ways they contributed significantly to changing the face of the Church. These communities included the Discalced Carmelites, the Visitandines, and the Ursulines.

A major breakthrough of the age was the tentative but successful introduction of several new communities of women. These congregations carefully made their way outside the straitjacket canonical definition of the role of women "religious" in the Church. These groups were comprised largely of women from modest social backgrounds and even the illiterate peasantry. They came together in community life with a fervent desire for personal holiness matched with a fervent desire to serve in fulfilling the Church's mission of charity.[36]

THE MISSION: THE POOR AND CHARITY

Seventeenth-century French society was haunted by the inescapable reality of the poverty and the desperate daily struggle for survival of the incalculable legions of the poor. Their presence and suffering were on a scale so unprecedented as to be truly harrowing to the poor themselves, and all but incomprehensible to the society in which they lived.[37] One could neither escape nor ignore the poor because they were everywhere. Whether in the streets of the city or in the fields of the countryside, one could not escape seeing their hunger and pain, their dirt and rags. Neither could one escape their insistent pleas for bread, alms, medicine, work, or shelter. One could do little to escape the poor, and even less to help them.

The traditional ecclesiastical sources of institutionalized, parochial, and personal charity dealt ineffectively with this new wave of poverty then submerging France. For its part, the state was about to embark on a campaign that treated the poor as a threat and dealt with them accordingly.[38] The poor and their poverty posed a challenge that urgently demanded a Christian response. They received one from the Catholic reform, which proclaimed as one of its central tenets the "Eminent Dignity of the Poor in the Church."[39]

One of the most important insights and preoccupations of the Catholic reform movement in France was that its urgent mission of bringing about the lasting spiritual and moral reconquest of the kingdom would remain incomplete and ineffective without a corresponding commitment to the renewal of Christian charity. The sad material and physical plight of the abandoned poor weighed heavily and personally on the collective conscience of the forces of the Catholic renewal in France. The thought of thousands of men, women, and children abandoned to the hopelessness of poverty was also more than the spiritually minded could bear. Out of their sense of personal responsibility came the development of a widespread and multifaceted charitable effort to serve the poor. This was to be integrated with the efforts of a parish-based spiritual and moral renewal.

Jansenism

As the reform and renewal of the French Church progressed in the opening decades of the century, the members of the spiritual elite became divided. They had unanimously agreed on the need for the reform and renewal of the French Church, but they split violently on the consistent theological, spiritual, moral, and political basis on which this reform should take place, and stay in place. The longstanding, divisive debate between the various theological schools within Catholicism on the all-important question of grace broke out furiously once again in France with the publication of Cornelius Jansen's *Augustinus* in 1640.[40]

In broad outline, on one side of this controversy stood a humanistic tradition in the Church, strongly supported by the Jesuits. It was "progressive, optimistic (concerning reconciling the problem of human liberty and God's grace), morally lenient (on those questions of divine law which did not command absolute certitude), favorable to the extension of papal centralization, and favorable to the autonomy of religious concerning the authority of local bishops." On the other side stood an older Augustinian tradition. This viewpoint was "conservative, pessimistic, morally rigoristic, and highlighted the role and authority of the bishops over the papacy."[41]

The strident rhetoric from both sides of this controversy and the politicization of the struggle made peaceful compromise all but impossible. As the seventeenth century progressed and the eighteenth century opened this battle escalated. In the process it misdirected and dissipated the spiritual energy of the Catholic renewal in France.

Conclusion

For those born during the tumultuous final decades of the sixteenth century, the picture presented by the condition of the French Church and state would not have been an encouraging one. If those same persons had been able to overcome the high demographic odds and live a long life well into the mid-seventeenth century, at their deaths they would have taken leave of a French Church and state that had been transformed, strengthened, and unified by the complex interplay of the forces of Bourbon political and Gallican-Tridentine religious absolutism. Two such people were Vincent de Paul and Louise de Marillac.

They did not, however, just silently witness to these decades of transformation in Church and state. Instead, they joined those in every age whose lives of holiness and service not only shaped and directed their own times, but in their transcendent value shaped later ages as well.

Vincent de Paul: His Life and Way

HUGH F. O'DONNELL, C.M.

Vincent de Paul said simplicity was his gospel. He might have added humility, for which he was famous. Love could as well be called his gospel, since he is the Apostle of Charity. The poor and the needy were his people, yet he also worked closely and intimately with royalty and the well-to-do. He was passionate to the end of his life, yet he was also gentle and fatherly, especially to his Daughters and those in need. Choosing not to tread on the heels of Providence, he accomplished more than those who acted in self-reliant haste. People worldwide easily recognize him pictured in the presence of orphans, galley convicts, and poor people, yet he desired to remedy the spiritual poverty of the people by the preaching and catechizing that was the passion of his life. Because it took him a long time to find the spiritual heart of priesthood in his own life, he was unflagging in his zeal to help brother priests fan into flame the cooling embers of their priestly identity. In a society fascinated with the practices of alchemy, he was himself a spiritual alchemist, who transformed the elevated spirituality of Pierre de Bérulle into an apostolic spirituality of God's presence in the poor. How he loved to see his co-workers changed into joyful apostles by the gift of the poor! Paris was his beloved city, but France, the rest of Europe, North Africa, and Madagascar constituted his mission field.

Simplicity may have been Vincent's conscious gospel, but the scope of his activities during the last thirty-five years of his life (1625–1660) and the tendency of biographers to focus on his works make it a difficult task to encounter the place in Vincent's heart where simplicity and single-minded love of God governed all. For

13

this reason, Vincent's life can be divided into two parts: Vincent I (1600–1625) and Vincent II (1625–1660).

Vincent II is the famous Vincent who became known as a father of his country,[1] and whose apostolic zeal sent missionaries and Daughters beyond the boundaries of France into Poland, Algeria, Madagascar, Ireland, and Scotland. Vincent II founded the Congregation of the Mission (1625) and, with Louise de Marillac, the Daughters of Charity (1633). Vincent II entered into an incredibly creative and fruitful relationship of collaboration and friendship with Louise de Marillac, a story just beginning to be appreciated and made known in our time. We are amazed by what Vincent II accomplished in the service of the Gospel, the poor, and the clergy. We are astonished, too, by the local, national, and international scope of his efforts; by the way he responded to needs of every kind; by the number and range of people he knew, corresponded with, called forth, and collaborated with; by the original spirit that guided the communities and confraternities he founded; by his missionary zeal; by the fire in his heart; by his immense energy even in the last decade of his life; and, finally, by the serenity and tranquility with which he acted in all these matters because of his absolute surrender to Divine Providence. The works of Vincent II formed the basis for his canonization and the esteem in which people have held him for three and a half centuries. Nonbelievers, too, have venerated him. Frederick Ozanam said, "Even the Revolutionaries admired Saint Vincent's charity. They forgave him the crime of having loved God."[2]

Where did this energy and genius come from? What fountain of living water gave life to all his works? The secret of his extraordinary zeal and influence lies with Vincent I, in the first twenty-five years of his priesthood, between the ages of nineteen and forty-five. In Vincent I we witness the gradual and beautiful transformation of his spirit. We discover that only over time did Vincent come to be in love with God. His was a somewhat hidden but entirely remarkable journey. We can call it Vincent's "journey to the poor," for indeed that is what it was: he came to vow his life to their service. In fact, his mystical perception of the role of the poor in Jesus' act of ongoing redemption in the world was decisive for his life mission. It is preferable, however, to call this part of his journey Vincent's "journey to freedom," because it reveals the personal and interior depths of his spirit, clarifying the way the spirit of God's love fashioned his apostolic genius.

VINCENT I: JOURNEY TO FREEDOM

Ambition ruled Vincent's early years in the priesthood. Among his chief reasons for becoming a priest was his desire to get an office in the Church from which he could obtain enough money to retire early, return home, and provide for his family. It was a reasonable goal for the times, but a long way from the trust in Divine Providence which would later become the quiet center of his incredibly active life.

He was born at Pouy in Gascony, in the south of France, in 1580 or 1581, the third of six children. His family was a solid peasant family capable of making ends meet only through hard work and frugality. His father encouraged and helped him toward the priesthood, to which he was ordained on 23 September 1600 at the age of nineteen or twenty. This was probably not exceptional since the decrees of the Council of Trent, which forbade such a early ordination, were not promulgated in France until 1615. While his ordination does not imply that he was corrupt or irresponsible, becoming a priest was part of a different design, namely, personal ambition. At this point, priesthood for him was more a career and a way forward than a vocation. All his hopes for advancement, however (two trips to Rome, promises of a bishopric, money from a will), came to nothing. As late as 1610 he wrote his mother apologizing for his singular lack of success in getting a satisfactory benefice.

Then he dropped out of sight for two years, 1605–1607. The only explanation of these years is a letter documenting his captivity in North Africa. He wrote that he had been returning by ship from Bordeaux when pirates captured him, took him to North Africa, and sold him into slavery. He records that he was a slave to four different masters. He converted or rather reconverted his last master, who had been a Christian but had apostatized, and together they escaped in a small boat back to France. Some historians and biographers say this did not happen. What is certain is that Vincent himself wrote the letter telling the story. When the letter was discovered toward the end of his life, he was embarrassed, distressed, and agitated, and wanted it destroyed. We ultimately do not know whether the events actually happened. If the captivity was an historical event, it in no way altered Vincent's desire for a benefice, because he wrote from Rome in 1608 that he had been promised an excellent one. If the story of the captivity was invented by Vincent in the spirit of a typical Gascon jest or perhaps to secure financial benefits from his former patron, it would reveal his own inner captivity during this time, his personal experience of unfreedom, and his eventual liberation. In this case, it can serve as an allegory of his interior journey to freedom.

Empty-handed and unsuccessful in his quest for the financial rewards of a Church benefice, he came to Paris in 1608. It was his first encounter with the city that was to be his home for the next fifty-one years. In spite of his best efforts as a man and as a priest, he had failed to achieve his life ambition of a good benefice and an early retirement. In this way his career began in failure, yet a new phase was about to begin. Winds of spiritual renewal and ecclesiastical reform were stirring the city. Vincent became acquainted with the people who were spearheading this movement, in particular Father (later Cardinal) Pierre de Bérulle, whom he took as his spiritual director. He also met Father André Duval, a professor of the Sorbonne, who was to be his "wise man" and counselor during the next three decades. Duval introduced Vincent to the *Rule of Perfection* written by the English Capuchin Benet of Canfield. From Canfield Vincent deepened his understanding of doing the will of God and the importance of waiting for God to lead. From him he learned the crucial truth of not treading on the heels of Providence.[3]

Vincent's arrival in Paris marked a turning point in his spiritual journey. Ambition was receding, and attention to God and vocation were advancing. He was not in Paris long when the judge with whom he shared living quarters accused him of stealing his money. Vincent was innocent, but did not defend himself. To be accused publicly and put out of the apartment humiliated him, yet he remained silent. Some years later the real thief confessed. This episode reveals in Vincent less concern with self-advancement and public image and an emerging resemblance to his silent Master.

Vincent had characteristically been a serious person. Joy and happiness flooded his life, however, when he became pastor of a parish for the first time in 1612. He was sent to the church of Saint-

Medard in Clichy, a poor rural parish just northwest of Paris. He loved the pastoral ministry, because the people, the poor people of the parish, touched his heart. He told the bishop he was happier than the bishop himself and even the pope. He called forth a new life of faith and practice from the people, and experienced the priesthood in a way unknown to him to that point. His stay, though fruitful, was short-lived. In less than a year Bérulle recalled him to Paris to become tutor and chaplain to the Gondi family and their children. Although sad to leave Clichy, he was to find the Gondis important in discovering his true vocation.

In these years, doubts of faith tortured a priest companion of Vincent's. He sought help from Vincent, who advised him, prayed for him, and eventually carried his burden, according to his first biographer. However this happened, the priest was relieved of his personal doubts and Vincent began a period of three or four years of doubt and darkness. This trial of faith was so severe at times that Vincent wrote out the Creed, put it in his cassock pocket, and when he could do nothing else, placed his hand over his heart and thus over the Creed signaling his own faith. Vincent came out of this trial either because of or at least concomitant with a promise to God to consecrate the rest of his life to the service of the poor.[4]

In this experience Vincent knew both the depths of his own poverty and the graciousness of God's mercy. This prolonged experience of anguish, desperation, and suffering raises the question: Who was the poorest person Vincent ever met? The answer that suggests itself is that he himself was. Vincent knew himself as the Poor One.

As a consequence, he would never be able to meet someone poorer than himself. Experientially aware of his own radical poverty, he was open to receiving every person, without judgment or disdain. In this there was an immense freedom, a freedom in himself and a freedom toward the neighbor, especially the poor person. A corresponding question also arises: Who was the richest person Vincent ever met? The same answer suggests itself: Vincent. The experience of his radical poverty was met by the gratuitous inflooding of divine mercy. His need for God was matched by the gratuity of God's mercy.

What the Providence of God had been preparing Vincent for first became evident in 1617. Without knowing it, Vincent preached the first sermon of the mission on the feast of the conversion of Saint Paul, 25 January 1617, in the parish church in Folleville. The sad state of spiritual neglect among the peasants on the estates of the Gondi family led him to it. Accompanying Madame de Gondi on a visit of her estates, he heard the confession of a man of good reputation who said he would have died in the state of sin had it not been for this opportunity to confess. Madame de Gondi was shocked to discover that this man's situation was not exceptional. She urged Vincent to preach to the whole parish, and he chose as his topic general confession. The response of the parish to Vincent's call for repentance and a general confession of their whole life was so overwhelming that he had to call the Jesuits from nearby Amiens. A large number of the parishioners received the sacrament of reconciliation on that first mission.

This experience had an unexpected and dramatic consequence. In the face of the spiritual need of the neglected peasants in the countryside, Vincent could no longer see himself confined to the service of a single family as chaplain and tutor. What did he do? He fled. It was the same eventful year of 1617. With Bérulle's help he left Paris and the Gondi family, and became the parish priest in Châtillon-les-Dombes in the southeast of France. He did not announce his departure or take leave of the Gondis. He could not risk their refusal, nor could he remain in that wealthy household any longer. The plight of the peasants had touched him profoundly. As in Clichy five years earlier, he was back among the people. Again Vincent's love for pastoral ministry and for the people became evident to all.

If the captivity revealed Vincent's bondage and deliverance (real, spiritual, or both), and if the trial of doubting the faith revealed Vincent, the Poor One, to be at home among the poor, his ministry at Châtillon-les-Dombes revealed the shape of his pastoral spirit.

The six priests living in the parish, legally prevented from doing anything pastorally for the people, lived idle and unedifying lives. Seeing that there was work enough for two good priests, Vincent went to Lyons and found a priest to become his assistant. The pastoral zeal and fidelity of Vincent and his associate called the other priests to a more regular life. They began to pray a half hour each morning and they dismissed their servants. Helping his fellow priests to a more faithful way of life was Vincent's first order of business, as it had been earlier in Clichy.

He divided his day between visits to the people, especially the sick, and time in the church and his residence. He was very much the apostle, going about the town for half the day. The other half he was the contemplative: studying, reading, and praying. In this quiet time he also mastered the dialect of the region and in a few weeks he taught catechism in it to the children he loved. He was always satisfied with whatever donation the people gave him, which astonished them in the light of their previous experience. In short, the parish was transformed in about six months.

Early in his pastoral work at Châtillon an incident occurred that led to the founding of the first Confraternity of Charity. In August 1617, as he was preparing for Sunday mass, a parishioner brought the news to him of the illness and destitution of an entire family in the parish. He preached on their need during the mass and that afternoon the people responded in overwhelming numbers by carrying them food and supplies.

Vincent then called a meeting of the women interested in assuaging the suffering in their parish. He urged them to put order into their generosity by taking turns. They decided to establish a group that would eventually become the first Confraternity of Charity, which gave rise to the Ladies of Charity, as the members were called in Paris. His style of working with the women was remarkable because he collaborated with them, helped them do what they agreed on, and drew up the charter. In other words, he made his contribution but the women organized themselves, and retained local autonomy.

Vincent would exhibit the same style of collaborative leadership later when he worked with the clergy of Paris to organize and establish the Tuesday Conferences for priests. He inspired and assisted the priests in organizing themselves. In both instances, Vincent showed a leadership style that was free, facilitating, enabling, focused, practical, and respectful of the call of others, both women and men.

The vocabulary of the charter of the first Confraternity of Charity reveals one of the most interesting things about Vincent's development, since throughout it he used the name Jesus instead of Christ. To that point in his life, as far as we know, he had not been accustomed to saying Jesus. He consistently used the personal name Jesus from that time forward until the end of his life to speak to and about the Son of God. This change reflects the growing personal dimension of his relationship to the Lord.

On the occasion of the organizational meeting, Vincent pointed out to the women that organizations like the Confraternity of Charity were accustomed to choose a patron and he asked who would be the patron of the confraternity. He advised, "Let us make Jesus our patron." In the rules of the confraternity he went on to say that when the women offered bread and soup to a sick person, they should offer it in the name of Jesus and his holy Mother, who had also been invoked as patroness. In this crucial year of 1617, therefore, Vincent was getting more and more in touch with Jesus at a personal level.

Meanwhile, Madame de Gondi found his absence from her household in Paris unbearable. She brought significant pressure to bear, through Bérulle and others, and eventually Vincent consented to return on condition that he would be free to preach missions and that someone else would tutor the Gondi children. He arrived at the front door of the Gondi household on 23 December 1617. Since his experience of the peasants had changed him for good, even in his return to the Gondis his life found a new focus. He preached missions in the towns and villages for the next seven years with the help of other interested priests. Appointed chaplain general of the galleys in 1619 by King Louis XIII at the urging of Monsieur de Gondi, Vincent became responsible for the spiritual well-being of all the galley convicts of France.

The year 1617, therefore, had been decisive in his journey of freedom in relation to the poor. It witnessed the dramatic change that had taken place in him and the steps in the process of conversion by which he became freely an instrument of God and a poor man for the poor. What a long distance he traveled in the space of nine years, from the humbled young priest who came to Paris in 1609 to the humble, zealous pastor of Châtillon for whom the name of Jesus came spontaneously to his lips!

During this period Vincent experienced a twofold conversion. First, he was being converted to the poor, who were becoming the center of his life. His early ambitions gave way to a world of faith in which he lovingly embraced the poor as a privileged presence of the saving power of Jesus' redeeming death. Second, he was also being converted to his priesthood. For many, this conversion of his has provided an unexpected insight into Vincent's journey. Priesthood for Vincent began as a career, a job, a way of getting an early retirement. The social and economic advantages available through priesthood preoccupied his thinking and governed his plans. Gradually he was being converted from priesthood as career to priesthood as personal relationship with Jesus.

An inner relationship existed between his conversion to the poor and his conversion to the priesthood. In discovering Jesus at the heart of his priesthood, he encountered the mystery of the poor. We can imagine that the people of Clichy, Folleville, and Châtillon deeply influenced the process. He was well on the road to becoming wholeheartedly a priest who loved the poor.

As significant and inspiring as his conversion to this point had been, the journey was not complete. Three events between the years 1617 and 1625, when Vincent founded the Congregation of the Mission, reveal the final stages of purification and freedom required for his life's work.

The first event occurred in 1621. Vincent's disposition was naturally moody and melancholy. He was not pleased with this emotional stance, and asked God to deliver him from it. For this purpose, he went to Soissons to make a retreat. His prayer was answered, maybe not immediately, but nevertheless it was answered and God delivered him from his moodiness. A few years earlier Vincent had met Francis de Sales and Jane Frances de Chantal, and a deep friendship sprang up among them. As Bérulle had played a strategic role in Vincent's earlier life, so Francis de Sales set Vincent's heart on fire with the love of God and impressed him with the power of gentleness. It is easy to suppose that their relationship set the stage for Vincent's retreat and contributed to his increasingly gentle style.

The second of the three events occurred in 1623. Because he had been unable to find a community willing to undertake the work with the poor, he had been preaching missions since 1617 in the towns and villages of the countryside with the help of other priests. As chaplain general of the galleys he brought the missions to the galley convicts. In 1623 he had scheduled a mission aboard the galleys in Bordeaux, which was near his hometown of Pouy. With the support and encouragement of friends he decided to visit his family. This would be his first visit home in twenty-three years. His parents were dead, but his family and relatives were doing well. He stayed ten days and rejoiced in being with his family again. On the final day he celebrated mass for his family. Afterwards, Vincent told them that he laid no claim to the inheritance or anything else that might be due him, but by the same token they should expect nothing from him. On his way out of town he wept bitterly and spent the next three months or so weeping. It became obvious that he had for a long time been carrying in his heart an unresolved relationship with his family. His parents had commissioned him many years before to secure a proper (*honnête*) retirement to take care of the family. This he had failed to do. His tears flowed from his affection for his family, which ran deep, in spite of his having been away from them so long. In time, he detached from them in his heart. At the end of several months his heart became peaceful and he was free to give all to the poor.

The final event occurred in late 1624 or early 1625. It was four or five months before the founding of the Congregation of the Mission. Vincent, anxious about the future of the missions, went to Father Duval, his old mentor, to bare his soul. He told Duval that Madame de Gondi had set aside money for a community to preach missions on her estates and had asked Vincent to find a community able and willing to do so. Since the Jesuits were unable to accept the conditions of the foundation, they could not do it. Other communities were also unable. In the meantime, Vincent, Antoine Portail, and some other priests had been preaching the missions and catechizing. God was evidently blessing their work, yet Madame de Gondi was increasingly anxious that a community be found before she died. Duval listened to Vincent. Then he told him that the will of God seemed clear: God was calling Vincent himself to do the work of the missions. Vincent accepted the call and founded the Congregation of the Mission to evangelize the poor people of the countryside (and, eventually, to help priests in their vocation). This took place in April 1625.

That is Vincent I. When Vincent founded the congregation, he was unconditionally free and open and his life's work lay clearly before him. It had been a long journey of seventeen years. From his arrival in Paris in 1608 until the founding of the congregation, he underwent an immense development of unconditonal freedom in his life, an unrestricted readiness to let the Holy Spirit work through him. The congregation, therefore, was to be God's work. That is where the energy of the next thirty-five years came from. Vincent's journey to the poor and to unconditional freedom were in reality a single journey. Once in touch with his own radical poverty and with the unconditional mercy of God, he entered into the freedom of the disciples of Jesus and became completely available to the Holy Spirit. This was the secret of Vincent: The experience of his own poverty and God's mercy were the sources of his incredible energy and achievements in the time of Vincent II.

LOUISE: THE UNEXPECTED GIFT

Independently of the transforming journey to freedom called Vincent I, God brought into Vincent's life the unexpected gift of Louise de Marillac. She came to him first for spiritual direction, and they later became co-workers and friends for the rest of their lives. Without Louise, the Lord had brought Vincent to a level of holiness and apostolic readiness for the evangelization of the poor that surely would have borne immense fruit in the second part of his journey. But, in fact, he was not to live it without Louise. She came into his life at that transitional moment when, having completed his interior journey to freedom (Vincent I), he was on the threshold of his public ministry (Vincent II). This may in part explain the initial uneasiness of their relationship. Vincent was reluctant to take on a time-consuming spiritual-direction relationship just as his life's work was falling into place. For her part, his peasant background and instinctive distance from high society clashed with her well-born and well-educated sensibilities.

The full extent of their relationship has yet to be discerned.[5] Their different social origins shaped their world views in ways that were unexpected and paradoxical. Vincent was a man of the earth; Louise was a woman of the city. She was ready to make things happen immediately, while Vincent believed everything had a time and a season. His more measured approach is evident in the first years (1625–1633) of his direction of Louise. Contrary to the widespread view that Vincent was calming down an excitable and worried Louise, there was a deliberate and deep purpose to Vincent's

23

guidance of her. From the time of her Pentecost experience in 1623, through which she knew she was to have a special mission that included living in community, she had no idea of the timing or details of her mission. In the face of her anxiety to get on with her mission, whatever it was to be, Vincent intentionally led her to trust in the gifts and timing of Divine Providence with complete peace and confidence. This was to be foundational for her mission.

Beyond their different world views, the symbols of their primary identities differed. Though they shared a common liking for order and a practical ability for organization and detail, Louise was the "head" person, the radical thinker, while Vincent was the "heart" person, the furnace of charity. As we read and reread the letters of Vincent and Louise, these primary symbols of head and heart may help us to read them in a new way.

The understanding of Vincent and Louise and the development of their relationship over time is rich and fruitful for our own understanding of mutuality, collaboration, and friendship in the kingdom and in the service of the poor. We can say that the collaboration and friendship that grew between Vincent and Louise bore fruit in an extraordinary responsiveness to all kinds of human needs. A new form of charity evolved in the way of loving poor people and in recognizing the role of the poor and how they carry the Mystery of Jesus. The poor, whom Jesus called blessed and Vincent called our masters and teachers, were approached as privileged mediators of redeeming grace. What Louise accomplished appears in the following section. What Vincent achieved follows now as Vincent II: Apostle of Charity.

VINCENT II: APOSTLE OF CHARITY

The foundation of the Congregation of the Mission in 1625 marked the beginning of Vincent's independent and public life. It was only with the foundation of the mission that Vincent's mission had a public and permanent basis. Until then, in spite of the wonderful interior journey and fruitful work, his life was defined in relationship to Bérulle and the Gondi family and temporary appointments arising from these relationships, such as his position as chaplain and almoner to Henry IV's former wife, Queen Marguerite de Valois; his service in the parishes of Clichy, Folleville, and Châtillon-les-Dombes; and his role as chaplain general to the galleys and missions on the Gondi estates. His one lasting initiative, prior to the founding of the Mission, was the establishment of the Confraternities of Charity beginning at Châtillon in 1617. With the founding of the Mission and the care of the Confraternities of Charity before him, his life's work was in place.

Once Vincent had accepted the donation of 45,000 livres from the Gondis to found the Congregation of the Mission, all his efforts went into obtaining official recognition. The archbishop of Paris recognized the new community on 24 April 1626. Seven years later, after considerable negotiation and a number of difficulties, the Congregation of the Mission received papal approval. The congregation grew slowly at first. In the beginning there were only three members: Vincent, Antoine Portail, and a third priest. In the early years of the congregation they had to rely on their neighbors to keep an eye on their residence, the Collège des Bons Enfants. By 1632 seven priests formed the congregation and they moved to larger quarters. The immense priory of Saint Lazare, the largest ecclesiastical property in Paris and far too big for them at the time, was transferred to them by its few remaining monks.

The first expansion of their work came in 1628, when the bishop of Beauvais decided to have a few days of retreat for priesthood candidates to prepare them for ordination. He had come to this decision in conversation with Vincent, whom he then asked to take responsibility for the retreat. This was a great innovation at the time, but from that time until the death of Vincent in 1660, 13,000 or 14,000 ordinands attended these retreats.

In 1633, in collaboration with some priests of Paris, Vincent established the Tuesday Conferences. Each Tuesday a group of priests would meet at Saint Lazare. Vincent chaired the meetings, and after a period of prayer the priests shared their thoughts and convictions about what it meant to be a priest. Their interaction was mutually encouraging; on leaving these meetings, all felt charged with renewed zeal. The Tuesday Conferences bore great fruit in promoting high ideals of priesthood and in fostering mutual support among the priests. Many future bishops attended the conferences, which gave Vincent an opportunity to become acquainted with them firsthand as it gave them an opportunity to deepen and purify their priestly commitments. The Tuesday Conferences grew to the point of having about 250 participants at the time of Vincent's death.

During these years, the development of the Confraternities of Charity occupied a place of primacy along with the development of the mission. From their beginning at Châtillon, the charities were organized at the local level and, consequently, had the flexibility to respond to new situations as they arose. Beyond caring for the sick poor, as they had been founded to do, they began to respond to the needs of beggars in 1621, then of prisoners and galley convicts, and eventually of young indigent couples and victims of famine and war.

The generosity of the rich women in the Charities was admirable, but as time went on two weaknesses became evident. For the charities to be effective, they would require supervision and personal involvement. The heartfelt interest and goodwill of the noble ladies no longer sufficed for the physical toil required to care for the sick and to clean and attend to the needs of the poor. Some of the Ladies of Charity, for example, delegated their work to their servants. But devotion could not be hired; what was needed was a heart, a soul, and an unconditional fidelity. In response to this need, Louise de Marillac recognized her mission and eventually, with Vincent, founded the Daughters of Charity. Vincent and Louise became father and mother to the Daughters of Charity.

Along with the ongoing supervision of the charities and the founding of the Daughters of Charity, Vincent devoted himself to the direction of the Sisters of the Visitation. He had received this mandate from the founders, Francis de Sales and Jane Frances de Chantal. Vincent directed the sisters in the spirit of these two saints and served as a living link between them and the sisters. As time passed he came to be in charge of four monasteries. The Sisters of the Visitation were always close to his heart because of his love for Francis and his relationship as spiritual director with Jane.

By 1633, then, the foundational works in the life of Vincent were complete: the Confraternities of Charity, the Congregation of the Mission, the Daughters of Charity, the retreats for ordinands, retreats for laity, and the Tuesday Conferences. From this time onward Vincent was called on to take an increasingly important role in ecclesiastical and civil affairs at the national level.

In 1638 he undertook a new and urgent work, the care of abandoned children. Each year more than 300 children were abandoned in the streets of Paris and at the Saint Landry shelter. Thousands of children died of hunger and neglect. In the beginning Vincent entrusted some of the children to Louise, and before long Vincent and Louise embraced the entire work. A dozen Daughters of Charity were assigned to this work and thirteen houses were built to receive the children.

At the beginning of 1639, Vincent began his first great crusade of charity. In January he became aware of the extreme distress of the province of Lorraine, ravaged by war, famine and plague. He appealed to the Ladies of Charity, and during the next ten years he did not stop sending help. Centers of assistance were set up and funded to provide food and shelter for the hungry and homeless and to nurse the sick. From Saint Lazare, Vincent exhorted, consoled, advised, and begged all to be patient. He organized missions for the refugees, received young women in danger, and mobilized assistance for the impoverished nobility of Lorraine. He also took advantage of his contacts with the prime minister, Cardinal Richelieu, and other influential people to plead for peace.

Devastation eventually spread to other areas of the country and, as it did, so did the response of the families of Vincent and Louise. Beyond the unrelenting support for Lorraine beginning in 1639, there were three other regions that called for help: Picardy, Champagne, and the Ile-de-France. The first two were plundered, burned, and devastated during both the Thirty Years' War and the beginnings of the civil war known as the Fronde. In 1652, a third front opened in Paris when sickness, murder, and pillage engulfed the Ile-de-France. Beginning in Lorraine in 1639, the cries of the poor led Vincent from province to province until his death in 1660.

The scope of the work is hard to imagine today. For example, in 1652 Saint Lazare provided soup twice each day for thousands of poor people gathered there. In June 1652, the Daughters of Charity fed 800 refugees at their motherhouse, located just a few steps away. In the parish of Saint-Paul, they fed 5,000 poor people and nursed sixty to eighty patients. The work was highly organized in a concrete and practical way. Donations of food and clothing were accepted and collected regularly. Suburbs were divided and assigned to various religious communities that ministered to the spiritual and material needs of the people. The Ladies of Charity met weekly and according to their own method divided up their visits to the poor. It was their plan to receive in each locale the requests that priests, religious, Daughters of Charity, and Confraternities of Charity relayed through the missionaries.

Abandoned ecclesiastics who roamed through Paris were gathered together by Vincent, who saw they received regular assistance. He rented a house for girls and women who wanted to leave their lives of vice, and entrusted them to Sisters of the Visitation. Women from the countryside received shelter, food, and protection in a house in the faubourg Saint-Denis. All this merely suggests the scope of the difficulties and the down-to-earth practicality of the response of charity.

In June of 1643, when Vincent was sixty-three years old, he undertook an entirely new set of responsibilities. After the death of her husband, Louis XIII, and during the minority of Louis XIV, Queen Anne of Austria formed the Council of Ecclesiastical Affairs, to which she immediately appointed Vincent. In these meetings Vincent exercised significant influence on the selection of good and worthy bishops, oversaw the renewal of monastic life, dealt with Jansenism, and was able to keep the plight of the people and the poor before the government of France.

Parallel to his consuming involvement in the affairs of France and his responsiveness to the urgent cries of the poor, Vincent attended to needs and invitations beyond the borders of France. The activity of the Congregation of the Mission extended beyond France to Italy (Genoa, Turin, and Rome), Sardinia, Ireland, and Scotland. He placed priests and brothers of the Mission on the French consulate staffs in Tunis and Algiers to bring spiritual assistance to enslaved Christian prisoners. In 1648 a group of missionaries left for Madagascar and, in 1651, another for Poland. In 1652 the Daughters of Charity were sent to Poland on request of its queen. Vincent also considered sending them to Madagascar in response to the pressing request of the missionaries for the Daughters of Charity in 1656. Vincent and Louise died, however, before this could take place, and only many years later did the Daughters arrive in Madagascar.

Meanwhile, the original work continued. The Tuesday Conferences grew to include Saintes, Marseilles, Alès, Turin, Le Puy, Angoulême, Angers, Bordeaux, and Val Richer. Priests from the provinces wrote to Vincent for advice. The ordination retreats and the seminaries flourished. He also freely welcomed thousands of laymen to Saint Lazare to make a retreat, nearly bankrupting the house in the process.

In keeping with his dreams and his prayer, Vincent did not die in bed. He died sitting up, fully clothed, as if fully armed, fighting for the poor. Since that day in 1617 when he sided with the poor, he had spent forty-three years fighting against sin, misery, fatigue, and sickness. A witness tells us, "At the moment of his death, he surrendered his beautiful soul into the hands of the Lord and, seated there, he was handsome, more majestic and venerable to look at than ever."[6] It was 27 September 1660, at 4:45 A.M., the hour for prayer.[7]

An account of his physical labors might read as follows. Between 1628 and 1660, 13,000 or 14,000 ordinands attended the ordination retreats. The house of Saint Lazare alone gave more than 1,000 missions. Twenty thousand retreatants were housed at Saint Lazare and the Collège des Bons Enfants. Almost 10,000 children were rescued from certain death. Hundreds of thousands of poor people were helped.[8]

The moral balance sheet goes beyond numbers. A new idea was taking shape during Vincent's lifetime. Vincent himself introduced an original form of religious life. He was one of the most able and perhaps the best of the reformers of the clergy. His innovations reached beyond the religious whom he encouraged and the episcopate he helped to reform. More than anyone, Vincent had restored good taste and simplicity to preaching, and, in a word, a new feeling for the power of the Gospel.

THE WAY OF VINCENT

Unlike Ignatius of Loyola, who gave to the Jesuits and to the world the *Spiritual Exercises*, Vincent did not outline his method or codify his spirituality. The one exception was *The Common Rules or Constitutions of the Congregation of the Mission*. They are a goldmine of spiritual wisdom, evangelical simplicity, discipleship, love of Jesus, practicality, experience, and common sense. He wrote them explicitly for the Congregation of the Mission only after the experience of living them for thirty-three years. The congregation has always jealously guarded them as part of its interior life. Their appearance in this volume marks the first time they have been published for a general readership. It may be that in making them public, the Congregation of the Mission will learn in a new way, as they are read with new eyes, what a treasure Vincent has given them, the fullness of which, we know, has not yet been lived out. Still, Vincent did not intend to write anything comparable to the *Spiritual Exercises* for the benefit of a public wider than his own community. We are left to distill his way from his life and letters.

The starting point for discovering Vincent's spiritual legacy is the recognition that Vincent did not have a *spirituality*. Rather, he had a *way*. This may at first seem like a mere verbal difference, but it is of crucial importance. Vincent was not a speculative person. His ideas were a consequence, not a source, of his love. Experience counted with him, and he habitually sought God's presence in events and the people involved in them. He had been led beyond Bérulle's elevations to the absolute conviction of God's presence in time, history, events, and people. His spiritual way was radically incarnational, historical, existential. "God is here," he learned from Benet of Canfield and Jan Ruusbroec. And he had the patience and trust to let God be God and to wait upon Providence. It is evident that organizing ideas into a spirituality was not his gift.

If this is true, how can we discover his way? His original biographer, Louis Abelly, and André Dodin, a contemporary French Vincentian who has devoted his life to distilling each day a bit more of Vincent's spirit, will guide us. Then, after the way of Vincent according to Abelly and Dodin, several of the practices Vincent gave us will be presented.

EXPERIENCE, FAITH, PRACTICAL WISDOM

André Dodin, C.M., in his classic *Saint Vincent de Paul et la Charité*, suggests that our best chance of grasping the shape of Vincent's originality comes from the three areas in which he felt most at home and was considered a master by his contemporaries: experience, faith, and practical wisdom.[9]

Vincent began with experience: his connection with reality, his contact with God. It was the vehicle of God's will for him. "Let us do the good that presents itself," he urged.[10] He was skeptical of grand ideas and schemes that did not rise out of events and circumstances. Events called him to respond and showed him the way in which God was leading him.

The confession of the dying man near Folleville and the concern of Madame de Gondi for the spiritual care of the country people opened the door to preaching the missions and the founding of the Congregation of the Mission. In a family's need and the generosity of some women, he sensed a call to organize regular assistance in the parish of Châtillon, which led to the first Confraternity of Charity. In the bold and confident initiative of Marguerite Naseau, the first to present herself in the service of the poor, Vincent recognized grace where no one had seen it before in the generous peasant women. In the pastoral desire of the bishop of Beauvais, he felt himself called to organize the first of the retreats for ordinands. Clearly, God revealed his way to him through circumstances and events.

Following closely on experience was action. Vincent noticed how in the Acts of the Apostles Jesus began to do before he began to teach (Acts 1:1). Living preceded teaching, action came before words. In the beginning of the *Common Rules* he urged the missionaries to imitate Jesus in letting the lived Gospel be the source of their preaching. Vincent always let the primacy of life and action guide him, for he found the living God there, in life and action.

From 1613 to 1617, as his significant experiences opened up to a deliberate pattern of life, Vincent formulated what he had begun to live. He paid close attention to events and even closer attention to the people who gave meaning to the events. As he underwent purification through grace and trials, he tried to decipher their meaning, and he made a response. When he discovered it was his mission to remedy the ignorance of the poor and the priests, he sought ways to respond. The rhythm and steps of his way are evident in these favorite words of his found throughout his writings: "It's necessary to give oneself to God (*se donner*) . . . in order to serve the poor . . . to go on Mission . . . to direct seminaries and ordinands." The worth of each human being resides in the action that gives truth to his or her existence. Such action for him consisted in rendering Christ present and letting him act in oneself, in making oneself present to Christ and in acting for him. *In nomine Domini*, "In his name . . . in the name of Our Lord Jesus Christ."

For Vincent, action had a radical meaning. We sense that he thought it perhaps was the only certain way to unite oneself to Invisible Reality, that is, to God and to God's will. "We have to sanctify our occupations by seeking God in them and by doing them to find God in them rather than to get them done."[11] For Vincent, God was present in activity. God is here to be sought in life and action. The Invisible God is alive and visible in our actions.

Vincent added faith to lived experience. He sought the invisible in the visible happenings and circumstances of life. His magnetic north in all things was Jesus. He sought at each moment to recognize the face of Christ and to live the concrete teachings and promises of the Gospel. "Nothing pleases me but in Jesus Christ," he said.[12] The missionary dimension of the life of Jesus focused his perception of the mystery of Christ. He saw how Jesus went around through the towns and villages proclaiming the good news. His eyes were always on the missionary Christ. In this he saw the unique quality of the Congregation of the Mission as a community moving from village to village throughout the countryside preaching the good news. He recognized also that the missionary activity of Jesus flowed from the very mission of the Word of God. The Father had sent him into the world so that at every moment Jesus was in the world on mission or as a missionary. Vincent understood that his vocation called him to associate himself with the missionary activity of the Incarnate Word. Jesus was sent on a redemptive mission that continues through us in the world today. It happened through the self-emptying (kenosis) of the Incarnation and the Passion and death of Jesus. This was Vincent's faith and, with eyes and heart shaped by this faith, he contemplated his experience.

Vincent's faith in the missionary Christ, radical and energizing as it was, led to an equally radical view of the Church. Vincent understood that the poor have a central place in the life of the Church and are privileged mediators of salvation. Although poor people appear disfigured by their deprivation, homelessness, hunger, anxiety, ignorance, judgment, or the condescension of others, Vincent said the situation is entirely different when we regard poor persons with the eyes of faith and "turn the medal over."[13] In faith we recognize their dignity as children of God, loved by God, but above all as living images of the life and death of Jesus. As he gave alms in the name of the former queen, as he met with people in Clichy and Folleville and Châtillon, as he knew himself to be a poor man, Vincent was led to be open to the faces of poverty and humility. He lived increasingly by the paradox that in order to live in Christ Jesus we have to consent to die in Christ Jesus and that we die in Jesus paradoxically through his very life. The mystery of the poor led Vincent along the road of detachment and humility and helped him see with the eyes of faith.

The third step for Vincent was practical wisdom. As someone who believed that personal value, dignity, and life were found in action, Vincent's life was shaped by three rules. The first was to act always with purity of intention and singleness of purpose. This had a concrete meaning for Vincent. He often repeated "it is necessary to begin with God, to look to God first, to ask for a share in God's spirit, a share in God's view of things."[14] He did not allow his purity of intention to be compromised by his own concerns. He said, "When we take care of God's business, God will take care of ours."[15]

The second rule was to consider an action as manifesting God's way when it effectively embraced the extremes. Affective love had always to be coupled with effective love, otherwise it would be an illusion. Love of God had to be expressed in love of neighbor. "It is not enough for me to love God, if my neighbor does not love God."[16] He brought the extremes of rich and poor together by helping the rich come to know the poor through generosity and service. As he was a mystic of action, Vincent's deep interiority and faith life were forever expressed and nourished in the life of zealous action. In all this he was a faithful disciple of his Master, who called the disciples to be wise as serpents and simple as doves.

The third rule was to mirror God's fidelity to his own being, and his great flexibility toward human beings. Vincent's rule of action was to be always firm and persevering in regard to goals, flexible and gentle in regard to means.

Vincent's commitment to experience, faith, and practical wisdom were all animated by the spirit of God's love. He said, "God is love and we must come to him by love."[17] God's love is not only the beginning and the end of all things; we must come to God by love.

The Way of Discernment

Louis Abelly will guide us on this part of the journey. In 1664 he cited Vincent:

> Among the multitude of thoughts and inclinations that incessantly arise within us, many appear to be good, but do not come from God and are not pleasing to him. How, then, should one discern these? We must look at them carefully, have recourse to God in prayer, and ask for his light. We must reflect on the motives, purposes, and means, to see if all of these are in keeping with his good pleasure. We must talk over our ideas with prudent persons, and take the advice of those placed over us. These persons are the depositories of the treasures of the widsom and grace of God. In doing what they suggest, we are carrying out the will of God.[18]

This paragraph gives a remarkable insight into Vincent's process of discernment. It has three moments to it. The first is unrestricted readiness, the second is weighing the evidence, and the third taking counsel.

Vincent advises us to begin in prayer and to ask for the gift of indifference. In the spiritual tradition the word *indifference* connotes a profound and life-giving disposition of complete openness in a disciple. It happens, however, that in our culture indifference has other and negative connotations. The French use the word *disponibilité*, yet we have no easy English equivalent. Indifference and *disponibilité* express the quality of a servant and can perhaps best be translated today as "unrestricted readiness." This is the first disposition of a disciple, to be ready to do the Lord's will without preconditions. Vincent was deeply convinced that following the Lord's will in all things and waiting on the lead of Providence was the way to life. For him, following one's own will and negotiating with God was an obstacle to the coming of the kingdom. The first requirement, then, is unrestricted readiness for whatever the Lord is calling one to do.

When our hearts are in a place of unrestricted readiness, we are prepared for the second step: to weigh the pros, the cons, the outcomes, the costs of a line of action, with detachment and openness. When we have a listening heart, it is no longer a question of marshaling the evidence in favor of or against a preconceived goal. Unrestricted readiness leads us to weigh the evidence from the Lord's point of view and with detachment from our own personal agenda.

The third and perhaps unique aspect of Vincent's way was to seek the counsel of a wise man or a wise woman. Vincent did this himself on many occasions. Father André Duval was Vincent's wise man until the former died in 1638. When Vincent founded the congregation, he went to Duval and presented his dilemma to him. It went something like this. "In 1617 Madame de Gondi set aside 45,000 livres and asked me to find a congregation to preach missions on her estates for the salvation of the souls of the people living there. Madame de Gondi is not well and she wants this matter settled before she dies. No congregation is able or willing to take up the work. However, Father Portail and I, and a few others, have been doing the work of preaching the missions. And God has been blessing our work a great deal." When Vincent finished presenting his quandry to Duval, Duval said to him, "The scriptures tell us that those who hear the word of God and do not heed it will receive many stripes." Rising from this interview, Vincent stopped looking for another congregation to do the work and founded the Congregation of the Mission. He also accepted the advice and guidance of Duval when the priory of Saint Lazare was offered to him. It was far too large for his modest purposes, so he was personally reluctant to take it. On Duval's advice he accepted Saint Lazare. Vincent believed God's will was revealed not only in the events and the circumstances of life but also in the counsel of the wise.

This was the substance of Vincent's way. It began with experience seen in the light of faith and moved toward action guided by the paradoxical principles of the Gospel. He entered on discernment by opening his soul to unrestricted readiness and, when his heart was ready, he examined the information, data, dangers, benefits and outcomes of the project. When this was done—in matters of significant moment—he sought counsel from one or two wise persons. Vincent's way was rooted in God's presence and activity in history. It was historical, existential, concrete, and dynamic. It was rooted in life and mystery. He sought God, not through theory, but by way of history and human existence. He had learned from experience that God is here and we are in God.

VINCENT'S CREATIVITY

The way of Vincent found concrete form in several innovative approaches to missions and common life. They are his method of preaching and prayer, repetition of prayer, silent prayer in common, and collaboration.

In response to the highly literary and flowery preaching style of the day, Vincent created what he called "the little method." It was simple, yet powerful and effective in the missions, and showed Vincent's practical spirit at work. The method had three steps: definition, motives, and means. The preacher was to begin by explaining to the people the meaning of the Gospel passage, virtue, or vice under consideration. Second, based especially on the Scriptures and practical experience, he was to present the motives for practicing a particular virtue or for avoiding a particular evil. Finally, he was to assist the people by suggesting practical means for living out the virtue in question or for avoiding the vice. In its stark simplicity, the little method had great power because it touched the mind, the heart, and the will. It restored the unction of faith and the power of conviction to the ministry of preaching. It also formed the core of his thinking about a method of prayer, which the Daughters of Charity adopted as one of their methods of teaching.

Perhaps Vincent's genius is most apparent in the development of "repetition of prayer." Vincent would regularly ask both the missionaries and the Daughters of Charity to share their prayer in the presence of the other missionaries or Daughters. He would ask a missionary or a Daughter, "Monsieur, or my Sister, what was your prayer this morning?" The person addressed was invited to share in a spirit of complete simplicity his or her prayer of the morning with the others in the group. Vincent would then respond by reflecting on it or praising and acknowledging what was said. Often deeply touched by what was shared, he manifested his appreciation. He then would continue to develop the topic. It was an original and wonderful practice, which became formalized over time. In many ways it has been lost, but efforts are being made to recover it. Vincent's practice of repetition of prayer, too, manifested his profound conviction that God is here. God is here in the prayer of my brother or my sister. God is here in the midst of all those who listen to that word shared in the spirit of simplicity.

Vincent called members of the Congregation of the Mission to pray for an hour each morning in common. He called the Daughters to pray a half hour in the morning and a half hour in the evening in the same way, in common. This was a call to silent, personal prayer. Remarkably, at the same time across the English Channel, George Fox, commonly considered the founder of the Society of Friends, or Quakers, was instituting a similar form of prayer: silent prayer in common. There is a mystical genius to this form of prayer, which escapes the insistence of logic that personal prayer is properly done in private. The power of this prayer is being rediscovered in our time.

Finally, Vincent's spirituality was entirely rooted in the sacrament of Baptism. Even his spirituality of priesthood was at heart baptismal. He saw that our vocation was to be baptized into the Body of Christ as members of one another, into the death of Christ and into the power of his resurrection. Because of this, Vincent was open to the gifts of many people. He had a wonderful gift for recognizing, acknowledging, and summoning the gifts of people from all different strata of society. It was, for example, a revolutionary moment when he recognized the gift of Marguerite Naseau, contrary to all cultural expectations of the time, and welcomed her as a servant of the sick poor. His ability was particularly evident in relationship to women. He recognized and honored their calling for new and innovative ways of participating in the Church's mission in the service of the poor. The gift of Louise de Marillac, of which we will hear in the following section, is the most dramatic instance

Vincent's way is of great importance today. Though Vincent was very much a man of the seventeenth century responding to the events and circumstances of his time, he leads us beyond the seventeenth century to our own, where we are called to be fully attentive and responsive to the God present in the events and circumstances of our day. If Vincent had a last word to say to us, he would perhaps offer us the bipolar paradox of waiting on Providence and acting wholeheartedly. In fact, he continually invites us to put our absolute confidence in the guidance of Providence, waiting until God leads, and then, as we recognize God's lead, giving ourselves unreservedly and with full hearts to the poor. For God is here.

Louise de Marillac:
A Spiritual Portrait

LOUISE SULLIVAN, D.C.

*F*ew names are as synonymous with charity as that of Vincent de
Paul. Believers and nonbelievers alike, across the world and
across the centuries, recognize the name and visage of the French
peasant priest who, together with his followers, the priests of the
Congregation of the Mission, the Ladies of Charity, and the Daughters of Charity, transformed the character of Christian charity in
seventeenth-century France by establishing works for health care,
education, and social welfare that continue to our day on six conti-
nents. But if Vincent de Paul's name has become a household word,
that of his friend and collaborator of thirty-six years, Louise de
Marillac, has largely remained hidden in his shadow.[1]

There have been many charismatic friendships in the history
of the Church, relationships between a man and a woman that are a
gift of God to the Church since their love for one another is fruitful
far beyond their mutual personal sanctification. Such, for example,
were the friendships between Jane Frances de Chantal and Francis
de Sales, and between Catherine of Siena and Raymond of Capua.
The charismatic graces uniting these saints flowed from their grace
of vocation and directed their general baptismal mission of love into
very special channels for the Church and her people. Only recently,
indeed in the past decade, have we discovered that the same sort of
charismatic friendship existed between Vincent de Paul and Louise
de Marillac.

Although the exact date of their first meeting is unknown,
(probably some time between the end of 1624 and the early part of
1625), it is certain that there was reluctance on both sides. Vincent's
can be supposed because of his earlier experience with the spiritual

direction of Madame de Gondi and his desire to devote himself to the missions, but Louise's is clear. She herself tells us, in her account of her Pentecost experience of June 1623, of her "repugnance" to accept any change in spiritual director.[2] But the day would come when, moved by the Holy Spirit, they would set aside their own desires and hesitations to enter fully into the divine plan.

The friendship between these two widely differing personalities, which began so inauspiciously, was to prove to be of incalculable significance to the Church and the poor. Many difficulties would have to be overcome but both Vincent and Louise would soon become conscious of the need each had for the other as they combined their gifts of nature and grace for a work as yet undefined except in the mind of God, who knew that Vincentian works would, as Louise's biographer, Jean Calvet, put it, "become what they were because Louise de Marillac put her hand to them."[3]

Subsequent to the charismatic grace bestowed on her by God on the feast of Pentecost, 4 June 1623, and her later meeting with Vincent de Paul, Louise de Marillac set out in earnest on a spiritual journey toward total union with God. The itinerary would prove arduous and painful and would be marked to an extraordinary degree by her temperament, her personal experience, and the period in which she lived.

LOUISE'S EARLY LIFE, TO 1633

What do we know of Mademoiselle Le Gras, as Vincent would always call her, when the two met? At the age of thirty-four, she had been profoundly marked by the dramatic, often traumatic events of her life. The natural daughter of Louis de Marillac,[4] she would never know, despite her father's affection for her, the love and security of family life. She never knew her mother, whose name, to this day, is unknown. Her health would always be delicate, due, no doubt, to the conditions in war-torn France at the time of her birth in 1591. As a member of the illustrious Marillac family, which held positions of power and influence in the courts of Marie de Medici and Louis XIII, she received her education at the royal monastery of Poissy near Paris, where her aunt, another Louise de Marillac, was a Dominican nun. There, she encountered the arts and the humanities, as well as liturgical prayer, spiritual reading, and the responsibility of the rich to the poor. Poissy also gave rise in her to the desire to enter the cloister.

The establishment of the Daughters of the Passion in Paris in 1606, with which her uncle, Michel de Marillac, was closely associated, seemed to provide Louise an ideal setting for living the life she felt called to by God. It is not difficult to imagine how devastated she must have been when Father Honoré de Champigny, provincial of the Capuchins, refused her request for admission. His reasons are not clear, but his words proved prophetic. He told Louise that God had "other designs"[5] for her life. This, however, is in hindsight. At the time, the shattered young woman could but accept the only option open to her, marriage.

The Marillacs, for their own interests rather than hers, arranged Louise's marriage to Antoine Le Gras, personal secretary to the regent, Marie de Medici. Nonetheless, it seems to have been a happy one, especially after the birth of their son, Michel, 18 October 1613. This happiness, however, would prove short-lived. The prolonged illness of her husband, leading to his death in December 1625, and the limitations of her child, who would always be a source of anguish for her, plunged her into the dark night of the soul. Relief would come only on Pentecost Sunday 1623 when her doubts would dissipate and she felt assured that one day she would be able to give herself to God as she desired. Louise carried with her throughout her life her hand-written account of the experience. Classified by Sister Goeffre, archivist of the Daughters of Charity, at the end of the nineteenth century as "Light,"[6] it is central not only to any understanding of her personal spiritual development but also to a realization of the revolutionary character of the Company of the Daughters of Charity, which she helped found. This community broke with the traditional form of religious life of the time since it would be a community in which there would be "much coming and going."[7]

When Louise met Vincent in 1624 or 1625, her spiritual storm had quieted. Nevertheless, she had yet to find the necessary balance between her considerable human talents and her personal mode of sanctification. A highly intelligent and decisive woman, an intellectual with a practical sense and remarkable organizational ability, capable of conceiving and actualizing vast enterprises in minute detail, Louise, paradoxically, experienced a need for nearly constant support in her spiritual life. Despite her physical frailty, this woman possessed seemingly limitless energy when confronted with the demands of the works for the poor or the needs of the incipient congregation of which she was superior. Nonetheless, she underwent periods of discouragement in her interior life and sought the presence and support of a spiritual guide to supply needed reassurance. Although Louise did not at first appear to believe that Vincent de Paul, ten years her senior, was the one to provide it, she "acquiesced," as she tells us.[8] Vincent did likewise and thirty-six years of friendship and collaboration resulted.[9]

It is well to examine, to the extent that such an examination is possible given the scarcity of documentation, the characteristics of this initial stage of Louise de Marillac's spiritual itinerary. When she met Vincent, she already had a regulated prayer life, knew the sacred Scripture well, had read many important spiritual writers such as Luis de Granada, Jean Gerson, Francis de Sales, and Pierre de Bérulle. She had also received spiritual guidance from Michel de Marillac, Jean-Pierre Camus, and possibly Francis de Sales. In a word, she was not a beginner in the spiritual life. It is essential to remember this, especially when considering her relationship with Vincent de Paul. Though contemporaries, they grew up and spent their youths in very different settings. More important still, their temperaments and life experiences varied radically. Louise would always place a high value on Vincent's guidance, but she did not absorb "Vincentian" spirituality to such an extent that her spiritual journey copied his. As Calvet contends, Vincent de Paul brought her a method rather than a doctrine. This method, however, would be the means that would enable her to reach her full human and spiritual potential.

When Vincent and Louise met, she had reached another turning point on her spiritual journey. She wanted to know, to understand, to see, to take control of her life of service to God, which she had promised in her vow of widowhood of 4 May 1625. Vincent knew that God was asking of her unconditional abandonment to his Providence, but peaceful abandonment was not in her character. Thus the challenge existed for both of them: how to prevent her from rushing headlong down the dangerous slope where self-questioning, self-analysis, and self-contempt were leading; how to enable her to fulfill the directive she had received years earlier in a letter from her then director, Jean-Pierre Camus, bishop of Belley, to turn her glance away from herself and fix it on Jesus Christ. Despite his considerable skill as a spiritual guide, Camus was not able to instill in Louise the confidence necessary to enter on the path of abandonment to the will of God. The wise Monsieur Vincent would do so.

The letters of Vincent to Louise, written between 1626 and the end of November 1633, the date of the founding of the Daughters of Charity, reveal his gentle, healing touch. The seventy-five letters of Vincent to her evidence the quiet wisdom with which he responded to her. Although we have only three letters from Louise to Vincent during this period, we know that she must have opened her heart to him. Though she was still an anxious, troubled, scrupulous woman, Vincent had come to understand that she had borne more than her share of suffering. Words, therefore, such as peace, abandonment, joy, and moderation recur like a leitmotif under his pen. At this early stage, he perceived that Louise's great gifts of nature and grace were contained in a fragile vessel. He knew that she needed neither the detached, cold reminders of human frailty she had received from Michel de Marillac nor the holy but ineffectual advice of Camus. Of her spiritual director, she required, rather, someone who would exercise in her life what she would later call "gentle persuasion."[10] Vincent de Paul was that person. Gently, he turned her gaze away from herself and toward Jesus Christ and the poor.

Little by little Louise learned to live as Vincent taught her, that is "content among [her] reasons for discontent."[11] As calm took possession of her soul, she began to see her vocation as a clear call from God to dedicate herself exclusively to the suffering "members of Jesus."[12]

Louise began what we may truly call her new life by a retreat around 1632. The graces she received fortified her. She felt confident enough to emerge from her solitude, to engage in personal charitable activity, and to assume increasing responsibility. Louise was sure of herself, and Vincent had the sign of the will of God that he had been seeking.[12a]

ACTIVE LIFE IN THE WORLD

The Confraternities of Charity, begun by Vincent in Châtillon-les-Dombes in 1617 to help the sick poor in their homes, had flourished at their beginning. With the passage of time, however, some had ceased to be effective. The spirit of the foundation was threatened. Someone had to visit them, study their activities, correct abuses, and revive in the members their original zeal. In the eyes of Vincent de Paul, no one seemed better suited to undertake this task than Louise de Marillac. So it was that he sent her out on 6 May 1629 to visit the Confraternity of Charity of Montmirail.

This was but the beginning of four years of intense activity in the service of the poor. She had found a work in which her human and spiritual gifts could flourish. She had at last broken the fetters that bound her. She could function as a free woman, confident of God's love for her and desirous of bringing that love to the poor. Furthermore, she was remarkably successful. In her *Spiritual Writings*, we find detailed accounts of her visits to the Confraternities of Charity, which reveal her keen intelligence, organizational ability, and capacity for leadership. Although she still relied on Vincent, particularly in her spiritual life, she had become his collaborator and equal, a woman of decision. Since this transformation was greater than Vincent could have hoped for, he was overjoyed. His letters from this period express his growing confidence in Louise. Not only does he tell her how pleased he is to hear that God is blessing her work; he also acknowledges that particularly difficult situations called for her skills.

Yet amid the normal trials and failures she experienced, Vincent was there to support her. The Louise de Marillac of this period, however, was a changed woman. She now had the inner strength to face difficulties and to deal with them calmly. She had found in union with God the courage she needed.

While visiting the Confraternities of Charity, Louise experienced the depth of human misery and discovered the resources of charity capable of alleviating it. With all her energy and talent, she sought to take up the burden of others instead of bewailing her own. In so doing, she broadened her horizons and expanded her heart. She discovered love in its widest dimensions and it set her free. She was no longer alone. Vincent had told her earlier, in a letter in 1630, "God is love and wants us to go to Him through love."[13] With this freeing love in her heart, she laid to rest the ghosts of the past. She took, once again, the name her father had given her, Louise de Marillac. As a Marillac she had the faith and confidence to believe that she could, with God's sustaining grace, rise above success and failure, joy and sorrow. The great undertaking is approaching. Louise, now forty-two, was in full possession of herself and ready, along with Vincent de Paul, to take the next step on the path along which God was leading them. The year is 1633.

The transformation that had taken place in Louise de Marillac over the nine years of her relationship with Vincent de Paul could never have occurred had she not prepared the soil of her soul to receive the gifts the Holy Spirit showered on her. In her prayer life as in everything else, Louise was marked by the era in which she lived. Because she was a seventeenth-century Frenchwoman, directly or indirectly her intellectual processes were influenced by Descartes and his philosophical method. Be they retreat meditations, acts of consecration, or "thoughts," they all have one element in common: They are reasoned.

Solid, profound, and often moving, her writings are always logical, and progress smoothly from point to point. Vincent would try to help her to become less reasoned and more spontaneous, to be more open to the infused gifts of the Spirit. As she herself admits, she would have to struggle to simplify the workings of her mind. Only toward the end of her life could she peacefully allow God to operate in her during her times of prayer. In a meditation on Holy Communion she exclaimed: "No desires, no resolutions, the grace of God will accomplish in me whatever He wills."[14]

Before reaching this mystical union with God, however, Louise would have to overcome her desire to become a saint by the sheer force of her will and the multiplicity of her prayers. Nowhere is this more evident than in her "Rule of Life in the World," written at the time of her husband's death in 1625.[15] In this three-page text, we find most of the major themes of Louise's spirituality that will develop and deepen with the passage of time. We also see the form her prayer life took during the early years of her widowhood.

The first thing that strikes the reader is the rigid structure that Louise imposed on her life in general and on her prayer in particular. From her first thoughts on awakening until retiring at night, she

45

accounted for every minute. She left no room for spontaneity. The Dominicans nuns or the Daughters of the Passion could hardly have lived a more regulated life. Indeed, it would seem that Louise was trying to turn the little apartment where she had moved after Antoine Le Gras's death into the cloister where she had been refused admittance years earlier. She set aside times to recite the hours of the Office of the Blessed Virgin. She fixed the time for assisting at Mass and the days for receiving Holy Communion. She established periods for meditation and spiritual reading, even indicating the titles. She specified fasting and penance, the hair shirt and the discipline. Finally came her devotions: the rosary, special prayers said at special times, and acts multiplied within certain periods of time. Surprisingly, despite all this, she found room in her schedule for household responsibilities and even limited social obligations, such as visits received and dinner guests. One is hard pressed, however, to see where her son, Michel, a thirteen-year-old boy, fit into her daily plan.

Nonetheless, despite the nearly stifling rigidity of this spiritual regimen, the broad lines of Louise de Marillac's spirituality are discernible: Jesus Christ, poor and suffering, honored and served; the mysteries of the Incarnation and the Redemption; the Eucharist; the Holy Spirit; the rhythm of the liturgical year; the Blessed Virgin; the service of the poor; the virtues of poverty, humility, gentleness, cheerfulness, trust, abandonment to will of God, fidelity, and, above all, love.

In light of her Rule of Life, certain letters of Vincent to Louise become clear. He knew that she was a soul called to perfection and he wanted to help her to reach it. Nevertheless he feared that she was as yet unable to let go enough of her desire to control her spiritual progress to heed his advice. Moreover, such a woman, bound to a regular schedule, was certainly not equipped to visit the Confraternities of Charity or to form servants of the poor. Thus it was that Vincent undertook to bring balance into her spiritual life. Father de Champigny had been correct: The cloister did not suit Louise de Marillac's character, since it was too prone to close in on itself. She needed, rather, to reach out and find her God in others. And so Vincent would urge her to moderation, peace, and calm. Given her scrupulous nature, he feared she would become anxious if she were unable to maintain the rule she had drawn up for herself.

He thus encouraged her not to hold herself bound to all her good resolutions[16] and to do whatever was necessary to preserve her health. In the same manner, Vincent furnished her with the outlines for her retreats but counseled her to go about her exercises "leisurely."[17]

Wise man that he was, Vincent also capitalized on Louise's remarkable powers of reasoning to help her overcome what he called her "indiscreet zeal"[18] and her "useless apprehension."[19] When she tried to do more than her health would allow, he reminded her that she was no longer a private individual but a person on whose well-being many others depended.[20] When old anxieties resurfaced, he chided for her "servile" fear, hard to justify in someone to whom God had given the "understanding of him" that he had given her.[21]

TRANSFORMATIONS

Through her service to the poor, God's grace gradually worked a cure in the heart, soul, and even body of Louise de Marillac. Together with Vincent de Paul, with whom she had been sharing her journey for nine years, she was ready to turn all her gifts toward the service of Christ in the poor. Each had but to allow the Spirit to act in and through them in the work for which God in his providence had been preparing them.

United in heart, in the heart of Jesus Christ, Vincent de Paul and Louise de Marillac sought to discover what God willed for them as the year 1633 was drawing to a close. Freed at last from the concerns of the past, Louise was living in the present, her eyes fixed on Jesus Christ suffering in the poor. Her zeal had given her renewed physical and spiritual strength as she devoted her energies to the works of the Confraternities of Charity. She was active, busy, and happy, but somehow convinced that God was asking yet more of her—a more total commitment to Jesus Christ in the poor. The Light of Pentecost 1623 had brought her the insight that one day Father de Champigny's words that God had other designs on her would be fulfilled, that she would at last make vows of poverty, chastity, and obedience in a small community where others would do the same and where she could help her neighbor.

Louise often reflected on this during her meditations and retreats. She knew that she had to abandon herself to the providence of God and await the manifestation of his will. Although she had progressed a long way on the path of abandonment to the will of God, waiting was not something that Louise readily did. She was a woman in a hurry. She was over forty, and her health was frail. The life span of the era did not encourage further delay. Yet Vincent insisted that they do just that until the designs of God became clear. Several of his letters to her from 1630 to 1633 reflect this. Examining them illustrates a discernment process in which two people are honestly and prayerfully striving to discover the will of God for them. We know from a letter of Vincent dated 19 February 1630 that he had begun sending girls to Louise to be trained to work under the direction of the Ladies of the Confraternities of Charity of Paris. The girl whom he mentions here is Marguerite Naseau. Vincent loved to repeat her inspiring story, since he considered her the first Daughter of Charity, although she died in February 1633, before its founding. In a letter of October of the same year in which Vincent speaks of Germaine, a young woman whom Louise had trained as a schoolmistress, he tells her that he had been "very much occupied" that morning with her and with the "thoughts Our Lord was giving [her]."[22]

By the spring of 1631, Louise had been eager to devote all her time and energy to forming the young servants of the poor. Vincent's letter to her on this subject is interesting.[23] Not only does he fail to find in her desire any sign of the will of God but he speaks of indications to the contrary. What did he mean? He was probably reluctant to see her take valuable time from her visits to the Confraternities of Charity. The poor served by them were perhaps the "more people" to whom he was referring in this letter. However, there appears to be something more. He speaks to her of the necessity of acquiring tranquility of heart. Without this, she cannot hope to be "fit and ready" to devote herself entirely to serve Christ in the poor and to form his new servants.

Guided by a saint over the years, Louise had gradually discovered the paternal love of God for her. Peace and confidence had quieted her agitated soul. As she spent her energies in serving the poor, she had come to realize, that, despite her weaknesses and complexes, she was called to bring the love of the Father to others.

Nevertheless, a point remained that prevented any long-term calm and threatened to block her ascent to the level of holiness to which she was drawn. This was her love for her son. Concern for him, which circumstances often justified, would plague all her life. Moreover, Louise de Marillac was a worrier. She did not so much cease to worry with the passage of time as to change the focus of her anxiety away from herself and, most importantly, to control it so that it no longer debilitated her. During the period prior to the founding of the Daughters of Charity, at least with regard to Michel, such was not the case.

Twenty-six letters from Vincent to Louise that deal with Michel Le Gras remain from this time. From them we learn that Vincent was supportive and helpful. Moreover, he also befriended the boy, welcomed him at Saint-Lazare, prevented him from being overly bled and purged, and, above all, saved him from studies for the priesthood, for which he had no calling. Though he sought to calm Louise's anxieties concerning Michel, he nonetheless chided her, sometimes humorously, sometimes seriously, for her inability to keep matters in perspective. And so he asked her to wait, while at the same time he continued his encouragement and sought to discern the will of God. It becomes increasingly evident, from his letters to her, that Vincent was aware that God was asking more of her.

WORKS OF THE DAUGHTERS OF CHARITY, 1633–1660

At Pentecost 1633 the discernment process seemed to be drawing to a close. Vincent wrote to Louise to tell her that a period of intensive prayer was called for concerning her future "employment."[24] In August he made his annual retreat, during which he sought light from God. Following it, he communicated his thoughts quite simply to Louise and promised that they would meet in a few days to make "a firm decision about the girls."[25]

Vincent was at last confident that God clearly wanted Louise to undertake the formation of the girls. The potentially paralyzing effects of her "excessive affection" for her son, which had, as Vincent thought, prevented her "from doing the will of God in other matters," had been brought within the bounds of reason.[26] The promised meeting took place. God had spoken to their listening hearts. On 29 November 1633, with Vincent de Paul's full approval, Louise de Marillac was at last free to consecrate herself and all her energies to the new undertaking. The founding of the Company of the Daughters of Charity, and Louise's later vow to dedicate herself entirely to its development and works, marks another turning point in her spiritual journey.

In 1645, when Vincent de Paul petitioned the archbishop of Paris, Jean-François de Gondi, to approve the young community, he wrote: "Works pertaining to the service of God come to an end ordinarily with those who begin them, if there is no spiritual bond among the persons involved in them."[27] With the guidance and support of Vincent, it had devolved on Louise de Marillac to create and sustain this spiritual bond among the young women. Vincent de Paul's conferences to the Daughters of Charity provided a rich source of spiritual formation for the infant community, but it must be remarked that there remain only 120 of them (although others may not have been preserved), covering a period of twenty-six years. Moreover, fifty-five of them are from the last five years of Vincent's life, 1655–1660. The spiritual as well as the professional formation of the sisters was, therefore, largely the task of Louise de Marillac. Other responsibilities certainly prevented Vincent from more direct involvement with what must surely have been his most consoling undertaking. Perhaps he also felt that the time had come for Louise to plumb the depths of her own spiritual resources and to employ them for the formation of others.

The form of consecrated life begun by Vincent and Louise with the Daughters of Charity has become the norm for most religious congregations. Though cloistered orders are alive and well, most religious women today live their lives in active apostolic communities. Such was not the case in the France of 1633. Francis de Sales had tried such an experiment earlier but it was not long before the Visitation nuns found themselves behind cloister walls. Vincent de Paul was well aware of the pitfalls of this singular sort of undertaking because he had succeeded Francis as superior of the Visitation in Paris. He and Louise, however, had few models of what to do. In this light, one can appreciate better the challenge presented by this radical break with tradition. The first Daughters of Charity, mostly peasant women, would transcend the strict class barriers of the day to work closely with the upper-class Ladies of Charity in their service of the poor. Moreover, excluded by lack of wealth and education from religious orders, they could enter into a new form of consecrated life calling them to unite contemplation and action. It had taken Louise de Marillac many years and much struggle to achieve that balance in her own life. She would now set about forming, both professionally and spiritually, "the good country girls" who came to her.[28]

At first the scope of apostolic activity of the Daughters of Charity was limited to the Confraternities of Charity of the Paris area. Beginning with Marguerite Naseau in the parish of Saint-Savior, the Daughters of Charity were soon found working under the direction of the Ladies of Charity in many other parishes of the capital. The Parisian Ladies of Charity were unlike the women of the Confraternities of Charity visited by Louise in the French provinces, in that they generally came from the nobility and the rich bourgeoisie. Their social position, it is true, provided them with great financial resources, but it also frequently limited their availability and occasionally their willingness for direct service. Thus Louise began to train the first Daughters of Charity to prepare the food and medicine, which, in collaboration with the Ladies and under their supervision, they would bring to the sick poor in their homes.

As the work spread, so did the reputation for quality service of the young women trained by Louise. Vincent would rejoice that "there are so many requests for them from everywhere" and, indeed, there soon would be.[29] First, on the instance of the powerful Genevieve Fayet, Madame Goussault, they assisted perhaps the most influential group of the Ladies of Charity in bringing food and spiritual comfort to the sick of Paris's oldest and largest hospital, the Hôtel-Dieu. The work undertaken by the Daughters there was one of collaboration. Soon they would be called on to take complete charge of hospitals around Paris and in the provinces. The first of these was the hospital of Saint-Jean in Angers in 1639.

Again, it was Madame Goussault who urged Vincent and Louise to accept responsibility for the work. She had a residence at Bourgneuf, a few miles from Angers, and she was fully aware of the plight of the sick poor—there were some two hundred—hospitalized there and "deprived of all care."[30] Finally the Daughters acquiesced. In January 1639, Louise herself accompanied the first three sisters on what, in those days, was a long and arduous journey. She remained a month negotiating with city officials and the administrators of the hospital, organizing the care of the sick and the running of the hospital, and setting up a simple residence for the sisters.

The "Rule for the Sisters of the Hospital of Angers,"[31] as well as subsequent rules for sisters employed in hospitals found in her writings, reveal her extraordinary organizational ability. She considered all aspects of care: food, medicine, maintenance of the sick room, dealings with doctors and employees as well as administrators and the Ladies of Charity. However, she also defined the spiritual dimension of service to the sick and the qualities with which they were to be served. So, too, she set down rules for the life of the sisters together and their relationship with God. The hospital at Angers is, consequently, the prototype of the care of the sick by active religious women. In many respects, it remains a model to be emulated, despite the evolution of health care.

Other hospitals would follow this one—Le Mans, Nantes, Fontainebleau, and Saint-Denis. Not all of them were successful, but Louise was able to inculcate in the sisters an esteem for their vocation and an awareness, as Vincent told them, of "the happiness which you have of being . . . engaged in assisting the poor,"[32] in whom the sisters "served Jesus Christ."[33] Everywhere their love and the training Louise had given them enabled them to bring care of high quality as well as a deep concern and respect for each sick person.

Meanwhile, as the numbers of the sisters increased, Louise began to look beyond the limits of the Confraternities of Charity of Paris toward the provinces. The beginnings were small. In 1637 Louise sent two sisters to Richelieu to visit the sick and to undertake the work she had initiated during her visits to the Confraternities of Charity, namely the instruction of poor little girls.

As the work of the hospitals and parishes of the provinces grew, another form of poverty was calling for the attention of Louise and the Daughters in Paris: the foundlings. The work of providing shelter for abandoned children was not new. La Couche, a house run by a woman and her two servants, had been accepting them for some time. However, as Vincent would attest to the Ladies of Charity in 1649, in a period of over fifty years not one child had survived.[34] Shocked by the horrors they had heard concerning the abuse of the infants at La Couche, Vincent, Louise, the Daughters of Charity, and the Ladies of Charity undertook the work of aiding them. Here, also, the beginnings were small. In 1636, Louise took two or three infants into the mother house. By 1640, the Ladies of Charity voted to commit to her and her sisters the responsibility for all the foundlings of Paris. Despite all the financial problems, the sisters of the young community showed great creativity in caring for these children. Faced with the ever-growing number of infants, Louise de Marillac had to create a whole new method of child care. Her response was to establish, for the first time in France, a program of foster care. There were other initiatives besides. In 1645 the weaned children were placed at Bicêtre, where Louise took great care to be certain that the schoolrooms were properly equipped and that the children were taught a trade. As for the newborns, an infant home, the first in France, was built in 1645 to improve their care. Until the end of their lives Vincent de Paul and Louise de Marillac would seek, along with their Daughters and the Ladies of Charity, to provide, despite nearly insurmountable obstacles, better service for these children whose souls a sister referred to in a conference as "roses," redeemed by the death of the Son of God.[35]

At the same period, another call—less appealing, but equally poignant—arose: the cry of the galley convicts. The royal prisons were like something from Dante's *Inferno*. No one knew this better than Vincent de Paul, who had been named Royal Chaplain of the Galleys in 1619. He had made an initial attempt to alleviate their miseries in 1622 by renting a house in Paris for a few of the prisoners. In 1632 he took over an abandoned building near the Porte Saint Bernard to shelter more of them. As funds were needed, he turned to Louise de Marillac. She was president at the time of the Ladies of Charity in the parish of Saint-Nicolas-du-Chardonnet. Since the shelter was located within her parish, Louise was able to interest the other members in the work. Their efforts were soon well known. In 1639 a wealthy banker left Vincent 60,000 livres to be used in the assistance of the prisoners. This permitted the Daughters of Charity to undertake their humble service: cleaning, washing, and cooking. Every day they brought food to the cells of the prisoners awaiting transfer to the galleys in Marseilles. It was arduous and the sisters often suffered physical and verbal abuse. The story of Sister Barbe Angiboust was well known. A prisoner had thrown soup and shouted obscenities at her, but the patience, gentleness, and respect with which she treated him and others served as a model for her companions. Indeed nothing seems to have dampened the zeal of these young country girls who went about trying to bring some comfort to those condemned to this antechamber of hell.

War, both civil and foreign, would open up yet another area of service for the Daughters of Charity. New cries of anguish touched the hearts of Vincent and Louise. They sent sisters to nurse the wounded on the battlefields of Châlons, Etampes, Sedan, Arras, Calais, and Metz. Some of them died there. Then, in 1650, the horrors of civil war, known as the Fronde, overtook France. Vincent and his sons, both priests and brothers, undertook almost immediate relief efforts for the refugees. The task was so enormous, however, that Vincent soon asked Louise for the help of sisters to be sent to care for the sick, the orphans, and the abandoned elderly. They also ran soup kitchens and distributed clothing. Despite the danger from plundering and rampaging armies, and from disease and famine, the sisters quietly and courageously reached out to the victims. This, too, would cost the lives of some of Louise's Daughters.

The Fronde finally ceased but the miseries of war continued. During the political struggles of 1652, soldiers pillaged the countryside. The population of entire villages fled to Paris, where there were already 100,000 beggars. Famine became a permanent condition. In the parish of Saint-Paul the sisters fed 8,000 poor people each day. At the mother house 1,300 poor were assisted.

In the outskirts of Paris, too, death and destruction ran rampant. In response, Vincent, Louise, and the sisters organized a charitable warehouse where they accepted gifts of money and goods. All the trade guilds of the city provided what they could for it. The sisters accepted everything. Also, they prepared packages to send to relief centers closer to the war-torn areas. Medical teams composed of a doctor and two sister nurses went to care for the sick and wounded in what remained of their homes. It is reported that this collective effort saved 193 villages.

In the work with the foundlings, Louise de Marillac had discovered misery in an institution that totally lacked the means to respond to the goals for which it had been created. She therefore reorganized the work, removed the children from La Couche, and placed them in a more appropriate setting. At the Hôtel-Dieu, too, she and her sisters had worked, along with the Ladies of Charity, as volunteers in an institution that, while good in itself, had failed to evolve with the times. The lessons they learned there would form the base for the health care they brought to the sick in the hospitals they would administer throughout France. The work with the aged at the Hospice of the Holy Name of Jesus, on the other hand, would be a completely new creation for Louise.

With funds given him by a wealthy and anonymous benefactor, Vincent purchased two houses "to receive forty poor persons in the hospital, twenty men and twenty women, whom he housed and fed."[36] These poor were not professional beggars, of which there were thousands in Paris, but rather elderly artisans. Lacking pensions or social security, they had been reduced by age and infirmity to destitution.

Louise de Marillac received full responsibility for organizing the work, as well as for providing sisters to serve the aged. She gave herself wholeheartedly to the task, striving to meet the bodily and spiritual needs of the residents in a pleasant, productive atmosphere. The documents we possess reveal Louise's organizational skill as well as her deep respect for each person. They also show her creativity, since she incorporated concepts that foreshadowed modern occupational therapy. For example, she reached out into the community to bring in craftsmen to set up workrooms. There the residents could be employed at tasks in keeping with their diminishing strength but still interesting and profitable. Although the institution provided for all their needs, they were allowed to keep a quarter of what they earned from their work for personal spending. This was a small sum, surely, but it enabled the elderly to retain the dignity of former days as well as a feeling of usefulness and independence. The work of the hospice never reached a large scale nor served many residents. Louise had deliberately decided that it should be as homelike as possible. Thanks to her creative genius, this hospice provides us with a prototype for the ever-expanding needs for care of the elderly.

In 1629, when Louise began to visit the Confraternities of Charity in the French provinces, she turned her attention beyond the visiting of the sick poor in their homes to the needs of young country girls. With no opportunity for schooling, their future seemed devoid of any possibility of escaping poverty. Moved by their plight, Louise tried to help them by giving pedagogical hints to the village school mistress, or where there was none, by remaining long enough to train someone for this role.

After 1633, when more young women joined Louise, she did not forget the little country girls. So it was that she sent the sisters, usually two by two, to distant towns to care for the sick and to teach young girls. In 1641, she turned her attention toward poor girls in Paris and petitioned the rector of the cathedral of Notre-Dame-de-Paris to authorize a school for them at the mother house. He granted her petition on 21 May 1641. The date marks the foundation of free elementary schools in the archdiocese of Paris.

Louise's great flexibility in adapting to local needs was the key to her success. Moreover, she sought to educate the whole person. Religious instruction was central to education, but it was not a sterile recitation of questions and answers. Her instruction offered a means for understanding life and one's relationship with God. Louise also integrated secular subjects with personal growth. The children were taught to read, to write, and to do basic arithmetic. They were also taught a trade such as lace making. For Louise, it was important to provide these young girls with a means for earning an honest living.

The sisters themselves, many of whom had little formal instruction, had first to be trained as teachers. Louise de Marillac undertook this responsibility, too, although other sisters would in time replace her. While she made no attempt to replicate the education she had received at Poissy, she did provide the sisters with both content and methodology. Moreover, she instilled in them the gentleness, respect, and availability they were to bring to this work. Historians are just beginning to recognize the great contribution of Louise de Marillac and the Daughters of Charity to the education of women in seventeenth-century France.[37]

As one examines the charitable activities of Louise de Marillac and the early Daughters of Charity, one is struck by their scope. Together with the Ladies of Charity, many of whom were Louise's personal friends, the Daughters became the hands of Providence for the poor in their homes and in hospitals, schools, orphanages, institutions for the elderly and for the mentally ill, in prisons, and on the battlefield. It would be difficult to find a group in need excluded from the charitable endeavors of Vincent, Louise, and the women with whom they shared their vision of the service of Christ in the poor. More striking yet is the realization that, prior to the deaths of Louise and Vincent in 1660, at no time did the Daughters of Charity number more than 200. Nevertheless, they transformed the character of Christian charity, thanks, in large measure, to the formation they received from their foundress and superior, Louise de Marillac.

Spirituality of Louise de Marillac

When reflecting on the extraordinary accomplishments of Vincent, Louise, and their Daughters, it is easy to be dazzled by the extent to which they discovered and alleviated the misery of the poor and, consequently, to lose sight of the unifying force behind it all: the vision of Jesus Christ suffering in the poor whom they served.

In his work on community, Thomas Dubay says that community is not built. Rather it happens as the result of two factors: a common vision and the burning pursuit of that vision.[38] It was the vision of Christ in the poor that had brought Vincent and Louise to collaborate in the Confraternities of Charity and later to found and work together for the Daughters of Charity. Let us now examine that vision as Louise de Marillac lived it and transmitted it to her spiritual daughters.

The centrality of Jesus crucified in Louise's spiritual evolution is evident from her earliest writings. Life had taught her that her vocation was to unite herself to Jesus on the cross. A text in her *Spiritual Writings*, dating from the period prior to 1633, is revealing. She wrote, "God, who has granted me so many graces, led me to understand that it was His holy will that I go to Him by way of the cross. His goodness chose to mark me with it from my birth and He has hardly ever left me, at any age, without some occasion for suffering."[39]

In 1643, when Louise began using the seal that would become the seal of the Company, it bore the image of a burning heart and

Jesus crucified surrounded by the words of Saint Paul as she had modified them, "The Charity of Jesus *crucified* urges us."[40] Late in her life, in a conference to the sisters entitled "On the Pure Love We Have Vowed to God,"[41] she urged her Daughters to respond unreservedly to the call of Christ on the cross, which they are to choose as their cloister and where they are to sacrifice everything that might prevent them from loving him with a pure love. Later in the same conference, Louise acknowledged that she had received a new light concerning the uncommon love Jesus wished to receive from those whom he had chosen to exercise the purity of his love on earth. She asked if she and the sisters could dare to hope for such a thing.

At this juncture, Louise de Marillac was, indeed, daring to call the good country girls of the company to the life of contemplation, which had previously been reserved to wealthy, educated religious. For Louise, it was the contemplation of Christ himself, who was to be their rule, their model, and the only object of their love. She urged her companions not to fear because God was asking all of them. As she had tried to do, they too would find comfort and strength at the foot of the cross.

If Louise de Marillac sought to fix the eyes of her Daughters on the suffering of Christ as the one whom they served in the poor, she also presented to them the entire life of Christ, "the source and model of all charity,"[42] as the example for the life of the true servant of the poor.

Louise's prayers and meditations followed the rhythm of the liturgical year. At each season she entered into what the Vincentian scholar André Dodin called "the mysterious adventure of the Incarnate Word."[43] During her advent retreats she reflected on the birth of Christ and the lessons of the crib. There she discovered love, simplicity, and humility—values she would later present as the fundamental virtues of the Daughters of Charity. The Christmas before her death, she would once again remind the sisters of the wisdom contained in this mystery. She assured them that from the example of the infancy of Jesus they would obtain all that they needed "to become true Christians and perfect Daughters of Charity."[44]

Meditation on the Incarnate Word led Louise de Marillac quite naturally to Mary, his mother, to whom she would consecrate the "Little Company," and whom she would designate in her spiritual

58

testament as its "only Mother."[45] We find Mary, in Louise de Marillac's writings, as the Mother of God, intimately united to her son in the accomplishment of the divine plan. Moreover, Louise's reflections on the role of Mary in the Redemption caused her to see, well before any definition of the dogma, the significance of the Immaculate Conception. Every aspect of Mary's life became a subject of prayer for Louise. She wished her spiritual daughters to turn daily to the Blessed Virgin. She asked them to recite the rosary while meditating on a single mystery and hailing Mary as "Daughter of the Father, Mother of the Son, and the Spouse of the Holy Spirit."[46]

Let us return now to Louise de Marillac's reflection on the life of Christ as the model of the life of a Daughter of Charity. From this perspective, the hidden life in Nazareth held special importance for her. In Jesus, the carpenter's son, the sisters could find the strength and courage to continue in their often humble tasks, knowing that, as he did, they were fulfilling the divine plan. With the coming of Lent, Louise de Marillac's prayer centered on the mystery of the Redemption. It was this aspect of the life of Christ, the suffering servant, that was, for her, the essence of the vocation of the Daughters of Charity. By their lives, they were called on "to honor His human life on earth."[47]

In Louise de Marillac's *Spiritual Writings*, we find the blueprint she offered her sisters, who were striving to learn from the example of Christ to be the servants of their "lords and masters," the poor. As Father Richard McCullen, C.M., Superior General of the Congregation of the Mission and the Daughters of Charity, put it in his preface to the 1991 edition of the writings, we often find in her letters "the deepest insight into the workings of [her] mind and heart" as well as a revelation of "the nobility of her soul."[48] The 377 remaining letters sent to the first sisters show the transformation of Louise's spirituality. A spirituality of the "we" gradually replaced the spirituality of the "I," of a God-and-I relationship, although it reached out to the poor. Jean Calvet, Louise's biographer, will speak of a "mysticism of the group."[49] It would be together that the aristocratic Louise and the "good country girls" would move toward union with God.

Few things show better than Louise de Marillac's letters the blending of the divine and the human, the supernatural and the practical, the contemplative and the active, that was to characterize this new form of consecrated life. Although Louise's remaining correspondence is less voluminous than Vincent's, her letters—whether addressed to the sisters, to Vincent, to Guy Lasnier, the Abbé de Vaux, vicar general of diocese of Angers and spiritual director of the sisters of the hospital there, or to several priests of the Congregation of the Mission who served as confessors and spiritual directors for the sisters—deal almost exclusively with the development of the nascent community and her own spiritual evolution. Moreover, the mails were slow and unreliable, so Louise profited from the opportunity to write to the sisters to include remarks and reflections on all aspects of their lives. The vocation of the Daughter of Charity, her consecration by vow, her service to the poor, her life in community, the virtues of her state, are intertwined with news of the sisters' families, recipes for medicines, and advice on how to pack pears and tend animals, or to keep books. A mystic with her feet solidly planted on the ground, Louise de Marillac called her spiritual daughters to a similar mysticism.

What are the aspects of the life and person of Christ of which Louise most often spoke? First, the will of God. Just as Jesus had come to accomplish the will of the Father, so the Daughter of Charity must strive throughout her life to know and to carry out God's will for her. This preoccupation appears some eighty-two times in her letters. For example, a remarkable letter of March 1644 to the dying Sister Jeanne Dalmagne reechoes Louise's concern that the holy will of God be accomplished in her, in her sisters, and in the company. After touching words of affection and comfort, she asks Sister Jeanne, when finally united with her Beloved, to "remember the needs of the poor Company to which God had called [her]" and to become "an advocate for it before the Divine Goodness so He may accomplish His plans for it."[50]

The second aspect of the life of Jesus emphasized by Louise is his status as exemplar for the fundamental virtues of the Daughter of Charity: humility, simplicity, and charity. Louise proposed to the sisters a supernatural humility leading to gentleness, respect, condescension, and forbearance. She warned them, too, of the consequences of a lack of such virtues. In a letter to Sister Madeleine, dated 27 June 1645, she went so far as to say that unless they strove to grow in these qualities, the work to which they were devoting themselves in the service of the poor would be "almost useless to them."[51]

The next of the true, solid, and essential virtues that Louise recommended repeatedly was simplicity. Frequently mentioned in conjunction with humility, simplicity was to be the hallmark of the Daughter of Charity, touching every aspect of her life: her relationship with God, with her superiors, with her companions, with the rich and with the poor. It was the means to preserve the primitive spirit of the company. A text in the "Thoughts" portion of her *Spiritual Writings*, written only weeks before her death on 15 March 1660, shows how strongly she felt about simplicity. The dying foundress reminded the sisters that the company "must never depart from . . . its poor manner of life." Should they find themselves with more than they needed to live in this way, they were to go to serve the poor "at their own expense." She then concluded, coupling humility and simplicity, "If this passes unnoticed, what does it matter, so long as our souls honor eternally the Redemption of Our Lord."[52]

The fire in the tone of this dying woman reveals an aspect of Louise de Marillac's character with which she had to struggle all her life. Since she spoke so often of gentleness and required "gentle persuasion" as an essential attribute of a superior, it was clear that she knew that she had a sharp tongue.[53] In her retreat of 1628 she resolved to combat her "frequent outbursts of impatience" and to acquire "gentleness" toward others.[54]

In her humility, Louise admitted this failing and asked the sisters to pray for her. As late as 1645 she acknowledged that she was still struggling against "deeply rooted habits" and needed their support and prayers.[55] The sisters did, indeed, know of her outbursts. The 1983 edition of her correspondence, which restored the original seventeenth-century French, shows flashes of it. For example, she warned Sisters Barbe and Louise in 1639 that their apostolic success had done nothing for their progress in virtue.[56] In a letter to Sister Andrée in Nantes in 1658 she cried out in exasperation, "For the love of God, learn to spell so that I can read your letters more easily."[57] She even occasionally chided Vincent, as when she told him in 1644, "You would recover more quickly from that cold if you went to bed earlier."[58]

If the sisters knew from experience that Louise could, at times, be harsh in her words, they were also keenly aware that she loved each of them individually and was deeply concerned about them and what was happening in their lives. As a child Louise de Marillac had been, as modern parlance would put it, disconnected. Her relationship with Vincent and with the first sisters, as well as with some of the Ladies of Charity, provided her with the connectedness she needed. The security flowing from this and from her ever-deepening relationship with God enabled her calmly and peacefully to deal with her own frailty. This in turn gave her the freedom to use her past experience to assist others. There can be no doubt that in the advice Louise gives her sisters in her letters she is drawing from her own sufferings and struggles and, as she told Sister Françoise Carcireux in 1656, "repeating . . . what [she] was told long ago."[59]

In this same letter we find echoes of the early letters of Vincent to Louise as she tells Sister Françoise that she cannot reach perfection by her own efforts and how counterproductive it is to analyze her soul and to be constantly seeking spiritual direction. Vincent de Paul's wise, patient, and loving spiritual accompaniment had borne fruit. Louise de Marillac was then able to accompany others in the same way along the journey toward union with God. The mysticism of the group was becoming a reality. Louise describes it in the conclusion of her letter to Sister Françoise, "I beg you . . . to help me by your prayers, as I will help you by mine, so that we may obtain from God the grace to walk simply and confidently along the path of His holy love."[60]

With humility and simplicity, Louise de Marillac was ready to enter the last phase of her spiritual journey, the stage given over completely to the third and most important virtue for the Daughter of Charity: love. The love of Jesus Christ crucified urged her on toward the love for total abandonment which is union with God. As love had become the driving force of Louise de Marillac's life, so she wanted it to be for all her Daughters. Over and over she urges them to be immersed in God in whose love they would "find nothing difficult."[61] The love to which Louise and the sisters were called was to be nourished by the qualities described by Saint Paul in 1 Corinthians 13. Calls to patience, kindness, humility, forgiveness, honesty, trust, and hope abound in her writings.

In addition to loving God, the sisters must also strive to love one another. Louise repeated this in season and out. While she recognized that this could be difficult at times, that it must always respect the individual, and that it often called for great virtue, she never tired of reminding them that it was this love they were called to and that without it the company could not endure. To explain this ideal of love to her Daughters, Louise chose, on numerous occasions, one of the principal themes of her prayer life: the image of the Blessed Trinity. But, as was her way, she led the sisters to concrete ways in which they could strive to image among themselves the unity of the Triune God. She urged them to remain united by "deferring to one another" and "by acquiescing, as far as possible to one another's opinions."[62]

The feast of Pentecost, celebrating the coming of the spirit of love into the Church and the world, also held special meaning for Louise de Marillac. To prepare herself for the coming of the Holy Spirit into her heart, she made a retreat each year between Ascension and Pentecost. The feast also reminded her of the special graces she had received on previous Pentecosts. On Pentecost Sunday, 4 June 1623, she received the Light that revealed her vocation to her. On the eve of Pentecost 1642, a ceiling in the mother house suddenly collapsed. There were no casualties. As in 1623, that feast of Pentecost marked a turning point in Louise de Marillac's spiritual journey toward union with God. She saw in the accident a sign of God's special protection for the company, but she also saw it as a call to her to sacrifice everything, to abandon everything to him, to make him "the unique object of all [her] affections."[63] The end was still a long way off. Much work, much growth was yet to come, but little by little she was detaching herself from all that was not God. In a letter to Sister Mathurine Guérin of 3 March 1660, in which Vincent de Paul informs her of the approaching death of Louise de Marillac, he writes, "Certainly it is the great secret of the spiritual life to abandon to [God] all that we love by abandoning ourselves to all that He wills."[64] It would be a wrenching separation for these friends of thirty-six years. But their friendship had freed and enriched both of them as well as bringing countless blessings on their spiritual children, their collaborators, and the poor. It was indeed charismatic, a gift of God to his Church.

Louise de Marillac is at last emerging from the shadows where she has remained hidden for over three centuries. The image of her now forming is one of a woman who transformed adversity into positive energy for the service of the poor, who used her deep, personal spirituality to grow in union with God and to form the first Daughters of Charity. Her writings present a new vision of Louise de Marillac, the woman, the foundress, the organizer, and the saint. As such, they speak across the centuries with a call to men and women alike to give themselves in love to God, to the poor, and to one another. Her message is, finally, being heard.[65]

The Legacy Unfolds

VIE THORGREN
AND FRANCES RYAN, D.C.[1]

INTRODUCTION

*I*n their passing, Vincent and Louise left an organic legacy of charity, a living reality received by others to creatively nurture and bring to fruition. The descendants of Vincent and Louise now comprise a global family including men and women in various communities and societies both religious and lay. Developing a genealogy of those groups that in some way trace their origins to the vision of Vincent and Louise is monumental. Because of their number and complexity, it may never be completed.

We can recognize, however, the further unfolding of their legacy in two of the many branches of the Vincentian family. The first branch, born of the inspiration of Saint Elizabeth Ann Seton, is credited with the development of Catholic parochial education and progressive health care in the United States. The second branch, a new lay society, resulted from the collaboration in France of Sister Rosalie Rendu, Daughter of Charity, and Frederick Ozanam.

ELIZABETH ANN SETON (1774–1821)

One branch of the Vincentian family took root in North American soil as a result of the life of Elizabeth Ann Seton, the first native-born saint in the United States.[2] Born in New York on 28 August 1774 to Richard and Catherine Bayley, she had much in common with Louise de Marillac. Like Louise, Elizabeth knew a mother-wound, as Catherine Bayley died 8 May 1777. The depth of the lifelong void experienced by Elizabeth is reflected in the

65

earliest memory she recorded in "Dear Remembrances," written in 1812. It concerns the death of her baby sister, Catherine, in October 1778, when Elizabeth was four years of age. "Sitting alone on a step of the door looking at the clouds, while my little sister Catherine, two years old, lay in her coffin; they asked me: Did I not cry when little Kitty was dead? No, because Kitty is gone up to heaven. I wish I could go too with Mama."[3]

Elizabeth adored her father, a respected physician, but, as with Louise, her father's marriage to Charlotte Amelia Barclay in 1778 left her outside the embrace of the complete affection she desired. Like Louise, Elizabeth spent a significant period of her childhood in the care of others. In her early years, too, she showed concern for the sick and the poor, and ministered to them with great compassion. Also like Louise, she was a wife, a mother, a widow, a single parent, and the foundress of a community of women who adapted the Rule of the Daughters of Charity. Elizabeth's adult life was marked by the same suffering over her husband's financial losses, illness, and early death, and maternal anxiety for her children's future.

During the final stage of her husband's illness, she accompanied him on a trip to Italy in a desperate attempt to prolong his life. Though her oldest daughter, Anna, accompanied them, this trip required leaving four of her children, the youngest only one year old, in the care of relatives in New York.[4] Ravaged by tuberculosis, the family disease, William Seton died shortly after their arrival in Livorno (Leghorn), Italy, on 27 December 1803.[5]

Their hosts in Livorno, the prosperous Filicchi family, became an important source of comfort and stability for Elizabeth and were instrumental in her later conversion to Roman Catholicism. Following her return to the United States, Elizabeth knew the sting of rejection by her Episcopal friends and extended family as a result of her conversion. During her lifetime, she also suffered the loss of her daughters Anna[6] and Rebecca.[7]

Through her relationship with Bishop John Carroll of Baltimore, and others, Elizabeth was invited to form a community of women religious. Father Samuel Cooper gave $10,000 toward its establishment, provided that the foundation be at Emmitsburg, Maryland. Elizabeth, appointed superior, made her first vows on 25 March 1809. The name of the community was the Sisters of Saint

Joseph.[8] During the years of growth at Emmitsburg, Mother Seton laid the foundation of the American Catholic school system. She trained teachers and prepared teaching materials, often translating books from French. In the Vincentian tradition, she also visited the sick poor in their homes.

Although suffering marked Elizabeth's life, her pain served to perfect her charity. Like Vincent and Louise, she discovered that humility paves the way for charity.[9] The love she extended to both critics and supporters did not depend on a loving response from them. She also absorbed the Vincentian lesson of not treading on the heels of Providence. Following her husband's death, when Elizabeth had to depend on the financial, emotional, and spiritual support of others, she frequently experienced time passing with excruciating slowness. Yet she was not disappointed. Through significant friendships, God provided for her return from Italy, for the important lifelines during her spiritual turmoil, and for the shelter and education of her children. During the early stages of the community she founded, Providence also led the way. In short, in all things Elizabeth Seton displayed the same commitment to God's will that had guided Vincent and Louise. She practiced daily her challenge to others to view "everything only in that one view *our God* and *our Eternity.*"[10]

God's will unfolded as she embraced an identification with the poor. Elizabeth knew that much of the opposition to Catholicism was class prejudice. Most of New York's Catholics were poor immigrants with somewhat rough manners. Although she had previously moved with ease in important social circles, she nevertheless chose to seek her salvation among the economically and socially disadvantaged. A reflection from 1814 reveals clearly that she knew her name to be written on the heart of Jesus, friend of the poor:

> These two words—"the disciple whom Jesus loved" and "Who leaned on his breast at supper"—We—not on his breast but he on ours indeed—our life in him—wrapt in him—for us he put himself in agony. Ah for *me*— myself—for me every stroke of flagellation—for me every thorn—for me the spears and nails on Calvary—that spear passed thro' my very name written on his heart—O written even as the name of his very disciples and good

shepherds—now from his tabernacle here—to our very heart![11]

Mother Seton's community grew quickly. During her lifetime, the sisters expanded to Philadelphia and New York. In 1846, a group of the sisters working in New York City formed the Sisters of Charity of New York. From this branch came two others, the Sisters of Charity of Halifax (1856) and the Sisters of Charity of Saint Elizabeth, Convent Station, New Jersey (1859). After her death, a union of the Emmitsburg sisters with the French community of the Daughters of Charity of Saint Vincent de Paul came about in 1850. Partly as a result of this union, Emmitsburg sisters working in Cincinnati formed a separate community (1852), which later gave birth to the Mother Seton Sisters of Charity of Greensburg, Pennsylvania (1870). This is only a partial listing of the many communities that look to Elizabeth Seton for their inspiration. The contribution of women in these various communities to the shape of contemporary Catholic education, religious formation, social work, and health care is inestimable.

Elizabeth Seton died in Emmitsburg, 4 January 1821, at age 47. The cause for her sainthood moved forward for many years, and Pope Paul VI canonized her on 14 September 1975.

ROSALIE RENDU, D.C. (1786–1856)

Jeanne Marie Rendu was born at Confort, a hamlet in the Jura mountains, on 9 September 1786.[12] She was the oldest of four girls, daughters of Jean Antoine Rendu and Marie Anne Laracine. Her mother loved the poor and showed hospitality to those who visited the family's farm. At age ten, Jeanne Marie lost, in quick succession, both her father and her baby sister, and thus her young life was marked at its beginning with loss and grief.

During the revolution of 1789 and its aftermath, Jeanne Marie witnessed the dangers her family embraced to help priests. For example, during the Terror, May 1793 to July 1794, Joseph Marie Paget, the bishop of Geneva, sought the Rendus' protection. He took refuge in their home and became known to the seven-year-old as "Peter," the gardener.[13] Her parents also hid their pastor and several other priests, and secretly attended mass at the peril of their lives. At one of these secret masses, their pastor gave Jeanne Marie her first communion. From Jeanne Marie's early years, therefore, her mother had taught her to care for others. During the revolution of 1830, remembering her mother's example, she in her turn gave refuge in her house to the archbishop of Paris, Hyacinthe Louis de Quélen.

Jeanne Marie briefly attended boarding school with former Ursuline nuns in Gex, and then, eager to help the sick and suffering, lived and worked in the hospital near her school. There, she met Armande Jacquinot, a girl from her own parish. Mademoiselle Jacquinot spoke to Jeanne Marie of her plans to enter the Daughters of Charity, who staffed the hospital. Jeanne Marie also felt called, but her mother found it difficult to let her fifteen-year-old leave home to join the Daughters of Charity, fearing she would never see her again. Jeanne Marie's mother was to live as long as she did, dying 3 February 1856, just four days before her daughter. Nevertheless, because of the rule forbidding the Sisters from making family visits, Marie Anne Rendu and her daughter met only once again for a few weeks' visit in Paris after Jeanne Marie entered the community.

On 25 May 1802, the two young friends, Armande Jacquinot and Jeanne Marie Rendu, entered the seminary [novitiate] in Paris.[14] Jeanne Marie received the name Rosalie. After just a few months of her novitiate, the new Sister Rosalie became ill. To restore and preserve her health, those in charge decided to have her continue the seminary elsewhere. They placed her in the suburbs of Paris under the direction of Sister Marie Madeleine Tardy at the Daughters' house on rue des Francs-Bourgeois-Saint-Marcel (now Boulevard Saint Marcel) in the Mouffetard district. Rosalie was destined to stay in that increasingly poor and crowded district for the rest of her life, fifty-four years.

In 1805, the French government authorized the Daughters of Charity to resume wearing the habit after the community's dissolution during the revolution.[15] At that time, Sister Marie Madeleine requested the habit for Sister Rosalie from the superior general: "I am very pleased with this little Rendu. Give her the habit, and let me have her."[16] Sister Rosalie made her profession in 1807, and in 1815, at age twenty-nine, succeeded Sister Marie Madeleine as the

Sister Servant, the community's title for local superior given it by Vincent de Paul.

When Napoleon Bonaparte reorganized works of public assistance in France, the Mouffetard house of the Daughters of Charity was one of several in Paris financed by his government to help the poor. Among the earliest works of Rosalie's house were a dispensary, a free school for children, a workshop, and a depot for clothes and linen for the most indigent. Besides bringing the poor to the convent, the sisters also visited the sick and the poor in their homes. As Sister Servant, Rosalie managed these growing works for the poor.

Another work, begun around 1840, sought to help poor young girls. Employed as apprentices in workshops and by dressmakers during the week, these girls would spend their holidays and weekends with the Sisters because they had no other suitable place to gather. The development of this work demonstrates Rosalie's ability to involve the poor in creating a community. It was so successful that it was imitated widely in Paris.

Sister Rosalie also provided for the graduates of the apprentices' association. She established for them the Association of Our Lady of Good Counsel, a society devoted to the care of the poor. Women who as girls had imbibed of Rosalie's love for the poor and outcast were thus able to continue in their adult years to reflect and pray while serving the poor. For example, some would read to a blind or old person, some would take meals to the sick, and others would mend and wash the clothes of poor elderly women. After the evening meal, members would then give and receive praise and encouragement from Sister Rosalie and the other members of their association. Besides these works, she also founded a workshop, an orphanage, and a home for the aged.

The following is typical of Sister Rosalie's advice: "A poor person is more touched by kindness than by material help. One of the best means of influencing them is to show them consideration. If you wish to be loved, you must love and if you have nothing to give, give yourself."[17]

In keeping with the Vincentian charism of active contemplation in the world, Rosalie generously shared with other established groups her experience of serving the poor. She worked with priests and seminarians, the Ladies of Charity, and religious communities, such as the Little Sisters of the Poor, the Augustinian Ladies of the Sacred Heart, and the Sisters of Our Lady of Zion. She is best known, however, for her guidance of Frederick Ozanam and the Society of Saint Vincent de Paul. Besides helping its first members to visit the poor in their homes, she often gave Ozanam practical advice on how to handle the difficult cases he and the society encountered. She helped him appreciate the life and work of their mutual patron, Saint Vincent de Paul, and continued her mentoring of the society until her death.

She also responded to calamities. During the revolution of 1830, as noted above, she gave asylum to the archbishop as well as to many other priests. During the cholera epidemic of 1832, she quickly gathered orphan children and had her Sisters care for them, thus beginning an orphanage.[18] By 1838, the Sisters' soup kitchen was providing some 2,000 poor with a daily ration. Expenses never seemed to worry Sister Rosalie as, indeed, she saw the open hand of Providence securing what was needed for God's poor.

During the revolution of 1848, her relationship with the poor inhabitants of the Mouffetard district was such that she was able to put an end to the bloodshed. Like another hero, Archbishop Denis Auguste Affre of Paris, killed by a bullet from the height of the barricades when he sought to end the revolutionaries' violence, Sister Rosalie fearlessly climbed to the top of the barricades in her district and addressed the crowd: "Do you think that I want to go on living when my children are being slaughtered? Stop this shooting! Haven't I enough widows and orphans to care for? Do you want to give me more?" Though the fighting continued elsewhere in the city, the struggle ceased there.[19] In 1852, to acknowledge her years of dedication, Emperor Napoleon III bestowed on Sister Rosalie the cross of the Legion of Honor. Seeing that she did not wear it, he sent, in 1854, a gold cross he hoped should would wear, since it contained relics of Saint Vincent de Paul.

Rosalie Rendu gradually lost her sight and contracted other illnesses. She died 7 February 1856, at age seventy, from the effects of pleurisy. She had given fifty-four years of her life to the care of the poor. Some 30,000 poor working persons crowded the streets of the quarter for her funeral and burial processions. Her gravestone reads: "To good mother ROSALIE [from] Her Grateful Friends, the Poor and the Rich."[20]

Veneration for her continues. The city of Paris named a street in the Mouffetard district after her. In 1936, a prayer was authorized for the beatification of this servant of the poor. In February 1951, the Daughters of Charity asked the archbishop of Paris, Cardinal Maurice Feltin, to begin the process for her canonization. An official study of her virtues and reputation for holiness, presented in March 1993 to the Congregation for the Causes of the Saints, continues the process for canonization of Sister Rosalie Rendu, Daughter of Charity.

Frederick Ozanam (1813–1853)

Antoine Frédéric Ozanam was born 23 April 1813 in Milan, Italy, the fifth of fourteen children born to Marie Nantas and Jean Antoine Ozanam.[21] His parents, French with Jewish heritage, both had great devotion to the poor. Jean Antoine, a physician, treated a third of his patients free of charge, while Marie, a nurse, visited the sick in their homes. On one occasion, they are reported to have surprised each other at the bedside of the same sick woman. They remained in Milan until after Napoleon's defeat when the Austrians regained control of city after the treaties of 1815. At that time, the Ozanams moved back to their native city of Lyons.

Amid financial difficulties, the Ozanam family experienced loss and grief in the deaths of eleven of their fourteen children. Of their three surviving children, Frederick contracted typhoid fever at age six, and endured frail health throughout his life. He felt intensely the loss of his many brothers and sisters, particularly his favorite, Elisa, age nineteen, who died when he was seven years old. He wrote:

On many occasions have I not seen my parents in tears; when Heaven had left them, but three children out of fourteen! But how often, too, have not those three survivors, in adversity and in trial, counted on the assistance of those brothers and sisters whom they had among the angels! Such are indeed also of the family, and are brought back to our minds in acts of unexpected assistance. Happy is the home that can count one half of its members in Heaven, to help the rest along the narrow way which leads there![22]

Frederick spent two years of rigorous classical studies in Lyons, 1828–1830, under the mentorship of Joseph Mathias Noirot, a priest and professor of philosophy. Noirot helped his young student through a crisis of religious doubt. Although this experience made Frederick determined to support the Church, he always appreciated the struggles of others. Following his father's wishes, Frederick moved to Paris in 1831 to begin his study of law at the Sorbonne. His father noted in his diary: "[Frederick] has refined, pure and noble sentiments; he will make an upright and enlightened judge. I venture to hope that he will be our consolation in our old age."[23]

During his student days at the Sorbonne, Frederick faced another crisis as he encountered antireligious sentiments in professors and fellow students. Strengthened by his growing friendship with Catholic leaders, Ozanam countered by helping to organize the first of the renowed Lenten conferences at the cathedral, Notre Dame de Paris, to affirm and defend the Catholic faith. In this way, Frederick took his place among the leaders of the Catholic revival in France.

At the same time, a greater challenge arose: to put the revived faith into practice. The Saint-Simonians had been gaining supporters at the university. These espoused a doctrine similar to a pantheistic socialism, derived from the writings of Claude Henri de Rouvroy, count of Saint-Simon. One of them, Jean Broet, belonged with Frederick to the Conference of History, a debating society. At one of its meetings, Broet challenged the Catholic members of the conference to put their historical theories into practice by working for the poor and oppressed as the Saint-Simonians were advocating for their own followers. Stung by the charge, Frederick recognized that the works of the Catholic members of the conference, while laudable, were often individual and unorganized, and that they should go to the poor.

For guidance in doing so, Ozanam turned to one of the foremost Catholic laymen of his time, J. Emmanuel Bailly. Besides being a professor of philosophy, director of the *Tribune Catholique*, and founder of the Conference of History, Bailly had developed a love for Saint Vincent de Paul. His family maintained a strong devotion to the saint and worked with the poor. Emmanuel's father, for example, treasured the large collection of manuscripts belonging to Vincent de Paul placed in his keeping during the revolution of 1789. His uncle was a Vincentian priest, and Emmanuel's son was named Vincent de Paul.[24] Bailly's wife, who shared Emmanuel's devotion to the poor, had undertaken, with a friend, visiting the poor of Sister Rosalie Rendu. Discouraged in the work by the reception she encountered, she agreed with her husband that "it was not women's work. Men, and young men, were wanted for it."[25]

Such young men, members of Bailly's Conference of History, were Félix Clavé, Jules Devaux, François Lallier, Paul Lamache, Auguste Le Taillandier, and Ozanam, all in their early twenties. They held the founding meeting of a Conference of Charity in May 1833. During early sessions of the conference, the members realized that they had no experience of finding the poor. They followed the advice of Monsieur Bailly, whom they elected their first president, and turned to the Daughters of Charity.

Bailly sent them to Sister Rosalie Rendu for advice and guidance. Rosalie accepted these volunteers, and located for each a poor family to visit. She also furnished her new volunteers with the chits that would allow these families to receive food and clothing, a practice the first Conference of Charity would later adopt as its own.

The conference originally had six or seven members, but one year later, in 1834, the total surpassed one hundred. Some rules needed to be drawn up to regulate the work of the emerging local conferences of this uniquely lay organization. For example, during the holidays, some members would not visit the poor in their homes, declaring it unnecessary. Ozanam responded: "Gentlemen, let us not forget that the poor have no holidays."[26] On 16 December, Ozanam further proposed that the society should divide into three sections, distinct, but linked together, for greater efficiency in reaching the poor.[27]

Despite opposition to this division coming from those who wished to preserve the original structure, Frederick enjoyed Sister Rosalie's support. On 24 February 1835, therefore, Bailly established the first two sections of the conference, and published the rule for the Society of Saint Vincent de Paul, to use its new name, 8 December 1835. Rosalie also fostered Frederick's growing interest in Vincent de Paul. Subsequently, from these conversations with her and from his readings, Frederick nurtured the conferences by emphasizing Jesus Christ in the poor. The life of Vincent de Paul gave focus to his writings:

> Vincent de Paul was not the man to build on sand or for the moment. The great souls who draw nigh unto God have something of the gift of prophecy . . . like all great Founders, he never ceases to have his spiritual posterity alive and active amid the ruins of the past.[28]

During the busy times of the beginnings of the society, Frederick continued his university studies. As his father had hoped, he finished his first law degree, in 1834, and began to practice and teach commercial law in Lyons. But since his first love was literature and history, he returned to Paris and received his first degree in literature in 1835, a doctorate in law in 1836, and a second doctorate, in literature, in 1839. His doctoral thesis on Dante and subsequent studies gave new impetus to critical study of the poet. Ozanam was later to become a foremost leader in Dante scholarship.[29]

At the beginning of 1840, Frederick received a chair in foreign literature at the Sorbonne, and the next year also taught part time at the famed secondary school, the Collège de Stanislas. Known as a popular teacher, he could often be seen enjoying friendly and animated walks with his students. In his personal life, he wrestled with his vocation. He explored with his friend, Henri Dominique Lacordaire, the possibility of joining him in the Dominicans. But his friends Lallier and Le Taillandier, fellow members of the society, had married and were settling down to family life. Ozanam, however, still doubted that married life was compatible with a life of good works. Father Noirot, his old mentor, never wavered in his view that Ozanam was not made for the life of a religious. He introduced Frederick to his future wife, Amélie Josephine Soulacroix. Married in 1841, Frederick had made a happy choice.

From 1841 to 1846, Frederick developed three main features of his life: the flourishing conferences, a growing love for teaching, research, and publishing, and his family. Ozanam had a way of bringing his vocation as a university professor to the marketplace by exercising a habitual concern for the poor. His example spread, and conferences of the Society of Saint Vincent de Paul began in Italy

(1836), spread over Europe, to the Americas,[30] the Middle East, and North Africa. By 1852, there were 2,000 conferences, with 500 outside France.

Ozanam's visits to the poor in their homes led him to pioneering reports to the society on the social evils of his time, and in his lectures he propagated Catholic social doctrine long before this was popular. His family life was blessed by the birth of his only child, Marie. His joy is clear in a letter to Théophile Foisset on 7 August 1845, "After a succession of favors which determined my vocation and re-united my family, yet another is added which is probably the greatest that we can have on earth: I am a father!"[31] Marie was the pride of his life.

Illness marked the years from 1847 to his death. At first, he had nephritis; later, pleurisy, accompanied by fever and a cough. To recover his health, the Ozanam family took several trips. During a visit to Italy, on 7 February 1847, they had an audience with Pius IX, and talked about Ozanam's research and the growing Society of Saint Vincent de Paul.[32] While traveling with his family, Frederick continued his research and publishing in Christian Latin, literature, and art.[33]

In 1852, Frederick visited the birthplace of Saint Vincent de Paul. He reported to his friend Alexandre Dufieux:

> There [in Pouy], we saw the old oak tree under which Saint Vincent de Paul, the boy shepherd, took shelter while herding his flock. That fine old tree is now held to the soil only by the bark, which is eaten into with age. But the branches are superb and even at the advanced season when we were there, the foliage was beautifully green. I saw in it the type of the foundations of St. Vincent de Paul which have no apparent bond of union with earth, but which nevertheless triumph over time and grow strong during revolution.[34]

He delighted in telling his brother Charles that the pastor of the village had had a branch of that dilapidated tree cut for him.[35]

On this same trip, Ozanam recounted another incident to his friend Lallier. At the shrine of Notre Dame de Buglose, Frederick had gone to confession to a holy priest. His simplicity and charity immediately reminded Ozanam of Saint Vincent de Paul, who, with his family, had once made a pilgrimage here. The priest spoke only of sufferings to be endured patiently, of resignation and submission to the will of God, "however hard that may be."[36] Such language surprised Ozanam, as he was feeling quite well at the time. But the advice was to come true in the last few months of his life.

Frederick traveled again to Italy for his health, but because of fading hopes for recovery, he took ship for his home in France. He died en route, however, in Marseilles, on 8 September 1853. It was the eve of the birthday of his collaborator, Sister Rosalie Rendu. He was just forty years old. Ozanam's cause for canonization continues; on 6 July 1993, Pope John Paul II declared Frederick Ozanam Venerable.

The lives of Rosalie Rendu and Frederick Ozanam were intertwined and similar in many ways. Their early experiences prepared them to found and spread the Vincentian ideals of caring for the poor. Both had exemplary parents who served the poor, even at risk to themselves. Both experienced grief as children. Their experience of the loss of siblings, parents, and health prepared them to share in some way the condition of the poor. Both were touched by the example of Saint Vincent de Paul. Following his spiritual way, they became contemplatives in the marketplace, he in the academic world, she in organizing and mentoring charity.

Generativity of the Legacy for Contemporary Times

VIE THORGREN

*I*n concluding this introduction, it is important to note the current relevance of such historical material. Men and women of the various Vincentian communities will value these documents as a personal and communal heritage. The great relevance of these texts however, lies in their generativity for anyone who seeks the freedom to love creatively.

Ultimately, Vincent de Paul and Louise de Marillac belong to all those who struggle with their own brokenness and limitations amid the demands of earning a living, nurturing the next generation, and deciding on their responses to the call of the Gospel. In the midst of modern fascination with productivity and success, these founders have much to teach about the enduring gifts of simplicity, humility, and love. Their contemplative reliance on Providence encourages those whose spirits have been deadened by a demand for action. Their own journey to the poor sheds light on the possibility of a deeper response to the sufferings and isolation of the poor and vulnerable today.

Vincent and Louise, then, offer not so much a systematic spirituality as a way. In developing this spiritual way, they turned to Jesus and took seriously his words that, in seeing him, we see the Father. Vincent and Louise grasped Jesus as the model for the truth of how God is in the world as well as for the deepest truth of who we are, beneath our brokenness and sinfulness.

Jesus showed in his own life and death the unconditional love of God working to befriend the needy, the outcast, and the oppressed. Throughout their lives, Vincent and Louise meditated on Jesus' humanity and then lived as he lived, and related as he related.

The heart of Jesus' ministry was good news to the poor, release to the captives, liberty for the oppressed (Lk 4:18). This was also the heart of theirs. Serving the poor was not simple human generosity; it expressed God's life in the world. Their lives call us to show forth the truth that Jesus revealed to us about ourselves. We are called to be the unqualified love of God for all.

This way to holiness is the vocation of every person. It is a holiness discovered in the world rather than apart from it; that is, it is a way that leads to an understanding of salvation as a reality for all. It is a way that fosters endless creativity in response to the signs of the time, and challenges us to explore innovative structures in response to changing needs. Lastly, it is a way that transforms us not individually but corporately through the gift of the poor.

For all those everyday persons committed to growth in the freedom to love creatively and to the spiritual and material assistance of the poor, Vincent and Louise hold up an ever new understanding of two important virtues. The first of these is humility, an attitude of the heart often misunderstood and devalued. In an age of psychological sophistication, when self-esteem is valued as a pivotal attitude in our ability to love, what are we to make of this virtue? Is humility an outmoded attitude, at odds with the ability to bring oneself to relationship? For Vincent and Louise, humility was the key that unlocks the door of love. They well understood that fear of our own limitations imprisons love within us. Humility, they remind us, is the means by which God revealed unconditional love to us. They draw our attention to the humility of a God who so esteems our humanity that he chooses to be one with us.

They remind us of the importance of the hidden years of Jesus' life—hidden within the womb and hidden in a village noted only for its insignificance. As early as 1626, Louise began a daily practice of meditation on Jesus within the womb receiving his flesh and blood, which became the means of our redemption. Recognizing the fruitfulness of this meditation, she offered it as an enduring legacy to the Daughters of Charity. By 1633, Louise had adopted the hidden years at Nazareth as a primary image for her service of others. Vincent shared her conviction that this honoring of the hidden life was essential.[1]

This insight of Vincent and Louise challenges an imitation of Christ that would focus solely on the years of Jesus' public ministry.

As Jesus reveals how God is in the world, he shows us God's esteem for the hidden ordinary life. It was in the midst of everyday persons that charity was conceived, born, fed and taught, and "advanced in wisdom and age and favor" (Lk 2:52).

This reflection on humility calls us to the truth that is our hidden potential. God knows us in our true selves as created in the divine image—an enfleshing of God's unconditional love for the world. Held in God's esteem, we are free to embrace each other in charity. Knowing ourselves as the poorest of the poor, we no longer hold some other as lesser than ourselves. Knowing our wealth in the richness of God's mercy, we no longer jealously guard the treasure of love. It may be poured out liberally in the hidden, ordinary moment.

In a time when the complexity of global problems tends to overwhelm us and causes us to question whether our individual actions can have any effect, the humility of God grasped by Vincent and Louise anoints us with individual and corporate confidence. All those hidden actions of caring for an elderly parent, shopping for and visiting with a homebound neighbor, raising a child with a handicap, extending hospitality to someone who is lonely, casting one's vote on election day, and quietly recycling out of respect for the environment, are expressions of a life esteemed by God.

Through this practice of humility, charity itself is discovered in its fullness. Vincent and Louise challenge our entrenched notions of charity as an act of generosity—as something we do for those more needy than ourselves. We begin to comprehend charity as a gift given to us—the privilege of feeding, healing, and comforting the very Body of Christ. In our concern for self-fulfillment, Louise's reflection on Jesus thirsting on the cross uncovers the basic thirst at the core of our being.[2] In her thinking, Jesus, belonging totally to our humanity and in complete abandonment, did not address the Father, but cried out in thirst for our faithful love. In this moment on the cross, Louise tells us, he revealed how God is in the world and who we are—full heirs to the Kingdom of Love.

The legacy of charity birthed in Vincent and Louise awaits fuller fruition in our own time. Those who read this volume will discover a living legacy. It is a legacy pregnant with meaning for those committed to Vincentian ideals and those who seek the gift of the poor. It is a way to holiness that belongs to the ordinary life.

VINCENT DE PAUL AND LOUISE DE MARILLAC

RULES, CONFERENCES, AND WRITINGS

Common Rules or
Constitutions of the
Congregation of the Mission

INTRODUCTION

"*H*ere at long last, my dear brothers, are the rules, or Common Constitutions, of our Congregation. You have been very anxious to have them and have had to wait a long time for them.*" With these words the founder opened his dedicatory letter to the rules. His confreres had to wait at least thirty-three years for printed rules. Vincent de Paul, a practical man of peasant stock, apparently did not mind putting off the publishing of his rules until the time which God had chosen.

As with many other communities, Vincent's Congregation of the Mission developed slowly, moving from informal to formal practices. The founder used, in time, the various legal means at his disposal to secure approbation by the state and the Church. The extant official documentation shows this progression. At the same time, his correspondence show his restless and probing mind at work, examining options (such as having vows or not), discarding some (concerning the import of the vow of poverty) and accepting others.

One of the most interesting and valuable texts coming from this preparatory period is now called the Codex Sarzana, Sarzana being a small town in northern Italy. The congregation has had a seminary there since 1734, and the community's archivist, Angelo Coppo, discovered this manuscript. It contains a draft of the Common Rules, as well as a much longer section on the constitutions and some rules of office. Its history is obscure, since it is the only manuscript to have survived with this material from the lifetime of

COMMON RULES OR CONSTITUTIONS

Vincent de Paul. At all events, the Codex Sarzana is authentic, and reflects Vincent's thinking in the years just before the publication of the rules in 1658.[1]

The Latin title page of the original *Common Rules* has the somewhat ambiguous title *"Rules or Common Constitutions"* (Regulae seu Constitutiones Communes). The Sarzana text is much clearer: *"Common Rules and Constitutions."* In this publication, the development of the text of the *Common Rules* of the Congregation of the Mission can be traced in footnote citations to the Codex Sarzana.

In addition to the *Common Rules*, so called since they pertained to all the members of the congregation, Vincent developed constitutions governing elections and similar matters. The primitive version appeared in Codex Sarzana. A later version did not appear formally until 1847. Even then, use of this material was severely restricted to only a few members of the community. In addition, there were particular rules governing the conduct of missions, seminaries, retreats for ordinands, and retreats for laity. A special document is the rules for the novitiate. Here, too, only a single manuscript remains. Its special value is that it contains the marginal annotations of the founder himself. Though not all of this material goes back in its entirety to Vincent de Paul, the *Common Rules* were uniquely his. The others are probably derivative, but at least reflect his teaching and pioneering spirit.

The *Common Rules* did not regulate every aspect of Vincentian life, being more hortatory and spiritual than prescriptive. Vincent drew his inspiration from meditation on the life and examples of Jesus. Vincent's organizational genius applied his biblical insights to the practical need of serving the neglected country poor and their neglected clergy. His rules emphasized the personal perfection his confreres were to attain through spiritual exercises and other activities, marked by wisdom and experience.

The *Common Rules* of the Congregation of the Mission continued to nourish the life of the community until 1954. In that year, constitutions were published, the first to be officially sanctioned by Church authority. Their publication was called for by the appearance of the Code of Canon Law of 1917. The constitutions of 1954 specified the role of the *Common Rules* as follows: "All should hold the common Rules given to us by our holy Father, Vincent, in the

84

highest esteem and veneration, since they constitute a code of perfection proper to our Institute" (Par. 219).

After the Second Vatican Council, new and definitive constitutions were published in 1984. These constitutions also addressed the same question: *"In order that, with God's grace, it might achieve its purpose, the Congregation of the Mission, which consists of clerics and lay persons, strives to be filled with the sensitivity and attitudes of Christ, indeed with his very spirit which is particularly clear in the examples from the Gospels explained in the Common Rules"² (Par. 4).*

Common Rules or Constitutions
of the
Congregation of the Mission³

VINCENT DE PAUL,
SUPERIOR GENERAL OF THE CONGREGATION OF THE MISSION
to my dear brothers in Christ

The Priests, Students, and Lay Brothers of the Congregation

Greetings in the Lord

Here at long last, my dear brothers, are the rules, or Common Constitutions, of our Congregation. You have been very anxious to have them and have had to wait a long time for them.

It is now about thirty-three years since our Congregation was founded, but I have not had our rules printed for you before now. There were two reasons for this. Firstly, I wanted to take our Savior as a model. He put things into practice before he made them part of his teaching. Secondly, delaying their printing has avoided many problems which almost certainly would have arisen if these rules or Constitutions had been published too soon. There could have been problems about living up to them later on, as they might have seemed too difficult or not so relevant. With the help of God's grace, delaying like this has saved us from such a risk. It has also made it possible for the Congregation gradually and smoothly to get

85

used to living the rules before having them in print. You will not find anything in them which you have not been doing for a long time, and I must say how pleased I am that you do live by them and that they have enabled you all to help one another.

So, my dear brothers, take these rules with the same affection which I have in giving them to you. Think of them, not as the product of human ingenuity, but as a gift from the Holy Spirit. Everything good comes from him, and we are not qualified of ourselves to claim anything as our own achievement. After all, can you find one single thing in them which will not be a help to you in avoiding evil, in growing in virtue, and in putting into practice the teachings of the gospels? And, as you can see, I have tried to base all the rules, where possible, on the spirit and actions of Jesus Christ. My idea was that men who are called to continue Christ's mission, which is mainly preaching the good news to the poor, should see things from his point of view and want what he wanted. They should have the same spirit that he had, and follow in his footsteps.

That is why, my dear brothers, I ask you very sincerely, in the Lord Jesus, to make a genuine commitment to basing your lives firmly on these rules. You can take it as absolutely certain that if you do this you will find them sound guidelines which in the long term will lead you safely to the goal you long for, happiness in heaven. Amen.

† JESUS, MARY, JOSEPH †

CHAPTER I

THE PURPOSE AND NATURE OF THE CONGREGATION

1. We read in sacred Scripture that our Lord, Jesus Christ, sent on earth for the salvation of the human race, did not begin by teaching; he began by doing. And what he did was to integrate fully into his life every type of virtue. He then went on to teach, by preaching the good news of salvation to poor people, and by passing on to his apostles and disciples what they needed to know to become guides for others. Now the little Congregation of the Mission wants, with God's grace, to imitate Christ, the Lord, insofar as that is possible in view of its limitations. It seeks to imitate his virtues as well as what he did for the salvation of others. It is only right that if

the Congregation is to do the same sort of work, it should act in the same sort of way. This means that the whole purpose of the Congregation is: (1) to have a genuine commitment to grow in holiness, patterning ourselves, as far as possible, on the virtues which the great Master himself graciously taught us in what he said and did; (2) to preach the good news of salvation to poor people, especially in rural areas; (3) to help seminarians and priests to grow in knowledge and virtue, so that they can be effective in their ministry.[4]

2. There are both clerical and lay members in the Congregation. The work of the former is to travel around through towns and villages, as Christ himself and his disciples did, breaking the bread of the divine word for the neglected, by preaching and catechizing. They also should urge people to make general confessions of their entire life and hear these confessions. Their ministry also includes settling quarrels and disputes, establishing the Confraternity of Charity, staffing seminaries which have been set up in our houses for diocesan clergy, giving retreats, and organizing meetings of priests in our houses. Their work also includes any other ministry which is supportive of those mentioned. The lay members help in these ministries like Martha in whatever way the superior wants them to. This help includes "prayers and tears,"[5] mortification, and good example.

3. If the Congregation, with the help of God's grace, is to achieve what it sees as its purpose, a genuine effort to put on the spirit of Christ will be needed. How to do this is learned mainly from what is taught in the Gospels: Christ's poverty, his chastity and obedience; his love for the sick; his decorum; the sort of life-style and behavior which he inspired in his disciples; his way of getting along with people; his daily spiritual exercises; preaching missions; and other ministries which he undertook on behalf of the people. There is something on each of these in the chapters which follow.

CHAPTER II
GOSPEL TEACHING

1. Let each of us accept the truth of the following statement and try to make it our most fundamental principle: Christ's teaching will never let us down, while worldly wisdom always will. Christ

himself said this sort of wisdom was like a house with nothing but sand as its foundation, while his own was like a building with solid rock as its foundation. And that is why the Congregation should always try to follow the teaching of Christ himself and never that of the worldly-wise. To be sure of doing this we should pay particular attention to what follows.

2. Christ said: Seek first the kingdom of God and his justice, and all these things which you need will be given to you as well.[6] That is the basis for each of us having the following set of priorities: matters involving our relationship with God are more important than temporal affairs; spiritual health is more important than physical; God's glory is more important than human approval. Each one should, moreover, be determined to prefer, like Saint Paul, to do without necessities, to be slandered or tortured, or even killed, rather than lose Christ's love. In practice, then, we should not worry too much about temporal affairs. We ought to have confidence in God that he will look after us since we know for certain that as long as we are grounded in that sort of love and trust we will be always under the protection of God in heaven, we will remain unaffected by evil and never lack what we need even when everything we possess seems headed for disaster.

3. A sure way for a Christian to grow rapidly in holiness is a conscientious effort to carry out God's will in all circumstances and at all times. Each one of us, then, should try to integrate into his life, as far as possible, these four principles: (1) We should conscientiously carry out what is ordered and avoid what is forbidden, when these orders or prohibitions come from God, from the Church, from our superiors, or from the Rules or Constitutions of our Congregation; (2) when there is choice open to us in matters neither ordered nor forbidden we should chose the less palatable rather than the more pleasing. This does not apply, of course, if the more pleasing things, being in some sense necessary, have to be chosen. Still, though, in such cases our motivation ought not to be that we like them, but simply that they are more pleasing to God. Finally, if when faced with a choice between things neither ordered nor forbidden there is no real element of personal preference between the options available, then any one of them may be chosen at random as coming from God's providence; (3) when something unexpected happens to us in body or mind, good or bad, we are to accept it

without fuss as from God's loving hand; (4) our motive for putting the above three principles into practice is that they are God's will. It is in this way that we can imitate Christ, the Lord. Christ always lived by these principles, and for that very motive. He tells us this himself: I always do what pleases the Father.[7]

4. Jesus, the Lord, expects us to have the simplicity of a dove. This means giving a straightforward opinion about things in the way we honestly see them, without needless reservations. It also means doing things without double-dealing or manipulation, our intention being focused solely on God. Each of us, then, should take care to behave always in this spirit of simplicity, remembering that God likes to deal with the simple, and that he conceals the secrets of heaven from the wise and prudent of this world and reveals them to little ones.

5. But while Christ recommends the simplicity of a dove he tells us to have the prudence of a serpent as well. What he means is that we should speak and behave with discretion. We ought, therefore, to keep quiet about matters which should not be made known, especially if they are unsuitable or unlawful. When we are discussing things which it is good and proper to talk about we should hold back any details which would not be for God's glory, or which could harm some other person, or which would make us foolishly smug. In actual practice this virtue is about choosing the right way to do things. We should make it a sacred principle, then, admitting of no exceptions, that since we are working for God we will always choose God-related ways for carrying out our work, and see and judge things from Christ's point of view and not from a worldly-wise one; and not according to the feeble reasoning of our own mind either. That is how we can be prudent as serpents and simple as doves.

6. We should make a great effort to learn the following lesson, also taught by Christ: Learn from me because I am gentle and humble in heart.[8] We should remember that he himself said that by gentleness we inherit the earth. If we act on this we will win people over so that they will turn to the Lord. That will not happen if we treat people harshly or sharply. And we should also remember that humility is the route to heaven. A loving acceptance of it when we are humiliated usually raises us up, guiding us, as it were, step by step from one virtue to the next until we reach heaven.

7. This humility was very often recommended by Christ himself, by word and example, and the Congregation should make a great effort to master it. It involves three things: (1) to admit in all honesty that we deserve people's contempt; (2) to be glad if people notice our failings and treat us accordingly; (3) to conceal, if possible, because of our personal unworthiness, anything the Lord may achieve through us or in us. If that is not possible, though, to give the credit for it to God's mercy and to other people's merits. That is the basis of all holiness in the Gospels and a bond of the entire spiritual life. If a person has this humility everything good will come along with it. If he does not have it, he will lose any good he may have and will always be anxious and worried.

8. Christ said: Anyone who wants to come after me must deny himself and take up his cross each day; and Saint Paul added, in the same vein: If you live according to your unspiritual nature you shall die, but if, by the Spirit, you mortify it you shall live.[9] Each one, therefore, should be most conscientious in accepting the overruling of his personal wishes and opinion, and in disciplining the gratification of each of his senses.[10]

9. In the same spirit each one is to avoid overattachment to relatives. Christ indicated this when he refused to have as a disciple anyone who did not "hate"[11] his father, mother, brothers, and sisters. He promised a hundredfold in this world, and eternal life in the next, to all who left family for the sake of the Gospel. All this goes to show what an obstacle to full Christian living blood relationships can be. Parents, of course, are to be loved in a spiritual way, as Christ showed.

10. Each one should show a great eagerness in that sort of openness to God's will which Christ and the saints developed so carefully. This means that we should not have a disproportionate liking for any ministry, person, or place, especially our native land, or for anything of that sort. We should even be ready and willing to leave all these gladly if our superior asks it, or even hints at it, and to put up, without complaint, with any disappointment or disruption this causes, accepting that in all this the superior has done well, in the Lord.

11. Christ, the Lord, wished to lead a communal style of life, so that he would be like other people and in that way win them over more easily to God, the Father. All of us, then, as far as possible,

are to maintain uniformity in everything; we should look on this as the safeguard of good order and of the holiness which comes from being together. In the same way we should avoid anything out of the ordinary, as it can be the cause of jealousy and disagreement. All this applies not only to food, clothing, bedding, and so on, but also to methods of direction, teaching, preaching, exercising authority, and even spiritual practices. Only one thing is needed for this uniformity to be maintained constantly among us, namely, the most exact observance of our Rules and Constitutions.[12]

12. Charitable behavior toward the neighbor should always be characteristic of us. We should try, then: (1) to behave toward others in the way we might reasonably expect to be treated by them; (2) to agree with others, and to accept everything in the Lord; (3) to put up with one another without grumbling; (4) to weep with those who weep; (5) to rejoice with those who rejoice; (6) to yield precedence to one another; (7) to be kind and helpful to one another in all sincerity; (8) finally, to be all things to all people so that we may win everyone for Christ. All of this is to be understood as in no way going against the commandments of God, or Church law, or the Rules or Constitutions of our Congregation.

13. If Divine Providence ever allows a house or member of the Congregation, or the Congregation itself, to be subjected to, and tested by, slander or persecution, we are to be extra careful to avoid any retaliation, verbal abuse, or complaint against the persecutors or slanderers. We should even praise and bless God, and joyfully thank him for it as an opportunity for great good, coming down from the father of lights. We should even pray sincerely to him for those who harm us and, if the opportunity and possibility present themselves, should willingly help them, remembering that Christ commanded us, and all the faithful, to do this: Love your enemies, do good to those who hate you, and pray for persecutors and slanderers.[13] And to get us to do this more willingly and more easily he said that we would be blessed in doing so and that we should be joyful and glad about it since our reward is great in heaven. And, more importantly, he was gracious enough to be the first to act in this way toward others so as to be a model for us. Afterward the apostles, disciples, and numberless Christians followed his example.[14]

14. We should follow, as far as possible, all the Gospel teach-

ing already mentioned, since it is so holy and very practical. But some of it, in fact, has more application to us, particularly when it emphasizes simplicity, humility, gentleness, mortification, and zeal for souls. The Congregation should pay special attention to developing and living up to these five virtues so that they may be, as it were, the faculties of the soul of the whole Congregation, and that everything each one of us does may always be inspired by them.

15. Satan is always trying to divert us from living up to this teaching by suggesting his own, which is the exact opposite. Each one of us, then, should be fully aware of this, and completely ready to oppose and overcome all those things. This applies especially to those values which conflict more obviously with our Congregation, such as: (1) mere human prudence; (2) the desire for publicity; (3) always wanting everyone to give in to us and see things our way; (4) the pursuit of self-gratification in everything; (5) attaching no great importance to either God's honor or the salvation of others.

16. The evil spirit often disguises himself as an angel of light, and now and then tricks us by his illusions. All of us must be ever alert for these tricks and should pay particular attention to learning how to recognize and overcome them. Experience has shown that the most effective and surest remedy in such cases is to discuss them as soon as possible with those appointed by God for this. So, if anyone feels himself troubled by ideas which seem to be in some way misleading, or upset by acute anxiety or temptation, he should tell his superior, or a director appointed for this, as soon as possible so that the matter can be competently dealt with. And he should accept with approval, as coming from God's hand, whatever solution is suggested, and put it into practice with confidence and respect. Above all, he should take care not to discuss it in any way with anyone else, whether a member of the Congregation or not. Experience has shown that this worsens the problem, causes similar trouble for others, and can, in the long run, even do serious damage in the whole Congregation.

17. God has told everyone to help others as members of the same mystical body. We, then, in the Congregation should help one another. So, if anyone is aware of someone else being greatly troubled by temptation, or of having been guilty of a serious fault, it will be his responsibility, promptly and in the best way possible, to see that effective remedies be suitably applied at the right time by the

superior. He must, of course, act from love and in the most practical way. Each one should accept it gratefully, as a means of spiritual progress, if his defects are pointed out to the superior in a spirit of love by someone who has noticed them outside of confession.[15]

18. Our Lord came into the world to reestablish the reign of his Father in all persons. He won them back from the devil who had led them astray by the cunning deceit of a greedy desire for wealth, honor, and pleasure. Our loving Savior thought it right to fight his enemy with the opposite weapons, poverty, chastity, and obedience, which he continued to do right up to his death. The little Congregation of the Mission came into existence in the Church to work for the salvation of people, especially the rural poor. This is why it has judged that no weapons would be more powerful or more suitable than those which Eternal Wisdom so tellingly and effectively used. Every confrere, therefore, should keep to such poverty, chastity, and obedience faithfully and persistently, as understood in our Congregation. And in order that each one might persevere until death in observing these virtues more certainly, easily, and meritoriously, he should try to the best of his ability to carry out what is prescribed about them in the following chapters.[16]

CHAPTER III
POVERTY

1. Christ himself, the Lord of all, lived in poverty to such an extent that he had nowhere to lay his head. He formed his apostles and disciples, his co-workers in his mission, to live in the same sort of way so that individually they did not own anything. In that way they were freer to combat greed for wealth in a better and more practical way, a greed which is ruining almost the whole world. That is why each confrere must try, weak as he is, to imitate Christ in developing this virtue of poverty. We must all realize that it is the unbreachable rampart by which the Congregation, with the help of God's grace, will be defended.[17]

2. Our ministry on missions could hardly be carried on if we lived in total poverty, since missions are to be given without charge. Nevertheless, we should try, in the Lord, to maintain poverty as an ideal and, as far as we can, in practice as well, especially as regards what is set out here.[18]

3. Members of the Congregation, individually and collectively, should understand that, following the example of the first Christians, all our belongings are common property and are given out by the superior to individual members, such as food, clothes, books, furniture, and so on, according to the needs of each. We have all accepted poverty, and so, to avoid any deviation from it, no one may, without the superior's permission, dispose of any of this sort of property belonging to the Congregation, or pass it on to others.[19]

4. No one, either, should have anything which the superior does not know about, or does not authorize, or which he is not prepared to give up at once if the superior says so, or even hints at it.[20]

5. No one should use anything as though it were his own personal property. No one should give away or accept anything, or exchange or lend anything, or go looking elsewhere for something, without the superior's permission.[21]

6. No one should take for himself what has been allotted to others or set aside for community use or abandoned. This goes for books as well. He should not pass on to someone else what has been assigned for his own use, without the superior's permission. Nor should he allow such things to deteriorate or get damaged through his own negligence.[22]

7. No one should go in for useless or exotic things. Each one, too, should keep his needs within moderate limits, and curb his hankering after such things, so that his life-style as regards food, room, and bedding is that of a poor person. And in this connection, and with regard to everything else for that matter, he should be prepared to put up with even the worst facilities in the house, willing to feel the bite of poverty in his life.[23]

8. And so that nothing which smacks of ownership to even the slightest degree may be seen among us, our rooms are not to be locked in such a way that they cannot be opened from the outside. And we should not have a safe in our rooms, or anything else locked with a private key, without the superior's express permission.[24]

9. No one moving from one house to another is to take anything with him without the superior's permission.

10. The virtue of poverty can be infringed by even the undisciplined craving for personal belongings. For this reason each one

should take particular care that this failing does not get a grip on him; and this includes wanting benefices, as being of spiritual value. No one, therefore, should covet any benefice or honor in the Church, under any pretext whatsoever.[25]

CHAPTER IV

CHASTITY

1. Our Savior showed clearly how highly he rated chastity, and how anxious he was to get people to accept it, by the fact that he wanted to be born of an Immaculate Virgin through the intervention of the Holy Spirit, outside the normal course of nature. Christ allowed himself to be falsely accused of the most appalling charges, following his wish to be overwhelmed with disgrace. Yet he loathed unchastity so much that we never read of his having been in even the slightest way suspected of it, much less accused of it, even by his most determined opponents. For this reason it is very important for the Congregation to be strongly determined to possess this virtue. And we must always and everywhere uphold it in a clear and decisive way. This should be more obviously our practice since mission ministry almost all the time brings us into contact with lay men and women. Everyone, therefore, should be careful to take advantage to the best of his ability of every safeguard and precaution for keeping this chastity of body and mind intact.

2. In order to succeed in this, with the help of God, we should be very careful to control internal and external senses. We are never to speak to women in a one-to-one situation in unbecoming circumstances of either time or place. When speaking or writing to them we should completely avoid using any words, even spiritual terminology, which smack of affectionate feelings toward them. When hearing their confessions, or when speaking to them outside of confession, we should not go too close to them nor take our chastity for granted.

3. And since intemperance is, so to speak, the nursing mother of unchastity, each one should be moderate with regard to eating. We should, as far as possible, use ordinary food, and wine diluted with plenty of water.[26]

4. Moreover, each of us needs to convince himself that it is not enough for missioners to have reached an above-average level in this

virtue. We must also try with every means available to prevent anyone having even the slightest suspicion of the opposite vice in any member of our Community. The mere suspicion of this, even though completely unfounded, would do more damage to the Congregation and its good work than the false accusation of any other wrongdoing, especially since it would result in our missions doing little or no good. Because of this we should use not merely every available ordinary means but even exceptional ones where necessary to prevent or remove this evil. For example, we should at times withdraw from some works, which in other respects are permissible and even good and holy, when in the judgment of the superior or director they seem to give reason for fearing such suspicion.[27]

5. And since a lazy life is the enemy of virtues, especially of chastity, each of us is to avoid being idle and should always make good use of his time.[28]

CHAPTER V

OBEDIENCE

1. Our Lord, Jesus Christ, taught us obedience by word and example. He wished to be submissive to the Most Blessed Virgin, Saint Joseph, and other people in positions of authority, whether good or disagreeable. For this reason we should be completely obedient to every one of our superiors, seeing the Lord in them and them in the Lord. In the first place we should faithfully and sincerely reverence and obey our Holy Father, the pope. We should also humbly and consistently obey the most reverend bishops of the dioceses where the Congregation has houses.[29] Furthermore we should not take on anything in parish churches without the approval of the parish priests.

2. Every one of the confreres should also obey the superior general promptly, without complaining, and unwaveringly in all matters not obviously sinful. This obedience is, to some extent, blind. It implies giving up our own opinion and wishes, not only with regard to what he specifically tells us but even with regard to his intention, since we believe that what he asks us to do is always for the best. We should always leave ourselves open to what he wants, like a file in the hands of a carpenter.

3. We are also to obey, in the same way, other superiors,

96

whether local or provincial, as well as lesser office-holders. Each one should also try to answer the call of the bell as Christ's voice, going so far as even to leave a letter unfinished as soon as the bell starts ringing.[30]

4. The Congregation wants to develop its commitment to this virtue quickly and smoothly. It should therefore try, as best it can, to see to it that the good practice of neither asking for, nor refusing, anything is always kept up among us. Of course when someone knows that something does not agree with him, or that he needs something, he should think about it in the presence of the Lord and make up his mind whether or not to tell the superior about it, without worrying about which way his answer will go. In this frame of mind he should put the matter to the superior. He should be convinced that the superior's response indicates God's will for him, and when he receives his answer he should accept it as God's will.

5. Each week there is to be a meeting, with the day, time, and place agreed, at which all can hear the superior's arrangements for the running of the house and put to him any suggestions they may have.

6. No one is to order anyone else to do something, or to reprove anyone, unless the superior has asked him to do so or he already has the duty to do so because of his work.

7. When someone gets a refusal from one superior he must not go to another superior about the same matter without mentioning the refusal and the reason for it.

8. No one is to abandon any work he has been given, even if impeded by other business that needs to be done, without telling one of the superiors in time, so that someone else can be appointed if necessary.

9. No one is to meddle in anyone else's work or ministry. But if asked to help out, especially by someone in charge of something, no matter how minor, he should readily do so if possible. If the work, however, would take a lot of time, this is not to be done without the superior's permission.[31]

10. No one is to go into anyone else's place of work without the superior's permission. If there is some need to do so, though, permission from the confrere in charge of the place is enough.

11. Letters can cause many problems, and not just minor ones. Because of this no one is to write, send, or open letters with-

out the superior's permission. When a letter is written it should be submitted to the superior, and it will be up to him whether to send it or not.[32]

12. Obedience should contribute to physical health. For this reason no one is to eat or drink outside the usual times without the superior's permission.[33]

13. Without the general or special permission of the superior no one is to go into anyone else's room, or open the door until he has heard "Come in," and while the two of them are together the door should be left open.

14. Without the permission of the same superior no one is to bring anyone else, especially anyone not a member of the Congregation, into his room.

15. No one is to write, translate, or publish a book without the explicit approval and permission of the superior general.

16. None of our lay brothers should want to study Latin or wish to become clerics. Their role is that of Martha. If any of them feel such an inclination, they should try to get rid of it at once as something suggested by the evil spirit, who perhaps is aiming at their ruin by disguising pride as zeal. They also need the superior general's explicit permission to learn reading and writing.[34]

CHAPTER VI
MATTERS CONCERNING THE SICK

1. One of the principal things Christ did was to visit and care for the sick, especially the poor. He very often recommended this to those he was sending into his vineyard. For this reason the Congregation should have a special care for helping and visiting the sick, whether outside or inside the house. We should help them physically and spiritually, as far as is practical, especially on missions. As well as this we should pay particular attention to setting up and visiting the Confraternity of Charity.

2. Wherever we visit a sick person, inside or outside the house, we should look on this person as Christ rather than as just a human being, since Christ said that he regarded any service done to such a person as being done to himself. For this reason on such occasions we should be considerate and speak in a low voice. And

what we say ought to console the sick person, put him in good humor, and help anyone else who is there.

3. Members of our own community who are sick should remind themselves that they are not kept in bed, or in the hospital, just to be nursed and brought back to health by medical help. They are also there, as if in a pulpit, to witness publicly to Christian virtues, especially patience and acceptance of the divine will, at least by their example. In this way they can make Christ present to those looking after them and to visitors. And through their sickness they themselves can grow in virtue. Obedience is one of the virtues most needed in the sick. They should be completely obedient to doctors and chaplains, as well as to the nurse and anyone else involved in their care.

4. To prevent any abuse creeping in, in connection with the sick, all who feel unwell should notify the superior, the person in charge of health, or the nurse. No one is to take any medicine, call in our doctor, or consult another one without the superior's permission.

CHAPTER VII

DECORUM

1. Decorum was such an obvious feature of the appearance, activity, and speech of Christ, the Lord, that he drew many thousands of people to follow him, even out into the desert. There they were pleased to be with him and to listen to the words of eternal life which he taught. They even forgot about the need for food and drink. Missioners should imitate this attractive characteristic of such a great teacher. Since we are obliged by our Institute to deal frequently with the neighbor, we should always fear lest the slightest impropriety on our part, giving bad example, destroy that which we have built up in the Lord by our work and ministry. For this reason all should carefully carry out what Saint Paul recommended to the first Christians: Let your modesty be known to all.[35] In order to be capable of living up to this we should be careful to put into practice the special rules dealing with decorum drawn up for the Congregation, especially the following.

2. First of all we should keep our eyes from all undisciplined

99

roving, especially in church, at table, and in public. We should see to it that there is nothing undignified or childish in our behavior, and nothing affected or mundane in our bearing.[36]

3. All should be careful not to touch one another, even in fun, apart from when it is normal to embrace as a sign of friendship or in greeting, for example when someone is leaving on a journey or just back from one, or has just joined the Congregation.

4. Each one should make an effort to keep neat and clean especially as regards clothes, completely avoiding, though, anything which is too elegant or stylish.

5. Each one is to keep clean, and look after, the modest furniture in his room, minimal though it may be. He should sweep his room every three days. In the morning, when he gets up, he should make his bed properly. In exceptional circumstances due to illness or work, someone else may be appointed to do this by the superior.

6. No one should come out of his room without being properly dressed.

7. So that we can more easily and readily witness to decorum when others are present, each one, when at home, even alone in his room, should pay particular attention to behaving with modesty, realizing that God is present. We should be specially careful not to sleep at night with nothing on or with insufficient bedclothes.[37]

CHAPTER VIII
GETTING ALONG WITH EACH OTHER

1. Christ, our Savior, formed apostles and disciples into a community and gave them guidelines for getting along well with each other. Here are some of them: love one another; wash each other's feet; seek reconciliation with a companion immediately after a disagreement; travel in pairs; and finally, anyone who wants to be the more prominent should keep in the background. There were other similar ones. Now our little Congregation wants to follow in the footsteps of Christ and the disciples, so it also should have the following regulations which concern good community living and communicating among us, and each of us should try our best to keep them.

2. Love, like that between brothers, should always be present

among us, as well as the bond of holiness, and these should be safeguarded in every possible way. For this reason there should be great mutual respect, and we should get along as good friends, always living in community. We should particularly avoid exclusive friendships, as well as any sort of ostracism, as experience has shown that these give rise to factions and destroy congregations.[38]

3. All should show the special respect due to superiors by uncovering their head to them. We should be careful not to interrupt them while they are speaking or, even more reprehensible, contradict them. All should also uncover their head to priests, and seminarists and students to their directors and professors. The priests should even try, in the Lord, to anticipate one another in showing this mutual respect. During meals, though, this gesture is to be made only to the superior or an important visitor. This is to prevent the roving eye and wandering mind.

4. Scripture tells us that there is a time for speaking and a time for keeping silent, and that in excessive talking sin is not lacking.[39] And there is plenty of evidence from everyday experience that the good work of any community dedicated to God is unlikely to last long if it has no guidelines about speaking and no provision for silence. We should keep silent, then, except during recreation. At other times no one should speak unnecessarily, apart from a brief passing remark in a low voice. This applies especially in the church, sacristy, sleeping quarters, and dining room, and particularly during meals. If someone at table, though, needs something, the person beside him should tell whoever is on duty, with a single word if a nod or other sign would not do. But no matter when we are speaking, even during recreation, we should avoid excessive argument and too loud a voice, since this could give bad example among ourselves or to visitors.[40]

5. Unless we have the superior's permission, none of us should speak to the seminarists or students, or to others, even priests, who are less than two years out of the internal seminary. Charity, though, may call for a brief passing greeting.

6. When anyone is in his own room, or is going around the house, especially at night, he should, as far as possible, avoid making noise, particularly when opening or closing doors. This will help in maintaining silence.

7. During recreation, and in other everyday matters, we

should aim at not letting good humor get out of control, mixing the useful with the agreeable. In this way we give good example to all. We will more readily achieve this if our conversation is usually about spirituality or theology for a missioner.[41]

8. When together like this, and at other customary meetings which take place from time to time, we should try to bring up for discussion, among other topics of conversation, mainly those which help our commitment to our vocation or our growth in holiness. Thus we might, for example, encourage devotion, mortification, obedience, or humility. Or another time we might gently, and with humility, defend them against people who belittle them. But if we dislike any of these virtues, we should make this fact known only to the superior or director, and take care not to reveal it to others either publicly or privately.[42]

9. We should take great care to avoid being in any way stubborn or argumentative in conversation, even if only in fun. We should even try, in the Lord, to prefer, as far as possible, other people's opinions to our own on all matters where freedom of opinion is allowed.[43] If someone, though, holds an opposite view to that expressed about something, he can put forward his point of view calmly and with humility. Above all, though, everyone should in conversation try to avoid anger or bad temper, or showing he is annoyed with someone, and no one should hurt another in word or deed, or in any other way.

10. Everyone must consider it a matter of prime obligation to maintain confidentiality, not only about matters of confession or direction, but also about what is said or done at chapter with regard to faults and penances. This also applies to other matters when we know confidentiality is requested by the superiors or is demanded by the nature of the case.[44]

11. No one should damage the reputation of others, especially superiors, in even the slightest way, or grumble about them, or criticize what is done or said in our Congregation, or in other communities.

12. No one is to snoop around, prying into how the house is run, or discuss this with others, or criticize explicitly or implicitly the Rules or Constitutions of the Congregation, or even its respected customs.

13. No one should grumble about food, clothing, or sleeping

accommodation, or even discuss them unless his assigned work calls for this.

14. No one should speak deprecatingly about other countries or provinces, as this usually causes no small trouble.

15. Disagreements and wars can take place between Christian rulers, and on such occasions no one should reveal a preference for either side. This is following the example of Christ, who did not want to adjudicate in a quarrel between brothers or decide about the rights of rulers. All he said was to give to Caesar what is Caesar's, and so forth.[45]

16. Each one should keep well away from discussions about national or international affairs, and other political matters, especially with regard to war and current disputes between rulers, and other similar rumors in the world. And each one should take care, as far as possible, not to write anything about all this.[46]

CHAPTER IX

GETTING ALONG WITH NON-CONFRERES

1. Besides the guidelines which our Savior gave his apostles and disciples about getting along with one another, he also gave certain instructions about how to behave toward other people, toward the Scribes and Pharisees and the authorities when brought before their synagogues and courts, how to behave when invited to meals, and so on. Modeling ourselves on him, then, it is right for us to have some guidelines for our behavior toward non-confreres, and we should try to live up to them.

2. By the very nature of our Congregation we are bound to come into frequent contact with lay people, especially on missions, but we should not seek such contact unless obedience or necessity calls for it. On such occasions we should keep in mind our Lord's words: You are the light of the world.[47] We should take the sun's light as an example; it gives both light and warmth, and is undiminished even when it beams on what is not clean.

3. Saint Paul wrote: No one in God's army gets involved in secular affairs.[48] Following this advice we should take great care not to be implicated in other people's lawsuits, nor to be executors of wills or involved in matrimonial or business negotiations or anything like that.[49]

4. No one should take on the administration of even religious business matters, or promise his help in dealing with them, or hint that he is available for them, without the superior's permission.

5. When at home in the house, no one should make himself available to strike up a conversation with strangers or become involved in getting another confrere for this purpose, unless the superior advises otherwise.

6. No one should invite non-confreres to a meal without the superior's permission.

7. No one should deliver messages, letters, or anything else, in either direction between confreres and others, without the superior's permission.

8. No one should show our Rules or Constitutions to non-confreres without the explicit permission of the superior general or the provincial. These Common Rules, though, may be shown to aspirants during a retreat with the permission of the local superior, and sometimes earlier on if he thinks it would be useful in the Lord.

9. No one should irresponsibly or pointlessly mention to non-confreres what has been, or is going to be, done in the house, nor should we discuss with them any matters which are not allowed in our own conversation, especially concerning the state or kingdom.[50]

10. When anyone is authorized to meet non-confreres, he should speak to them only about what needs to be said, or what can promote the salvation and spiritual development of either party, or of both, and with a sense of what is serious, religious, and moderate, according to circumstances of persons, places, and times.[51]

11. When anyone goes out of the house, he is to follow the superior's wishes as regards manner, time, and companions; it is for the superior or his delegate to designate a companion. The person designated as a companion should defer to the other and be a willing listener.

12. When anyone asks permission from the superior to go somewhere, he should also explain where he wants to go, and why, and as soon as he gets back report to him on what he did.

13. Everyone should use the usual door for leaving or entering the house, unless either necessity or the superior's permission allows otherwise.

14. When leaving the house, even when it is allowed to go and

come by the back door or through the church, we are to mark ourselves "out" and let the doorkeeper know when we will be back so that he can inform callers. We should not go out in the morning before daylight, and should be back before nightfall, and, as soon as we get back, mark ourselves "in."

15. Except while traveling, no one is to eat while out of the house without the superior's permission.[52]

16. If, while traveling, anyone passes through a place where the Congregation has a house, he should stay in that house rather than anywhere else. While in that house, he is to be answerable to whoever is in charge and should not do anything while there without his advice and direction. This also applies to someone coming to such a house on business.[53]

CHAPTER X

SPIRITUAL PRACTICES USED IN THE CONGREGATION

1. Christ, the Lord, and his disciples had their spiritual practices, such as going to the temple on certain days, sometimes going off to be by themselves for a while, giving time to praying, and other such practices. It makes sense, then, for this little Congregation to have its own spiritual practices. It should prefer conscientious fidelity to these rather than to any others, unless necessity or obedience rules this out. Moreover, these spiritual practices help us more effectively to keep the other Rules and Constitutions and to grow in holiness.[54]

2. According to the Bull which established our Congregation, we are bound to honor in a special way the Most Holy Trinity and the Incarnation, mysteries beyond words. We should therefore try to carry this out most faithfully and, if possible, in every way, but especially in these three ways: (1) frequently honoring these mysteries by a prayer of faith and adoration, coming from our inmost heart; (2) dedicating certain prayers and good works each day to their honor and, above all, celebrating their feast days with special dignity and the greatest possible personal devotion; (3) trying constantly, by our teaching and example, to get other people to know these mysteries and to honor and worship them.[55]

3. There can be no better way of paying the best honor possible to these mysteries than proper devotion to, and use of, the

Blessed Eucharist, sacrament and sacrifice. It includes, as it were, all the other mysteries of faith and, by itself, leads those who receive Communion respectfully, or celebrate Mass properly, to holiness and, ultimately, to everlasting glory. In this way God, unity and trinity, and the Incarnate Word, are paid the greatest honor. For these reasons, nothing should be more important to us than showing due honor to this sacrament and sacrifice. We are also to make a great effort to get everyone else to pay it similar honor and reverence. We should try, to the best of our ability, to achieve this by preventing, as far as we can, any lack of reverence in word or act, and by carefully teaching others what to believe about so great a mystery, and how they should honor it.[56]

4. Because this Bull also expressly recommends it, and for other reasons as well, we should likewise have special devotion to the Most Blessed Virgin Mary. Confreres, therefore, both individually and collectively, should, with God's help, try to carry this out perfectly: (1) by specially honoring every day this preeminent Mother of Christ, who is also our Mother; (2) by putting into practice, as far as possible, the same virtues as she did, particularly humility and chastity; (3) by enthusiastically encouraging others, whenever opportunity and means permit, to show her the greatest reverence and always to serve her loyally.[57]

5. We should take the greatest care to pray the divine office properly. We pray it in the Roman rite and in common, in a middle tone of voice, even when on missions. We do not sing it, so as to leave more time for helping others. Exceptions to this would be houses where we are bound to Gregorian Chant because of obligations accepted, or students preparing to receive orders, or seminaries for diocesan students, and other suchlike commitments. No matter in what place or at what time we pray the canonical hours, we should remember the reverence, attention, and devotion with which we should do so, since we know for certain that we are at that moment praising God in our celebration, and therefore sharing in the role of angels.[58]

6. One of the most important ministries on our missions is to encourage people to receive the sacraments of penance and Eucharist frequently. It is right, then, that we ourselves should, with greater reason, give good example to them in this matter, or even far more than just good example. We should therefore aim at giving

good example in the most perfect way possible. And since every-thing should be done in an orderly way, the priests are to go to confession twice a week, or at least once, to one of the confessors appointed for the house, and not to anyone else without the supe-rior's permission. They are to celebrate Mass every day unless something prevents this. Those who are not priests, though, are to go to confession every Saturday and on the eves of the main feast days to one of the above-mentioned confessors, unless the superior has appointed someone else, and they are to receive Communion, with the advice of their director, every Sunday and on the above-mentioned feast days, and are to go to Mass every day.[59]

7. Christ, the Lord, in addition to his daytime meditations, sometimes used to spend the whole night in prayer to God. We cannot fully follow his example in this, though we should try to do so while making allowance for our weakness. All the confreres, therefore, should conscientiously spend one hour a day in mental prayer, and the custom of the Congregation is that this is to be done together and in the assigned place.

8. Each one should see to it that he does not let a day pass without reading from some spiritual book suited to his own needs, spending at this whatever length of time the superior or director indicates. As well as this the priests and all the students are to read a chapter of the New Testament, reverencing this book as the norm of Christian holiness. For greater benefit this reading should be done kneeling, with head uncovered, and praying, at least at the end, on these three themes: (1) reverence for the truths con-tained in the chapter; (2) desire to have the same spirit in which Christ or the saints taught them; (3) determination to put into practice the advice or commands contained in it, as well as the examples of virtues.

9. All of us are to make two sorts of examination of conscience every day so as to have a clearer understanding of our failings and, by doing so, to make up for them with God's help and to sharpen our sensitivity in this matter. One is to be made briefly before the midday and evening meals, focusing on some virtue to be acquired or on some failing to be overcome. The other is a general review of all the day's activity and is to be done shortly before going to bed.[60]

10. So that we may show reverence for Christ's withdrawal from the crowds, especially the forty days which he spent out in the

desert, all those entering the Congregation, clerical and lay, are to make a retreat, and a general confession of their whole lives up to then, to a priest designated by the superior. Those already members are to make a similar retreat, with a general confession covering the period since their last one. The seminarists are to do both every six months and the others once a year.[61]

11. It is hardly possible to make progress in the spiritual life without the help of a spiritual director. So, unless a directee sometimes talks about the state of his interior life to his personal director, as he should, it is extremely difficult for him to reach a level of holiness appropriate for him. Each one of us, therefore, should with complete openness and due reverence give an account of his conscience to the superior, or someone assigned by him, in the manner customary in the Congregation. We should do this every three months, especially when on retreat, and as often as the superior thinks necessary.

12. Everyone is to be particularly conscientious about being present at the spiritual conferences which we have once a week. These should usually cover topics like yielding in our own personal wishes and opinions, the practice of following God's will in everything, getting along well together like brothers, zeal for personal holiness, and progress in other virtues, especially those which make up the spirit of the mission.

13. So that we in our weakness can to some extent imitate Christ's self-humiliation and his willingness to be ranked with sinners, each one every Friday in the presence of the others is to acknowledge his failings to the superior or someone replacing him. This applies both at home and on missions. We should take in good part whatever corrections and penances are given. The brotherly custom of asking in chapter to be publicly admonished about our failings is to be kept up, and each one therefore should take great care to give this type of admonition in a spirit of charity and humility.[62]

14. As well as this we should make an effort to accept uncomplainingly whatever humiliations come our way, even apart from chapter or, for that matter, at any time. In this way we deepen more quickly a willing acceptance of the experience of rejection, and accordingly advance more and more along the path to holiness. When, therefore, at the end of mental prayer or a conference, the superior indicates to someone that he wishes to point out to him

some failing, the person concerned should kneel down at once, listen to the admonition willingly, in a spirit of humility, and without comment, accept any penance given, and faithfully do it.[63]

15. The continuous work of missioners is such that we cannot be obliged by any rule to undertake severe physical mortifications and austerities. In spite of this, though, each one should value them highly and always have a leaning toward them and even, health and important work permitting, make use of them. We have as examples Christ and the early Christians, and even many lay people conscious of the need for penance. No one, though, should take on any such penances without consulting the superior or director, unless they are imposed in confession.

16. Every Friday each one is to be satisfied with only one course at the evening meal, a course of vegetables of either leaf or bean variety. This does not apply on missions or while traveling.

17. On the Monday and Tuesday before Ash Wednesday we are to abstain from meat if at home, honoring God by this minimal self-discipline at a time when many Christians seriously offend him by their licentiousness and gluttony.

18. Moreover, the timetable which is customary in the Congregation is to be strictly followed by everyone, whether at home or on missions, particularly as regards the times for getting up and going to bed, prayer, the divine office, and meals.

19. There is to be spiritual reading in the dining room all through the meal, both at home and on missions, so that the mind may be nourished as well as the body.

20. We should also keep up other worthwhile practices customary in the Congregation, such as to visit the chapel immediately before going out and after coming in, greeting Christ in the Blessed Sacrament; to catechize the poor, especially beggars, particularly while traveling, if the opportunity occurs; to kneel down on entering and on leaving our rooms in order to invoke God before doing anything and to thank him afterward.[64]

21. If anyone wants to take on any spiritual practices over and above those prescribed in these Rules, he ought to discuss it with the superior or director and should do only what they authorize with regard to them. If he were to do otherwise, he might perhaps be doing his own will, or even the devil's. Thus, as punishment for his imprudence or disobedience, he might be tricked by the devil

into something with only the appearance of being worthwhile and, in the long run, do himself spiritual harm.[65]

1. Our Lord, Jesus Christ, gave his disciples rules for giving missions. He told them to ask the Lord of the harvest to send workers to his harvest, and he indicated the peoples to go to, how to behave on the way, what houses to stay in, what to preach, what to eat and, finally, how to deal with those who did not welcome them. We want to follow in their footsteps, as far as our limitations allow, so we should be careful to live up to the following rules, and to the advice usually given in the Congregation. These indicate the proper program and method for our missions and other ministries.[66]

2. Each one should try, as the occasion arises, to help people by advice and correction and to encourage them in good works. No one, though, should become anyone's director, except during re-treats, on missions, in houses where we have pastoral ministry, or on other occasions when appointed by the superior. But even in these circumstances no one is ever to give any instructions or rule of life in writing without the superior's permission and approval.

3. To avoid our missioners having Saint Paul's words justly quoted against them, How can they preach unless they are sent?,[67] no one is to preach in public or catechize from a pulpit without both approval from the provincial and appointment to it by either the same provincial or the local superior. On missions, though, the director of the mission may make temporary changes of preachers and catechists by substituting others when he judges in the Lord that it is necessary, and when waiting for a written answer from the superior would cause problems. He is, however, to tell the superior as soon as possible why he made such changes.[68]

4. None of us is allowed to hear confessions, either of members of the Congregation or of others, without approval by the ordinary. To avoid any abuse, though, those who have such approval should not engage in this ministry unless they have been designated for it by the provincial and appointed to it by the same provincial or the local superior.

5. Those who are going on missions are always to bring with them the mandate of the most reverend bishops in whose dioceses the missions are being given, and should show it to the pastor or whoever is in charge of the churches to which they are going. Before they go home at the end of the missions they should report to the bishops on what they did, if the latter wish this. But the superior is first to be consulted so that he can indicate how this is to be done and who is to do it.[69]

6. At the beginning and end of each mission all should ask for the blessing of the pastor or, if he is absent, of the assistant, and they should not do anything of importance without first mentioning it to him, and be careful not to proceed with anything to which he objects.

7. Saint Paul and his co-workers used to do manual work night and day so as not to impose on the people to whom they were ministering. Following their example we are not to impose on anyone during our missions and all our ministry is to be done gratuitously. We do not accept any money as stipend or for food. There is nothing wrong, though, in accepting an offer of furnished lodgings.[70]

8. Everyone should sincerely wish to be appointed to visiting the sick, or settling quarrels and disputes, especially on missions and even, when the situation calls for it, ask, with humility, to be appointed to this. Charity, however, should be properly regulated by obedience, so no one is to take on this sort of caring ministry without the superior's permission.[71]

9. Much prudence and care are called for when problems about cases of conscience from confession are discussed, in order that the person concerned may never be identified. To avoid the harm which can be caused by this no one should bring up for discussion problems arising from any case of conscience of any importance heard in confession without first consulting the director of the mission.

10. The name missioners, or Priests of the Mission, clearly indicates that the work of missions is the primary and most important of all ministries to people. And we did not invent this name for ourselves, but popular usage, reflecting Divine Providence, gave it to us. For this reason the Congregation should never replace missions with other ministries apparently more effective. Each one,

rather, should have a deep commitment to them and be always ready to go on missions when obedience calls.[72]

11. The direction of nuns could interfere quite a lot with missions and other ministries of our Congregation, so each one of us should abstain completely from directing them. No one should call on them or preach in their convents, even during missions, without previous explicit permission from at least the local superior. And although our Congregation was appointed to direct the Daughters of Charity right from their foundation, no confrere is to take on their direction, or go to them or even talk to them, without the same superior's permission.

12. Finally, confreres, individually and collectively, are to understand that the plea of missions should not mean neglect of the ministry to clergy who are not members of our Congregation, especially ordinands and seminarians, as well as to other people on retreat, carried on in our houses. Though our preference is for missions, giving them should not mean omitting our work for the clergy whenever we are asked to do this by bishops or superiors. The reason is that by the nature of our Congregation we are bound almost equally to both. Also, everyday experience shows that no matter how effective these missions may be there will be no lasting effect without the help of the pastors, to whose holiness the above-mentioned ministries contribute quite a lot. Each one should therefore give himself ungrudgingly to God in such ministry, bringing care and devotion to it. And to do this more easily and effectively we should make an effort to follow out exactly the instructions usually given by our superiors about this.

CHAPTER XII

SOME USEFUL MEANS NEEDED FOR PROPERLY AND EFFECTIVELY
CARRYING OUT THE MINISTRIES JUST MENTIONED

1. In the beginning of these rules or constitutions the Congregation took Christ, the Lord, as a model, as someone who did not begin by teaching but by doing. In this last chapter, therefore, it is equally necessary to point out that he is a model also for doing all things well, because whatever good we may do deserves blame rather than praise if it is not done well. For this reason it is right to add these few guidelines and means helpful for properly carrying

out the ministries just mentioned. All our missioners should make a real effort to put them into practice.[73]

2. Each one, in every single thing he does, especially in preaching or other ministries of the Congregation, should make an effort to have, to the best of his ability, as pure an intention as possible of pleasing God alone. We should renew this intention many times, particularly as we begin more important activities. We should be careful above all not to indulge any wish for human approval or self-gratification. Such a wish can infect or spoil the holiest action, as Christ taught it: If your eye is evil your whole body will be full of darkness.[74]

3. Saint Paul says that it can sometimes happen that though we begin in the Spirit we end up in the unspiritual.[75] This usually happens when our activity leads to a certain foolish self-congratulation which we are stupid enough to feed on if it went off well with people praising us. Or it can happen when we feel so downhearted and distressed that we cannot in any way find peace, if our activity has not gone well. We should, therefore, take every care never to fall into either of these faults. In order to counteract the first we should keep in mind this truth, that all the glory is to be given to God and nothing to ourselves but embarrassment. On top of this, if we were vainly gratified with that sort of praise, we should be very much afraid of hearing these words of Christ: I tell you, you have received your reward.[76] The cure for the second is this: to turn at once to genuine humility and the willing acceptance of the experience of rejection, which is what God asks of us in such circumstances. After that, to reflect carefully on the fact that very often we can hope for as much glory for God's name and usefulness for others from this type of disappointment, patiently put up with, as from sermons which please people and are apparently beneficial.

4. Since these two evils, foolish self-congratulation and disproportionate disappointment, which corrupt preachers, usually stem from praise on the one hand and criticism on the other about this type of public activity, no one should praise any confrere, especially in his presence, for exceptional natural gifts or talents, above all with regard to eloquent sermons which have attracted public attention. On the other hand, no one should unfavorably criticize anyone for lack of eloquence or knowledge or any similar shortcomings noticed in his preaching. But if anyone needs a bit of encourage-

ment to boost his lack of confidence, or a warning to curb his itching vanity, it is up to the superior to give it, or to delegate someone to do so, with prudence and in private. It is not wrong, though, to praise others for acts of humility, mortification, simplicity, or other such virtues, even with regard to preaching, provided that this is done in their absence, with restraint and discernment, and with God in mind.[77]

5. As simplicity is the principal and most characteristic virtue of missioners, we should show it at all times and in all circumstances. We should be more careful to practice it during missions, especially when we proclaim the Word of God to country people, to whom, because they are simple, God speaks through us. For this reason our style of preaching and catechizing should be simple and suited to the people, and in line with the simple method which the Congregation has used up to now. Each one, therefore, is to avoid completely speaking with too much tenderness or with affection. We should take care not to preach any far-fetched or too subtly contrived ideas, or pointless distinctions, from the pulpit of truth. We should remember that Christ, the Lord, and his disciples made use of a simple way of speaking and, because of this, reaped a much better harvest with a most abundant yield.[78]

6. Those who are appointed to seminaries for students not of our Congregation, to direction of ordinands, to conferences with pastors and other clergy, and similar ministries should also use this simple ordinary way of speaking. And they should take special care, by word and example, to urge all those to whom they minister to develop their spiritual lives as well as their learning. Our missioners should try especially to behave with great humility, gentleness, respect, and cordiality toward them. Those who are giving retreats should, as far as possible, do the same.[79]

7. Since novel or merely personal opinions usually harm both their originators and their followers, all confreres should be careful to avoid such novelties and personal opinions. In fact we should always be in agreement, as far as possible, on doctrine and in what we say or write so that we can, as Saint Paul says, be united in spirit and ideals, and even in speech.[80]

8. Saint Zeno says, Curiosity makes a person guilty, not learned,[81] and Saint Paul says: Learning puffs up.[82] This is especially so when his other advice is overlooked: not to think more

highly of oneself than one ought, but to estimate oneself soberly. All of us, therefore, but especially the students, should always be alert in case undisciplined craving for learning insidiously invades our heart. We are not, though, to neglect the dedicated study which is needed for the proper carrying out of the work of a missioner, as long as our primary aim is to acquire the learning of the saints, which is taught in the school of the cross, so that we may preach only Jesus Christ, following the example of Saint Paul, who also admitted frankly, when writing to the Corinthians, that he had decided that when among them he would speak of nothing except Jesus Christ, and of him crucified.[83]

9. Of all the guidelines in the Gospel needed by those who work in the Lord's vineyard, this is the one that should appeal most to us: Whoever wishes to be the greatest among you, let him be like the least and the servant of the others.[84] For, the moment the Congregation gives up following this advice, with uncurbed ambition taking over, it will be completely ruined. It is because this desire, slipping easily into minds which are by nature inclined toward ambition, urges them on to many evils. In particular it urges them to hope for appointments of distinction, to envy those who receive them, or to congratulate themselves if they have received such appointments. And so, lured on and deluded by the false glamour of superficial fame, which is the only thing they set their eyes on, they do not notice the nearby cliff and end up disastrously by falling over it. That is why it should be a prime concern of ours to get away from the monstrosity of pride. But if it already has a place in our hearts, then a suitable way to get rid of it immediately, following the Lord's advice already quoted, would be to try, through genuine humility, to have a less inflated opinion of ourselves and to want always to have the lowest place. If it should happen that we notice traces of foolish self-congratulation in ourselves because of the prominent duties or works we carry out, the remedy is to ask the superior immediately, though with respect for his authority, to relieve us of these duties and to appoint us to some unremarkable work of his choice.[85]

10. All of us should as well make a particular effort to repress the first feelings of envy which can arise when the reputation, public estimation, and prominent works of other congregations are better than ours. We must definitely convince ourselves that it does

not matter by whom Christ is preached, as long as he is preached, and that as much—sometimes even more—grace and merit come to us when we are pleased at other people's good work as would come if we had done it ourselves with self-congratulation or from a less worthy motive. For this reason everyone should try to have Moses' way of thinking. When he was asked to stop some people from prophesying, he retorted: Would that all the people were prophets. Would that the Lord might bestow his spirit on them all.[86] As well as this we should think of other congregations as being far worthier than our own, though we should have greater affection for ours, just as a well-brought-up child will have far greater love for his own mother, poor and unattractive as she may be, than for any others, even if they are outstanding for wealth and beauty. All should realize, of course, that this feeling of affection is only for the persons, virtues, and grace found in the Congregation, and not for anything it has which is attractive and brings public acclaim; that is something we should make a special effort not to give in to and to shun. And this is not just for the individual with regard to himself, but applies to the Congregation as a whole. This means that not only do we not seek publicity or applause for it, but even that we want it disdained and kept unobtrusive in the Lord, remembering that it is the mustard seed, which cannot grow and bear fruit unless it is sown, hidden underground.

11. In the same way, all should be on their guard against two further vices, from opposite extremes, both militating against the whole purpose of the mission. They are all the more dangerous because it is not immediately apparent that they are vices, as they insidiously assume so different an appearance that they are very often taken to be real virtues. This pair are laziness and undisciplined enthusiasm. The first vice, under the guise of the prudent care of health needed for better worshiping God and helping others, gradually infiltrates our way of thinking and makes us look for bodily comforts and excuse ourselves from the effort which virtue demands. Laziness suggests to us that this effort is far greater than it really is, so that virtue, which in itself should be universally loved, strikes us as repugnant. This vice draws down on us the curse fulminated by the Holy Spirit against the sort of workers who do God's work carelessly or fraudulently. The second vice, on the other hand, masking our self-love or anger, impels us to act harshly

toward both sinners and ourselves, and to take on more work than we can manage, even against obedience, resulting in damage to physical and mental health, involving us later in a frantic search for cures, so that we end up sluggish and sensual. For these reasons all of us should make every effort to shun these two extremes, always steering a middle course. And there is no doubt that we will find this middle course by carefully keeping our Rules and Constitutions,[87] properly understood, and by listening to those guardians of wisdom in whose hands God's special providence has placed us, but only if, when necessary, we humbly and trustingly look for a ruling from them and accept their direction totally and unreservedly.

12. We must remember, above all, that although we are always to be guided by those virtues which make up the spirit of the mission, we should be armed with them to the fullest possible extent when the time comes for us to minister to the country people. At that time we should look on them as the five smooth stones with which, even at the first assault, we will defeat the Goliath from hell in the name of the Lord of Armies and bring the Philistines, that is, sinners, under God's rule. But this will happen only if we first lay aside Saul's armor and make use of David's sling. In other words, we must go out preaching the Gospel like Saint Paul, not with a show of oratory or philosophy, but grounded in doctrine, and in the power of the Spirit, even if eloquence is lacking. We should remember that since, as the same apostle says, God chose those who, by human standards, are weak, foolish, and contemptible in order to rout and destroy those who, by the same standards, are learned and powerful, we can hope that in his boundless goodness he will give us the grace to cooperate in our own way in his work of saving people, especially the poor in country areas, even though we are the least deserving of workers.[88]

13. All should foster a special respect and love for our rules or Constitutions, including even the ones which do not seem to be all that important, regarding all of them as means given to us by God himself for growing in the holiness which our vocation calls for, leading to our working with greater ease and efficacy for people's salvation. All should therefore fervently make a deeply felt self-giving commitment to living according to them. As regards any points we find intellectually or psychologically distasteful, we should keep on trying to overcome self-centeredness and to defeat

the merely natural, remembering that, according to Christ's words, the kingdom of heaven suffers violence and the violent bear it away.

14. Each one is to have his own copy of these Rules or Common Constitutions, and also of the particular ones concerning his own duties, and should read them through, or hear them read, every three months. That is so that they will be more deeply rooted in our memory and mind, and therefore more completely lived up to. We should try to understand them correctly, and on a few occasions during the year we should each humbly ask the superior to impose some penance for faults against them. By this humbling of ourselves we will more easily obtain forgiveness from the Lord for our faults, and be strengthened against further ones in the future. The fidelity with which we do this will, in fact, be an indication of our fidelity in following these Rules or Constitutions, and of our commitment to growth in holiness. However, if anyone notices that he has made some progress in living up to them, he is to thank Christ, the Lord, for it and should ask him to give him, and the whole Congregation, the grace to live up to them even more completely in the future. As well as this, we must get it firmly into our heads that when we have carried out all we have been asked to do, we should, following Christ's advice, say to ourselves that we are useless servants, that we have done what we were supposed to do, and that, in fact, we could not have done anything without him.[89]

Conferences of Vincent de Paul to the Congregation of the Mission

INTRODUCTION

*I*n great contrast to the efforts made to preserve, with the aid of modern technology, every word of wisdom uttered by contemporary spiritual guides, the men and women inclined to save the spiritual vision verbally shared by Vincent de Paul toiled not only under the limitations presented by the elementary tools at hand for recording his insights, but also under the burden of an even greater obstacle—the saint's repugnance at the idea that anyone should place a value on his words.[1] Although Louise de Marillac was able to impose on Vincent's humility for the welfare of the country girls who were the first Daughters of Charity (as well as for the multitude of women who followed in their footsteps), most of the members of his "little company" accepted his dedication to virtue through their own practice of "holy indifference."

Fortunately, Brother Bertrand Ducournau, Vincent's faithful secretary for thirteen years, took matters into his own hands late in the summer of 1657, just three years before Vincent died.[2] After receiving from Father René Alméras, at that time assistant superior of Saint Lazare, tacit permission to undertake the task, Ducournau made an effort to preserve as much as he could of the saint's remaining discourses to the priests and brothers of the Mission.[3]

It should be noted that the holy founder had the invariable custom of addressing the community during the exercise known as the repetition of prayer on Sundays, Wednesdays, and on each of the major feast days of the year. He also spoke to his confreres twice each Friday, that is, at the morning chapter and at the evening conference.[4] Thus, simply in terms of volume, the foresighted brother's task was an imposing one.

Of the many discourses given before 1657, only synopses and extracts have been preserved. However, as a result of Ducournau's effort, a major portion of Vincent's talks from his last years were collected in "two or three large" manuscript volumes after the saint's death. These discourses were reconstructed from the secretary's notes and recollections, as well as the notes and recollections of one or two other members of the community. Unfortunately, the original manuscript of only one conference, that of 30 May 1659, has survived to the present day. Nevertheless, the erasures and corrections found in this original have testified to Ducournau's dedication to authenticity.[5]

Copies of the remainder of Brother Ducournau's manuscripts were preserved in two volumes housed in the Congregation's archives in Paris. The excerpts and full conferences (thirty-one, with notes for a thirty-second) contained in these volumes do not duplicate one another. Conference material contained in the work of Louis Abelly, Vincent's first biographer, complements them. Many of the conferences which he records can be found in no other source.

Interestingly, Abelly possessed "a more complete collection of the conferences" than those in the archives; however, there are significant differences between his version of several conferences and the version of the same conferences as contained in the copy of Ducournau's manuscript. While these differences would seem to cast more shadows than light on the ipsissima verba of Saint Vincent, scholarly opinion holds for the greater authenticity of the archival copies, based on a consistency of style and contents shared with other conferences, as well as on Abelly's tendency to take liberties with quotations.[6]

The first printed version of the conferences was privately published in 1844 for the members of the Congregation at the direction of its "second founder," Jean Baptiste Étienne.[7] Thirty-seven years later, a one-volume edition intended for a wider readership was published at the request of the then superior general, Father Antoine Fiat.[8] In his effort to provide twentieth-century devotees of Vincent de Paul a complete edition of these materials, Father Pierre Coste worked with the 1881 edition as well as further archival

manuscripts and Abelly's extracts. The fruits of his labor constituted the second part (Volumes 11 and 12) of his fourteen-volume
collection, Saint Vincent de Paul: Correspondance, Entretiens,
Documents (1920–1925), the premier contemporary source for
those wishing to touch the mind and heart of Saint Vincent.

The most recent edition was undertaken by André Dodin, to
mark the tercentenary of the death of the founder. To the previous
edition of Coste, Dodin added "Paroles," utterances taken from
Abelly's 1664 biography. In addition, Dodin rearranged the texts of
the conferences and gave them a new enumeration.[9]

As presented in Coste, Vincent's conferences to his confreres
bring to life not only the spiritual insights he wished to share, but
also, in many instances, a sense of the setting in which he gave his
talks. Stage directions, as it were, accompany the words of the
saint. These are necessary to explain the background of that which
has been preserved only as excerpts from larger discourses. In other
cases, such notes aid the reader in understanding tangents or developments in Vincent's train of thought as he either became aware of
the further ramifications of ideas he wished to share, or interacted
in some way with his listeners.[10] The existence of such commentary
points to two critical characteristics of these conferences, that is,
their extemporaneous nature and their dialogical framework, characteristics they share with Vincent's conferences to the Daughters of
Charity.

Coste underscored the first of these qualities in noting that as
Vincent spoke, "everything poured forth as if from a spring."[11] It
became immediately clear to the reader that Vincent did not base
his reflections on a planned text. The frequent exclamations of "O
my God," "O Savior," and "O gentlemen and my brothers!" indicate the spontaneity of many insights. Even the phrasing in the
present written texts demonstrates that they originated as oral decla-
mation. The temptation is ever present to add further punctuation
to make the flow of ideas more readily understandable to the reader.
Sometimes, too, the flow of ideas filled the time allotted more
rapidly than Vincent could have imagined.

The saint's penchant for turning a conference into a dialogue
with his listeners can be seen in the rhetorical questions he often
directed to them, and those he directed to himself, as though they
had come from his audience or other members of the community,

those not present, or yet to join. [12] On occasion the dialogue might involve a request for assistance in the completion of a thought, or the correct presentation of a passage of Scripture.

Because of the foregoing characteristics, what Vincent's conferences may have lacked in organization (they do at times reflect a certain amount of repetition), they made up for in liveliness of spirit; it is hard to imagine that many of his confreres dozed off while Vincent was speaking. The conferences clearly reflected the humility, simplicity, warmth, and good humor of the saint himself. In their spontaneity they model the simple method of speaking that Vincent called his missioners to make the keystone of their preaching. As they sought to bring to the confreres' minds examples of the types of speech or behavior members of the community should avoid, Vincent himself, in true humility, became their focal point. Likewise, their humor often came as Vincent poked fun at himself. In some instances, the remarks accompanying the conferences indicate that Vincent also added humor through facial expressions, as well as hand and body gestures. [13] Such expressions and gestures, however, never appeared out of place, or distracted his listeners from the spritual message he intended to impart.

Overall, the conferences reflect Vincent's warm affection for his brothers in the "little company." In this regard, many examples might be given of those conferences in which he gave over a portion of the discourse to a heartfelt report on the work of his confreres on mission in Tunis, Madagascar, Poland, and Ireland. These talks, some including letters from the missionaries themselves or witnesses to their work, preserved valuable information on the early history of the Congregation of the Mission. More importantly they captured the great value Vincent placed on the virtuous lives of those missionaries as seen in his distress at their pain, and his joy at any earthly success they achieved, but much more so at the glory he knew would be theirs as they strove to walk in the footsteps of Christ, the evangelizer of the poor.

Nevertheless, the excerpts and conferences offered in this volume in chronological order have been chosen as they give witness to that warmth and affection from a different direction. Ostensibly they have been selected as they provide evidence of Vincent's spirituality, particularly his insights on the virtues he believed the members of the community must live if they were to remain true to the mission Christ had entrusted to them. These selections present the roots of the origins of the Vincentian mission in space and time, as well as, and more importantly, in the spirit at the heart of what can be called the Vincentian charism. That spirit is the spirit of simplicity, meekness, humility, mortification, and zeal in love for the forgotten of society as lived by Christ.

The selections at hand, however, also reflect Vincent's love for the "little company" as they contain the various details of what might be called an extended last will and testament to his brothers. For here he speaks of the realization that the time for sharing his insight and further encouragement to fidelity in living the Common Rules would be limited. [14] Although at times touched with anxiety and concern, his words project a sense of the future and a vision, mostly filled with hope, that the work begun well would continue. As Vincent reflects on the future of the community and provides warnings against the threats that would inevitably come, his wonderment at the goodness of God, already experienced in so many ways, overwhelms his fears. He embraces his brothers, and the generations of men and women who have shared his vision, with a warmth and affection born in his own faith experience of the "living hope" and "indescribable . . . glorious joy" to be had by those who, while tested like gold in the fire, find their "praise, glory and honor" in the person of Jesus Christ among the poor. [15]

REPETITION OF PRAYER, 25 JANUARY 1655[16]
(On the Origin of the Congregation of the Mission)

Vincent provides the first recorded explanation of the origin of the Congregation of the Mission. In doing so he speaks directly of the role of Françoise-Marguerite de Silly, Madame de Gondi. Focusing on that lady's experience of priests poorly trained in their sacramental duties, Vincent tells how it led to his first "mission" sermon, as well as the second end of the Congregation: the proper formation and education of the clergy.

(Monsieur Vincent told us, at the end of the repetition of prayer, that the Company should go to Holy Communion for three ends: first, to return thanks to God for the Company in general seeing that he was pleased to call the Congregation of the Mission into being on

123

such a day as the feast of the Conversion of Saint Paul, for the first sermon was preached by himself, at the request of the wife of the General of the Galleys, to induce the people to make a general confession. God bestowed many blessings on that sermon.)

Ah! my confreres, no one had ever thought of that; nobody knew what missions were; we were not thinking of them at all, and we did not know what they were. That is the sign by which we may recognize a work of God, for that in which men have no part is something done by God, something that proceeds immediately from him, and he then makes use of men to do his work. Now there were two things that moved the General's wife to have those poor people provided with an opportunity to make a general confession, of which one was . . . If I mention it to the Company I shall be calling attention to a certain family: shall I mention it, O my God?

(Here he paused a little and then said:)

Yes, I will, I must tell it because no member of that family is now alive; they are all dead and so too is the parish priest of whom I am about to speak; and I have also heard that one of the man's relatives, who was an excellent person who came here to see me some time ago, also died recently, and he was the last living member of that family. Now, the fact is that the late Madame [de Gondi], while going to confession one day to her parish priest, noticed that he did not give her absolution; he mumbled a few words between his teeth and did the same thing on other occasions when she went to confession to him. This disturbed her somewhat so that one day she asked a religious who was paying her a visit, to let her have the formula of absolution in writing, which he did. And this good lady, on returning to make her confession, requested the said parish priest to pronounce over her the words of absolution set down on the paper, and he did so. She continued to do this every time she went to confession to him, handing him the paper, because he was so ignorant that he did not know the words which he was supposed to pronounce. When she told me this I too was on the watch and I paid more particular attention to those to whom I confessed and I found, as a matter of fact, it was quite true that some did not know the words of absolution.

Now this good lady was only a girl when this happened to her. She recalled the incident and, considering the danger in which all those poor souls stood, made up her mind, in order to remedy this evil, to have a sermon preached to them on the way to make a good general confession and on the necessity of making one at least in the course of one's life. This proved to be a success as I have said, so that, as I was unable to hear the confessions of all the people who came flocking in from every direction, I had to send to the rector of the Jesuits in Amiens and beg him to send me some help. He came himself, but remained only until the next day, because he had something to do, and he sent some of his priests to help us. Afterward, seeing that this proved a success, we thought about the means of arranging for some persons to go from time to time to the estates of the said lady to give a mission. I was charged with the task of speaking to the Jesuit fathers and of asking them to accept this foundation. I went to Father Charlet.[17] They told me they could not accept this foundation, and that it was contrary to their institute. The result was that, when this was seen and when nobody could be found who was willing to undertake the preaching of missions, it was resolved that an association of some good priests should be formed.

The other reason which moved the lady was, as has been said, the peril in which the majority of her poor country subjects stood with regard to their salvation, for want of having made a good general confession.

And that too is the primary reason which had caused us to give ourselves to God to prepare candidates for ordination, to ensure that all priests shall be well instructed in those matters necessary to their state of life, such as knowing how to pronounce the formula of absolution, and all those other things absolutely necessary to administer the sacraments of the Church. Ah! my brothers, who would then have thought that God intended, by means of the Company of the Mission, to bring about all the good which by the grace of God we now see it doing? Ah! who knew that he meant to make use of it to seek out on farms, even in remotest Barbary, those poor Christian slaves, to rescue them, if not indeed from hell at least from purgatory? And who knew that it was his will to make use of it in many other places, as we see he does?

The first reason then (as I have just said) for which we should go to Holy Communion today is to thank God for having established the Mission; the second is to ask his forgiveness for all the faults which the Company in general and each of its members in particular has committed up to the present; and the third is to ask him for the grace to correct these faults and to perform our duties better and better.

CONFERENCE, 17 MAY 1658[18]
On the Observance of the Rule

Preserved with its own detailed introduction, this conference provides an intimate reflection of Vincent's feelings as he distributed the first copies of the Common Rules to the Congregation, as well as of the spirit by the first confreres, the spirit that lay at the heart of the title used by Vincent in calling them the "little company."

Although missionaries are always bound to collect, if possible, all the words of Monsieur Vincent, because there is not a single one of them that does not convey instruction for themselves and their posterity, nevertheless, this obligation is especially urgent when he speaks to them as a father, treats them as his dear children, and addresses them on some important topic. Hence, as his discourse at the conference held on Friday, 17 May 1658, when he distributed the book of our rules, was replete not only with good and useful teaching, but also with fatherly sentiments he felt for the Company, some persons[19] have endeavored to collect them with the greatest possible fidelity, and even to describe all that then happened that those who were absent might participate in the edification and special consolation of those who had the happiness to be present.

The subject of the conference was the observance of rules and it contained two points: first, the motives; second, the means of observing our rules well. Monsieur Vincent arrived in the conference room while a brother was speaking. Dealing with the first point, the brother said that if the rules were not well observed now, with far greater reason they would not be observed in a hundred or two hundred years time. Monsieur Vincent asked him to repeat this, and then, after allowing him to finish, spoke himself in almost the following words:

My confreres, God has not given me the grace of inspiring me with such urgent motives for the observance of our rules, nor with means as good as those that have been mentioned, and that I have just heard. Blessed be God! May his holy name be blessed for ever.

(Here he paused for a short time.)

A motive that should urge us to observe our rules well, my confreres, is, so it seems to me, that by the grace of God all the rules of the Mission tend to withdraw us from sin, and even from imperfection, to gain the salvation of souls, to serve the Church, and to give glory to God. It seems to me that they all, by the grace of God, tend so well to this end that whoever will observe them as he should will be in the state which God asks of him will be exempt in his person from vice and sin, will be useful to the Church, and will render to our Lord the glory he expects from him. What a motive, gentlemen, for the Company to observe its rules well, to be free from defects, so far as human weakness permits, to glorify God and to labor that he may be loved and served on earth. O Savior, what happiness! I cannot reflect on it enough.

A good servant of God once said to me, alluding to the book [of Saint Francis de Sales] entitled *Introduction to the Devout Life*: "Consider that whoever would exactly observe everything contained in this book would attain great perfection, although it would appear that all the practices recommended are ordinary and accommodated to human weakness." May I not say the same of our rules? Though they prescribe only a fairly ordinary sort of life, they still are enough to lead those who practice them to high perfection, and not only to personal perfection but also to destroy sin and imperfection in others. And indeed, gentlemen, how can those who will not observe them labor for their own perfection and that of their neighbor? And what glory will they give to our Lord? On the other hand, if, by the grace of God, the Company has made some progress in virtue, if each one had left the state of sin and advanced in the state of perfection, is it not the observance of the rules that has accomplished all that? If the Company, by the mercy of God, does some good on the missions and for ordinands, is it not our rules also which effect it? And without our rules, how would we have been able to do it? Oh, we have great reason then to observe them inviolably. Happy will the Company be if it remains faithful to them!

Another motive for exact observance of our rules is that they are all taken from the Gospel, as you will see, gentlemen, as you will see. They all tend to conform our life with that which our Lord led on earth. Our Lord came, sent by his Father to preach the

Gospel to the poor. *Pauperibus evangelizare misit me. Pauperibus,*[20] to the poor. Gentlemen, to the poor, as, by the grace of God, the little company strives to do.

A great reason for the Company to humble itself is that hitherto there has never been a Company, it is unheard of, that had for its end to do what our Lord came into the world to do, namely, to preach the Gospel to the poor alone, to the abandoned poor: *Pauperibus evangelizare misit me.* For, you see, that is our purpose, and one which a short time ago God was pleased to bequeath to the Company as a monument and as a memorial for posterity.

The queen,[21] having heard of the want of faith and of certain disorders that reigned in the city of Metz, even among the clergy, decided, some time ago, to have a mission given there. She had word conveyed to me by two prelates that I should go and see her about it. I went, and Her Majesty told me of her devout design and that she wished the Company to go to Metz to give a mission there. I replied: "Madame, Your Majesty is then unaware that the poor priests of the Mission are only for poor country people, but we have another company of ecclesiastics who meet every Tuesday at Saint Lazare and who are well able, if Your Majesty is agreeable, to carry out the work more worthily than we." The queen replied that until that moment she had been unaware that our company did not exercise its functions in cities, that she would be very sorry indeed to divert us from our Institute, and that she gladly consented to the priests of the Tuesday Conferences giving a mission at Metz. They have done so, by the grace of God, with great blessing and will soon be home.

My confreres, our inheritance is the poor, the poor; *pauperibus evangelizare misit me.* What happiness, gentlemen, what happiness! To do that for which our Lord came from heaven to earth, and by means of which we too shall go from earth to heaven, to continue the work of God, who shunned cities and went to the countryside to seek out the poor. That is what our rules are concerned with, to help the poor, our lords and masters. O poor but blessed rules of the Mission, which bind us to serve them to the exclusion of cities! Consider that this has been unheard of, and how blessed are those who observe them, because in doing so they shall conform their life and all their actions to those of the Son of God. O my God, what a motive have we here for the Company to observe its rules well: to do what the Son of God came on earth to do! That there should be a Company, and that it should be the Company of the Mission, made up of poor folk, entirely devoted to that end, going here and there through towns and villages, leaving cities behind it, something never done before, and going about to announce the Gospel solely to the poor, and yet our rules consist in that.

But what are those rules? Are they those which the Company has had in its hands up till now? Yes, but it has been found advisable to explain them a little, and to have them printed, so that each one may have them in a more commodious form. We will distribute them this evening to the Company. You have been waiting for them a long time, gentlemen, and we have put off giving them to you for a long time for good reasons. First, to imitate the example of our Lord, who began to do before he began to teach: *coepit Jesus facere et docere.*[22] He practiced the virtues for the first thirty years of his life and spent only the last three preaching and teaching. And so the Company has striven to imitate him, not only by doing what he came on earth to do, but also by doing it in the way he did, for the Company can say that too, namely, that it has first done and then taught, *coepit facere et docere.* It has been thirty-three years or so since God gave it a beginning, and during all that time the rules we are now about to give you have, by the grace of God, been practiced. And so you will find nothing new in them, nothing that you have not been doing for many years with great edification.

Second, if we had given the rules first, it would have been difficult to avoid certain inconveniences which would have ensued. The delay has, by God's grace, preserved us from them. If the Company had been given rules which it had not practiced at all, it might have experienced some difficulty in observing them, but by giving it rules which it has carried out and practiced for so many years with edification, and in which it found no element of difficulty in the past, there is nothing in them that the Company should not find equally easy in the future. We have acted like the Rechabites mentioned in holy Scripture who, by tradition, kept the rules their ancestors had given them, although they had not been set down in writing.[23] Now that we have ours written out and printed, the Company will have nothing to do but to maintain itself in possession of what it has held for many years, and continue to do always what it has hitherto done and practiced.

Third, gentlemen, if we had given rules in the beginning, before the Company had put them into practice, there would have been reason to think that such conduct might have savored more of the human than the divine, that it might have been a plan adopted and developed in a human way and not a work of God. But, gentlemen, I do not know how all these rules, and all that you see done here have come into existence, for I never thought about it. It has all been introduced little by little, without anyone being able to say what the cause was. Now, it is a principle of Saint Augustine that, when the cause of a thing cannot be discovered, it should be referred to God, and he should be recognized as its principal and author. According to this rule of Saint Augustine, is not God the author of all our rules, all of which have been introduced I know not how, and in such a way that no one can explain when or how?

O Savior, what rules! Where have they come from? Did I ever think of them? Most certainly not, because, gentlemen, I never even thought of our rules, or of the Company, or even of the word "Mission." God has done all that; men have had no share in it. As for myself, when I consider the manner which God has been pleased to employ in bringing the Company to birth in his Church, I confess I do not know where I am, and it seems to me that all I see is a dream. Oh, this is not human, this is from God. Would you call that human which the human understanding had not foreseen, which the human will had neither sought, nor desired in any way whatsoever? Poor Father Portail never thought of it; nor did I. It has all come about contrary to all my hopes and without my ever having thought of it in any way.[24] When I consider this and see what the Company is doing, it truly seems to me to be a dream, and I think I am dreaming. I cannot explain it to you. It is like the poor prophet Habakkuk. An angel seized him by the hair of his head and carried him off to a far distant place to console Daniel, who was in the lions' den. Afterward, the angel brought him back to the place where he had been seized, and the prophet, seeing himself in the same place from which he had set out, thought he had dreamed it all.

Would you call the origin of our missions human? One day I was called to hear the confession of a poor man who was dangerously ill. He was regarded as the best man, or at least one of the best men, in the village. And yet he was burdened with sins he had never dared to mention in confession, as he himself afterward declared aloud in the presence of the late wife of the General of the Galleys. He said to her: "Madame, I was damned if I had not made a general confession on account of the grave sins I had never dared to confess." The man died shortly afterward and the lady, having thereby perceived the necessity of general confessions, desired me to preach a sermon on this subject the following day. I did so, and God bestowed so great a blessing on it that all the inhabitants of the place made a general confession. There was such a throng of people that I had to send for two Jesuit priests to come help me to hear confessions, to preach, and to catechize. This led to our continuing to carry out the same exercise in all the other parishes on the lady's estates for many years. In the end she wished to support and maintain priests to continue these missions, and, for this purpose, secured for us the Collège des Bons Enfants, to which Father Portail and myself withdrew.[25] We associated with us a good priest to whom we paid fifty *écus* a year. And so the three of us used to go preaching and giving a mission from village to village. When we set out, we used to give the key to one of the neighbors, or asked him to sleep in the house overnight. However, wherever I went I had only one sermon, which I manipulated in a thousand different ways: It was on the fear of God.

That is what we used to do and in the meantime God was doing what he had foreseen from all eternity. He bestowed a certain amount of blessing on our labors and, seeing this, some good ecclesiastics joined us and asked to remain with us. O Savior, O Savior! Whoever would have thought that that would have come to the state in which it is now! If anybody had said it to me then, I would have thought he was ridiculing me, and yet that was the way in which God deigned to start what you now see. Well, my confreres, would you call that human which no one had ever thought of? For neither I nor poor Father Portail ever thought of it. Ah, we did not think of it; ah, such an idea was far from our minds.

Did we ever think of the works in which the Company is now engaged, for instance, the ordinands, who are the richest and most precious deposit the Church could entrust to our hands? Such an idea never occurred to us. Did we ever think of the Confraternity of Charity? How was it that we undertook to rescue poor foundlings? I do not know how all this came about. As for me, I would be unable to say. Father Portail here can testify to you that nothing was farther from our thoughts than all this.

And the Community exercises, how were they introduced? Just the same, little by little, I don't know how. Conferences, for instance, of which this may be perhaps the last I shall hold with you, we never thought of them. And repetition of prayer, a thing hitherto unheard of in the Church of God, and one that has since been introduced into several well-regulated communities in which it is now practiced with blessing, how did the idea of it occur to us? I don't know at all. How did the idea of all the other exercises and functions of the Community occur to us? Again, I haven't the faintest idea.

It happened as if by itself, little by little, one thing after another. The number of those who joined us increased, everyone strove to acquire virtue, and as the numbers increased from one day to another, so, too, good practices came into existence, so that we might live closely united together and observe uniformity in all our works. These practices have always been observed and, by the grace of God, are still observed today.

Lastly, it has been found advisable to set them down in writing and embody them in rules, and those are the rules which we shall now distribute to the Company. Now, gentlemen, there are two sorts of rules: The first are special rules for the superior, the assistant and the other officers, and those should be given only to those who hold office, as is the custom in all well-regulated communities. There are others which are suitable to all, priests, clerics, and brothers. It is these we have printed and are now about to give you. I hope, gentlemen, that as the Company has always loyally and sincerely observed them, I hope, I say, that it will accept them, now that we have gathered them together, with its usual loyalty, sincerity and simplicity, and that it will not regard them as proceeding from men but from God, and coming from his Spirit *a quo bona cuncta procedunt*,[26] and without which *non sumus sufficientes cogitare aliquid ex nobis.*[27]

O my Savior, O gentlemen, am I asleep? Am I dreaming? Me, giving rules! I don't know how we have managed to get here. I could not imagine how this has happened, and it always seems to me as if I am still in the beginning. The more I think of it, the more it seems to me removed from human invention, and the clearer I see that God alone inspired the Company with them, yes, gentlemen, the Company. For if I have contributed anything to them, I am afraid it is my little contribution which prevents them from being well observed and from producing all the good they would have accomplished. All that now remains to be done, gentlemen, is simply to imitate Moses who, when he had given God's law to the people, promised all those who would observe it all kinds of blessings: in their bodies, their goods, and in all things. And so, my confreres, we should hope for all sorts of gifts and blessings from the goodness of God for all those who shall faithfully observe the rules he has given us: blessings on their persons, blessings on their projects, blessings on all they carry out, blessings on their coming in and their going out, in short, the blessing of God on all that concerns them.

But also, just as Moses threatened the vengeance and the curse of God on all those who would not keep his holy commandments, so too is there reason to fear, great reason to fear, that those who will not observe these rules, with which God has inspired the Company, may incur his curse. A curse on their bodies and souls, a curse on all their plans and on all their undertakings, a curse in the end on all that concerns them.

But I have confidence in the grace of God and in your own goodness, gentlemen, that all of you will on this occasion renew the fidelity with which you have observed them, even before they were written, and that he whose exact observance stood at three degrees will henceforth stand at four, and that he who had four degrees will in future have five or six. And so, gentlemen, I hope that the fidelity with which you have kept these rules in the past, and the patience you have shown in waiting for them for so long, will obtain for you from the goodness of God the grace to observe them still more easily in future.

(Monsieur Vincent asked that the books of rules be brought to him and went on as follows:)

O Lord, who has so abundantly blessed certain books (as, for instance, the book now being read at table)[28] that well prepared souls draw great profit from them for divesting themselves of their defects and advancing in perfection, grant, O Lord, your blessing to this rule, and may your Spirit anoint it so that it may produce in the souls of all those who read it removal from sin, detachment from the world and all its vanities, and union with you.

(He then said that he would distribute the books only to the senior priests, and that the scholastics would be given their copies on the following day, and that there would be two or three copies in the Seminary,[29] which should be for the use of all, so that everyone would be able to read them. As for our lay-brothers, seeing that they did not understand Latin, the rules would be printed in French for them, and then they too would be given copies. He afterward requested the senior priests to approach him for their copies, saying that, if he were able, he would exempt them from this trouble, and would go and bring a copy to each one in his place. He concluded as follows:) Come, Father Portail, come here, you have always been patient with my limitations; may God bless you.

(He then gave copies to Fathers Alméras, Bécu, and Gicquel, who were nearest to him on either side, and said that the others should approach according to the order in which they were seated.[30] Each one received the rules on his knees with great devotion, kissing, out of respect, both the book and the hand of Monsieur Vincent, and then the ground. Monsieur Vincent meanwhile addressed a word or two to each one:) Come, Father, may God bless you.

(When the distribution concluded, Father Alméras knelt down and asked for his blessing in the name of the whole Company, which also knelt down. After this Monsieur Vincent prostrated himself and also added the following words:)

O Lord, you who are the eternal law and inimitable reason, who govern the whole universe by your infinite wisdom, you from whom all the governance of creatures and all the laws of the good life have emanated as from their living source, be pleased to bless those to whom you have given these rules and who have received them as coming from you. Grant to them, O Lord, the grace necessary to observe these rules always and inviolably even unto death. In this hope and in your name I, a wretched sinner, will pronounce the words of blessing: *Benedictio Domini nostri Jesu Christi descendat super vos et maneat semper, in nomine Patris et Filii et Spiritus Sancti, Amen.*[31] When he had finished, he began the prayer *Sancta Maria* and so forth,[32] and the Company withdrew.

(Monsieur Vincent delivered this discourse in a medium, humble, gentle, and devout tone of voice and in such fashion as to make the hearts of all those listening to him feel the paternal affection of his own. It seemed to those who heard him that they were with the apostles listening to our Lord speaking, especially at the last sermon he preached to them before his Passion, when he too gave them his rules by giving them the commandment of love and charity: *Mandatum novum do vobis; hoc est praeceptum meum ut diligatis invicem, sicut dilexi vos.*[33] Several could not restrain their tears, and all felt in their souls various sentiments of joy aroused by what they had seen and heard, of love for their vocation, of a renewed desire to advance in virtue and a firm resolve to observe their rules faithfully. And, if it had been permitted that evening, each one would have repeated the words that some had said to others, especially those words of the Gospels of Saint Luke and Saint Matthew: *Beati oculi qui vident quae vos videtis;*[34] *Beati aures vestrae, quia audiunt,*[35] blessed are the eyes that see what you see, and your ears because they hear it.)

CONFERENCE, 6 DECEMBER 1658[36]
On the end of the Congregation of the Mission.
(Common Rules, Chapter 1, Article 1)

Indicating that the ends of the Congregation are rooted in imitating Christ's mission on earth, Saint Vincent calls the confreres to a consistent and persistent effort for personal perfection as essential to achieving those ends. He focuses on each of the ends, providing answers to rhetorical objections to particular works and warning against the challenges that he believes would be raised to the mission of the "little company" after his death.

My brothers, we shall not converse together this evening in the usual way, that is, by way of a conference at which each one mentions his thoughts on the subject proposed. We have thought it advisable to talk about explaining the rules of the Company. Because, wretched man that I am, I do not observe them myself, I am very much afraid I do not realize, as I should do, the importance of this observance of rule. Consequently, I am unable to say anything tending to the glory of God and the explanation of the spirit of the rule so as to make it understood. However, we shall make an attempt, and see if it is necessary to continue the explanation, either by myself or others, and in the way we have begun.

We must read the rules if we are to discourse on them.

(And, when he had the lamp brought over to him and opened a book, he said:)

Here is the first rule with which reason teaches us to begin. I will read it in French for the sake of our brothers who do not understand Latin:

> We read in sacred Scripture that our Lord, Jesus Christ, sent on earth for the salvation of the human race, did not begin by teaching; he began by doing. And what he did was to integrate fully into his life every type of virtue. He then went on to teach, by preaching the good news of salvation to poor people, and by passing on to his apostles and disciples what they needed to know to become guides for others. Now the little Congregation of the Mission wants, with God's grace, to imitate Christ, the Lord, insofar as that is possible in view of its limitations. It seeks to imitate his virtues as well as what he did for the salvation of others. It is only right that if the Congregation is to do the same sort of work, it should act in the same sort of way. This means that the whole purpose of the Congregation is: (1) to have a genuine commitment to grow in holiness, patterning ourselves, as far as possible, on the virtues which the great Master himself graciously taught us in what he said and did; (2) to preach the good news of salvation to poor people, especially in rural areas; (3) to help seminarians and priests to grow in knowledge and virtue, so that they can be effective in their ministry.

Those, my brothers, are the first words of our rules, and they let us see God's design for the Company and how from all eternity he had the idea of the spirit and the services of this Company. Now the rule contained in the words we have just heard, if rule it can be called, says, at the end of the paragraph, that the little Congregation should make use of the same means as those which our Lord practiced to correspond with his vocation, namely: first, to strive after its perfection; second, to preach the Gospel to the poor, especially those in the country; and, in the third place, to serve ecclesiastics. That is the rule. It follows the practice of the general councils; for, before drawing up a canon, the cardinals and prelates state the doctrine and set forth not only the matter from which they should compose the canon, but also their reasons for doing so. The part that precedes our rule states that our Lord, having come on earth to save men, began to do and then to teach. He did the former by practicing all the virtues. Now all the actions he performed amounted to the numerous virtues appropriate to God who had made himself man to be an example to other men. He practiced the latter by teaching divine truths to the poor people, and by imparting to the apostles the knowledge necessary for the salvation of the world for the guidance of nations and for making them most happy.

The Company intends to imitate our Lord as far as poor and wretched persons can do so. What does that mean? It means that the Company has proposed to conform itself to our Lord in its line of action, its deeds, its works, and its ends. How can one person represent another, without having the same features, characteristics, size, manners, and looks? It can't be done. And hence it is necessary, if we are resolved to render ourselves like this divine model and feel in our hearts this desire and holy affection, it is necessary, I repeat, for us to strive to conform our thoughts, our words, and our intentions to his. He is not only *Deus virtutum*,[37] but he came to practice all the virtues. As his actions and inactions were so many virtues, we too should conform ourselves with them, by striving to be men of virtue, not only with regard to the interior, but by acting virtuously so that what we do or do not do is done or not done according to this principle. That is how the preamble to the rule should be understood.

It was only fitting, my brothers, to begin this rule by a declaring the end toward which the Company tends, in what and how it shall render service to God. That was the procedure adopted by Saint Augustine, Saint Benedict, and all those who have founded companies. They stated in the first place what they proposed to do and began by defining their institute. And therefore it was only fitting that we should place at the beginning of our rules the bull's eye or mark at which we aim. If we are asked, "Why are you in the Mission?," we should recognize the fact that God has established it so that we may labor: first, for our own perfection; second, for the salvation of the poor; and in the third place, to assist priests, and therefore say: "I am in it for that purpose." O my confreres, what do you think of this end? Could our Lord give us a more holy and a more sanctifying end, one in greater conformity with his infinite goodness, and more in keeping with his providence in the care it takes in leading men to their salvation? Our end, therefore, is to strive after our own perfection, to preach the Gospel to the poor, and to instruct the clergy in the knowledge and virtues suitable for them.

As to this first end, the Gospel invites us to it. It sets before priests and all Christians a rule of perfection, not indeed any sort of perfection but one like to that of the eternal Father. What a wonderful command from the Son of God! "Be perfect," he said, "as your heavenly Father is perfect."[38] That is a high aim, who can reach it? To become perfect as the eternal Father! Nevertheless, that is the standard. But as all Christians do not strive to attain it, God, by certain ways which men should admire, beholds the negligence of the greater number, and raises up some who offer themselves to his divine Majesty to undertake, with his grace, to become perfect themselves and to lead others to perfection.

In what does this perfection consist? It consists in making us pleasing in the eyes of God, in possessing sanctifying grace and in possessing it unceasingly. That is what renders all our thoughts, words, and actions pleasing to God. And even what we leave undone, all is pleasing to him. Oh, what happiness! Oh, what happiness has a missionary who makes it his chief endeavor to render himself pleasing to God, who strives to rid himself of all impediments and to acquire what he lacks! This labor makes us pleasing to God. Well now, gentlemen, this implies that to labor at acquiring virtues is to labor at rendering oneself pleasing to God. It is essential therefore to labor at it unceasingly, to receive grace unto that end. It is essential to be always advancing *plus ultra*.[39] And if, in the morning, we have reached six degrees [of perfection], let us reach seven in the afternoon, by doing all our actions as perfectly as possible. What does a priest or brother do who, in the morning, raises his soul to God to offer him all his actions of the day, in union with the actions and intentions of our Lord, who renounces vanity, self-complacency, and all self-interest? He performs an act of perfection which renders him more pleasing to God than he was on the preceding evening. What does he do who considers his inclinations to evil, who takes means to combat them, who excites himself to sorrow for his sins, to a love of humiliations, sufferings, and zeal?

He performs an act of perfection which renders him more pleasing to God today than he was yesterday. And as that is so, gentlemen, we render ourselves more pleasing to God the more perfectly we practice virtue. That is what our rule leads us to. Let us give thanks to God for our happy lot. O Savior, O my brothers, how happy are we to be in the way of perfection! O Savior, grant us the grace to walk straightforward therein and to walk therein without growing weary.

In a word, what does our perfection consist in? It consists in doing all our actions well; first, as reasonable men, by leading a good life with our fellow men and in observing justice toward them; second, as Christians, in practicing those virtues of which our Lord has given us an example; and lastly, as missionaries, in carrying out the works which he did and, in the same Spirit, as far as human weakness allows, which God knows well. That is what we must tend toward. Accordingly, my brothers, a missionary who would think only of learning, of preaching well, of doing wonders in a province, of moving all to sorrow, and of all the other good done by missions (or, to speak more correctly, by the grace of God)—is such a man who neglects mental prayer and the other exercises of his rule a missionary? No, he lacks the chief requisite, his own perfection. It is only right that persons called to such an important state as that of serving God in the way we do, and who have received of his goodness the grace of responding to the call, should render themselves agreeable in his sight and make a special profession of pleasing him. Should not the spouse please her husband so that there is nothing in her displeasing to him?

Moreover, we are the mediators who are to reconcile men with God. Now to succeed in this, the first thing we should do is to strive to please God, as, when one wishes to negotiate with a nobleman, a prince, or a king, one chooses a person who pleases him, who will be listened to, and in whom nothing can be found that will hinder the granting of the expected favor.

So then, gentlemen, we should strive unceasingly after perfection and the proper performance of all our actions that they may be according to the good pleasure of God and that we, by this means, may be made worthy to come to the help of others. A superior, therefore, who would neglect spiritual exercises and good order on the missions, who would allow things to go according to the whims of each individual, and who would not make his own advancement his chief concern would be wanting in the first point of this rule, which directs us to render ourselves perfect. Hence one of the resolutions we should make is to give ourselves to God that we may make it our chief concern to perform our ordinary actions well and in such circumstances as will render them pleasing to God. Our perfection consists in this; otherwise, *quid prodest homini si mundum universum lucretur, animae vero suae detrimentum patiatur?*[40] What will it profit us to have done wonders for others and to have neglected our own souls? Our Lord, after withdrawing from the crowds, gave himself to prayer and desired that his apostles, after having completed their external duties, should retire into solitude, like himself, so as not to omit their spiritual exercises. Their perfection, too, consisted in the performance of both these sorts of duties.

The second thing which the rule directs us to do is to instruct people in country places; we are called to this. Yes, our Lord asks us to preach the Gospel to the poor. That is what he did, and that is what he desires to continue doing through us. Here we have great reason to humble ourselves, seeing that the eternal Father applies us to the works of his Son, who came to preach the Gospel to the poor and who gave this as a proof that he was the Son of God, and that the long-awaited Messiah had come. What a great obligation we have then to his infinite goodness, seeing God has chosen us from so many, many others, more worthy of this honor and more capable of succeeding in it than we are.

"But, Monsieur, we are not the only ones who instruct poor people. Do parish priests do anything else? What else do preachers do in towns and in the country? What do they do for Advent and Lent? They preach to the poor and they preach better than we." That is quite true, but there is not in the Church of God a single company which has the poor for its portion, and which gives itself so wholly to the poor as never to preach in large cities. This is what missionaries profess to do. It is their special characteristic to be, like Jesus Christ, devoted to the poor. Our vocation then continues his, or, at least, it is in harmony with his in its circumstances. Oh, what happiness, my brothers, but what obligations we have to love it.

A great motive, then, for us is the dignity of this work. To make God known to the poor, to announce Jesus Christ to them, to tell them that the kingdom of heaven is at hand and that it is for the poor. Oh, how great that is! But that we should be called to be associated with, and to share in, the works of the Son of God surpasses our understanding. What, to render ourselves—I do not dare to say it—so great, so sublime is it to preach the Gospel to the poor, for it is above all else the office of the Son of God. We are applied to it as instruments by which the Son of God continues to do from heaven what he once did on earth. Great reason have we, my brothers, to praise God and to thank him unceasingly for this grace!

Another motive for devoting ourselves entirely to this function is its necessity. You know, gentlemen, how great it is. You are aware of the almost unbelievable ignorance of the poor people, and you also know that there is no salvation for those who do not know the necessary Christian truths, truths that must be known, according to the opinion of Saint Augustine, Saint Thomas, and others, who think that a person who does not know who the Father is, nor the Son, nor the Holy Spirit, who is ignorant of the Incarnation and of the other mysteries, cannot be saved. And indeed, how can a soul that knows not God, nor what God has done for love of it, how can that soul believe, hope, and love? And how can it be saved without faith, hope, and love? Now God, seeing this necessity and the accidents that have occurred in the lapse of time, through the negligence of pastors and the rise of heresies, which have caused such great losses to the Church, has willed, in his great mercy, that missionaries remedy this, sending them to place those poor people in a state of salvation.

Other theologians find this opinion too severe, although based on these words of our Lord: *Haec est vita aeterna ut cognoscant te solum Deum verum quem misisti Jesum Christum*[41]—this is life eternal that they know you the one true God, and Jesus Christ, whom you have sent. From this it may be deduced that those who know not the unity of God, nor the Trinity, nor Jesus Christ, shall not possess eternal life.

So, then, some say that no one can be saved without this knowledge, and others maintain the contrary. In this state of doubt, is it not better to follow the safer opinion? *In dubiis tutior pars est tenenda.*[42] And is there anything in the world more commendable than to instruct the ignorant in these truths, as truths necessary for salvation? Does it not seem to have been part of God's goodness to remedy this need? O Savior, O my Lord and my God, you have raised up a company for this purpose. You have sent it to the poor, and it is your will that it should make you known to them as the one, true God, and Jesus Christ whom you sent into the world, so that, by this means, they may have eternal life. This it is which should make us prefer this occupation to all earthly conditions and works and consider ourselves more happy therein. O my God, who can comprehend it?

Another reason for helping the people deals with those who do not make good confessions and who knowingly conceal mortal sins, because such persons do not receive absolution from them and, dying in this state, are lost forever. And yet how many do we find who conceal their sins through shame! They do not cease from going to confession and communion, but they turn all those good actions into so many sacrileges.

I once knew a man guilty of a horrible sin which he had never had the courage to confess. During an illness in which he was in danger of death, he went to confession to his parish priest without telling this great sin, although he knew quite well that, by not mentioning it, he was committing a sacrilege and would be lost if he died in that state, and yet he would not mention it to his confessor. After his recovery, and during a mission given near his home, he came to it, made his confession, and declared to us all that I have been telling you.

Now, as that is the case, please observe the reason we have for praising God for having sent us as a remedy for this evil, and how we should set our hearts on fire with the love for this work of helping the poor people and of devoting ourselves to it in earnest, seeing that the need for it is extreme and that God expects it of us.

Such being the case, those break the rule who do not wish to go on missions or who, having gone on them and suffered some inconvenience, do not wish to return to them, or who, taking pleasure in working in seminaries, do not wish to leave them or who, taking pleasure in some other work, are reluctant to exchange it for that of the missions, which is so necessary. Surely it is worthy of a missionary to have and to preserve this desire of going on missions, to be keen on this work of helping the poor people in the same way as our Lord himself would help them if he were still on earth, and, lastly, to form his intention to live and die in this holy exercise. This is what should be done, and difficulties should not make us afraid. It is God's work, and it deserves our overcoming repugnances and resisting temptations. They beset all those who would follow our Lord; what then? Was not the Son of God subject to them? He overcame them, and he will undoubtedly give us the same grace if we wish to combat them as he did. Something which will greatly help us toward this is to render ourselves indifferent to the kind of work we do.

The third end of our little Institute is to instruct ecclesiastics, not only in the doctrine they are bound to know, but also in the virtue they should practice. What do you accomplish by teaching them the former without the latter? Nothing, or almost nothing. They need both mental ability and a good life. Without the latter, the former is useless and dangerous. We should excite them equally to both, and God asks this of us. In the beginning nothing was farther from our thoughts than to train ecclesiastics; we thought only of ourselves and the poor. How did the Son of God begin? He hid himself, he seemed to think only of himself, he prayed to God, and seemed to act only as a private individual. Nothing more happened, and then he preached the Gospel to the poor.

But, in the course of time he chose apostles. He went to the trouble of instructing, warning, and forming, and lastly of animating them with his spirit, not for themselves alone but for all the nations of the earth. He also taught them all the maxims for the formation of priests, to administer the sacraments and to discharge their ministry. It would take me too long to go into details. And so, in the beginning, the Company concerned itself only with itself and the poor. At certain times it withdrew to its own work, and at others it went forth to instruct the poor country people. By the permission of God nothing else but that was apparent to us. In the fullness of time, however, he has summoned us to contribute to form good priests, to give good pastors to parishes, and to show them what they should know and practice. Oh, how noble is this employment! How sublime it is! Oh, how far above us! Who ever thought of the retreats for ordinands and of seminaries? This undertaking never occurred to our mind until God showed us that it was his pleasure to devote us to it. He has therefore led the Company to those works without choosing them, and yet he requires us to apply ourselves to them earnestly, humbly, devoutly, constantly, and in a manner that corresponds with the excellence of the work.

That, gentlemen, is the heart of what I wished to say to you in explaining this rule. Let us now examine the difficulties it may present. First, the Son of God might be asked: Why have you come upon earth? To evangelize the poor. That is the order of your Father; why then do you form priests? Why do you give them power to consecrate, to bind and to loose, and so forth? It may be said that, by coming to evangelize the poor, we do not mean to come merely to teach them the mysteries necessary for their salvation, but also to accomplish what the prophets and the figures of the Old Law predicted to make the Gospel effective. You know that in ancient times God rejected sacrilegious priests who had profaned holy things; he held their sacrifices in abomination and said that he would raise up others who, from the East to the West, from the North to the South, would cause their voice and their words to be heard: *In omnem terram exivit sonus eorum.*[43] And by whom did he fulfill this promise? By his Son, our Lord, who has formed priests, who has taught and trained them and given them power to ordain others: *Sicut misit me Pater et ego mitto vos.*[44] And he did so that through them he might do for the ages what he himself had done during his life, for the salvation of all nations by instruction and administration of the sacraments.

Someone in the Company might say: "Monsieur, I am in this world to preach the Gospel to the poor and you sent me to work in seminaries. I wish to be free to do what I came here to do, namely, to give missions in the country and not to shut myself up in a town for the service of the clergy." It would be an illusion, a great illusion, for a man not to be willing to be training good priests, all the more so as there is nothing greater than a priest, to whom is given all power over the natural and mystical Body [of Christ], the power to forgive sins, and so forth. O my God, what a power! Oh, what a dignity! This consideration, therefore, obliges us to serve this state which is so holy, so exalted.

But there is another [consideration], which is the Church's need of good priests who will repair all the ignorance and all the vices that cover the earth and who will rescue this poor Church from a state so deplorable that all good Christians should weep tears of blood.

Some are inclined to think that all the disorder we see in the world should be imputed to priests. This may scandalize some. But the subject I am dealing with demands that I should show, by the greatness of the evil, the importance of the remedy. Several meetings were held on this issue, which was treated thoroughly, to discover the reasons for all those disasters. The result was that it was decided that the Church had no worse enemy than priests. It is from them that heresies have originated. Consider for example those two heretical priests, Luther and Calvin.[45] Because of priests, heretics have prevailed, vice has reigned, and ignorance has set up its throne among the poor people. This is due to the disorders of priests and to the fact that they have failed to oppose with all their strength those three torrents which have deluged the world.[46]

What a sacrifice, gentlemen, you offer to God by laboring to reform them, that they may live according to the sublimity and dignity of their state and that, by this means, the Church may be rescued from the disgrace and desolation in which she now is.

"Monsieur, granted that we should do this, but why should we serve the Daughters of Charity?" Did not the Son of God come to preach the Gospel to the poor, to ordain priests, and so forth? Yes. Did he not consent to have ladies associated with him? Yes. Did he not direct them to perfection and to help the poor? Yes. If then our Lord has done that, he who did all things for our instruction, shall we not think we are doing what is right by following him? Is there anything that seems contrary to his manner of acting in taking charge of those young women who assist the sick poor? Did not the apostles undertake the government of women? You know that even then deaconesses were appointed. They did wonders in the Church of God, and their duty was to arrange the women in order and to teach them how to observe the ceremonies at assemblies. In this way, both sexes served God equally. And shall we think that it is not for the [Congregation of the] Mission to see that both sexes honor and serve our Lord? Are we not imitators of this divine Master who seemed to come into the world only for the poor and who, nevertheless, directed a company of women? Observe, my confreres, what a blessing from God it is to find ourselves in the state in which the Son of the eternal Father found himself, and to direct women, as he did, who render service to God and to the public in the best possible way that poor young women are capable of doing.

"But," someone will say to me, "why burden ourselves with a hospital? Look at the poor people in the Hospital of the Name of Jesus who interfere with our work. Is it necessary to go there to say Mass, to instruct them, to administer the sacraments and at the same time to provide them with the necessities of life? Why go to the frontiers to distribute alms, to run the risk of so many dangers and to turn aside from our proper functions?" Eh! gentlemen, can one without impiety find fault with these good works? If priests devote themselves to care for the poor, has not that been the office of our Lord and of many great saints, who have not only recommended the poor to others, but have themselves consoled, comforted, and healed them? Are not the poor the afflicted members of our Lord? Are they not our brothers and sisters? And if priests abandon them, who do you think will help them? So then, if there are any among us who think they are in the [Congregation of the] Mission to preach the Gospel to the poor but not to comfort them, to supply their spiritual but not their temporal wants, I reply that we ought to help them and have them aided in every way, by ourselves and by others, if we wish to hear those consoling words of the Sovereign Judge of the living and the dead: "Come, beloved of my Father; possess the kingdom that has been prepared for you, because I was hungry and you gave me to eat; naked and you clothed me; sick and you visited me."[47] To do this is to preach the Gospel by words and deeds, it is to do so most perfectly and it is also what our Lord did, and it is what those who represent him on earth, in office and in character, such as priests, should do. I have heard it said that it was almsgiving which helped bishops to become saints.

"But, Monsieur," someone may say to me, "is it our role to admit the insane to Saint Lazare and troublesome youths, those young demons?" To such a one I will say that our Lord willingly surrounded himself with lunatics, demoniacs, the insane, persons tempted and possessed. They were brought to him from all parts to be healed and set free, and he endeavored to supply a remedy for them. Why find fault with us, who strive to imitate our Lord in the way in which he has testified is pleasing to him? If he received the insane and the possessed, why should we not receive them? We do not go out looking for them, they are brought to us; and how do we know if his providence, which has so ordained it, does not wish to make use of us to heal the illness of those poor people, an illness which he so much loved in them that he seemed to have taken it upon himself? It was his will, after all, to appear as it were in a state of madness and lunacy, to sanctify this state in his sacred person. *Et tenuerunt eum, dicentes quoniam in furorem versus est?*[48] O my Savior and O my God, grant us the grace to see these things with the same eye as you regarded them.

"But the abandoned children, why burden ourselves with them? Have we not enough to do ourselves?" My brothers, let us remember what our Lord said to his disciples: "Let the children come to me,"[49] and let us be very much on our guard against hindering their coming to us for, otherwise, we shall be opposed to him. What friendliness did he not show to children, even taking them into his arms and blessing them with his hands! Is it not from children that he took an occasion to give us a rule for our salvation, commanding us to become like them, if we wish to enter the kingdom of heaven?[50] To take care of children is, in a way, to become a child. To take care of foundlings is to take the place of their fathers or, rather, that of God, who has said that if a mother should forget her child, yet he would not forget it.[51] If our Lord were still living among us and saw fathers and mothers abandoning their children as these are, do you think, gentlemen, do you think, my brothers, that he too would consent to abandon them? It would insult his divine goodness to entertain such a thought, and we would be unfaithful to his grace, which has chosen us for the direction of this hospital, if we were to shrink from the trouble we find in it.[52]

I am mentioning these difficulties to you, my brothers, before they arise, because it may be that they will arise. I shall not be able to work much longer. I shall soon be leaving. My age, my infirmities, and the abominations of my life will not allow God to let me remain longer on this earth. After my death, then, there may come those with a spirit of opposition, and lazy ones who will say, "Why bother ourselves with looking after these hospitals? How can we help so many people ruined by the wars and go visiting them in their lodgings? What is the good of bothering ourselves with so many undertakings and so many poor? Why direct these Daughters who attend the sick and waste our time on lunatics?" There will be some who will oppose those works, have no doubt about that. Others will say that it is far too much to undertake sending men to distant lands, to the Indies, to Barbary. But, my God, but, my Lord, did you not send Saint Thomas to the Indies and the other apostles throughout the world? Did you not entrust them with the care and guidance of all the peoples of the world in general and of many persons and families in particular? No matter, our vocation is *Evangelizare pauperibus*.[53]

"We are quite willing to give missions here at home. There is enough to be done here without going outside. That is what I am willing to work at, but please don't talk to me about foundlings, the old people in the Hospital of the Name of Jesus, and persons confined here [Saint-Lazare]." Some day men of such perverse mind will be seen. They will decry the good works God has led us to undertake and to carry on with his blessing, have no doubt of that. I warn the Company of it that it may see things as they really are, as works of God, confided to us by God, without our having intruded ourselves into a single one of them, without our having contributed in any way to have the care of them confided to us. God gave them to us, either through those in whom the power of doing so resides, or by pure necessity, and these are the ways by which God has engaged us in these undertakings. And so everybody in the world believes that this company is from God because people see that it flies to the relief of the most urgent and the most neglected needs.

Yet, for all that, there will always be some to find fault. I warn you of it, my brothers, before I leave you, in the spirit in which Moses warned the children of Israel, as Deuteronomy tells us.[54] I am going away; you shall never see me again;[55] I know that many shall rise up among you to lead the others astray; they will do what I have forbidden you to do, and they will not do what I commend to you on behalf of God.[56] Take great care not to let yourselves be ensnared because, if you act like them, evils will come upon you that will destroy you while, on the contrary, if you perform the works of the Lord without omitting any, you shall be blessed with all kinds of blessings. *Post discessionem meam*, said Saint Paul, *venient lupi rapaces*.[57] After I have gone away, there shall come ravening wolves, and false brethren shall rise up among you. They will proclaim perverse doctrines and teach you the opposite of what I have taught you. Do not listen to them; they are false prophets. In the same way, my brothers, there will be corpses of missionaries who will work to introduce false maxims to ruin, if they can, these foundations of the Company. Such men must be withstood.

I do not know if I shall be saying too much if I relate what Saint Benedict said before he died. There were even then, in the houses which he had instituted, discontented religious who were saying: "Why this and why that?" They were murmuring against the rule and condemning the practices established in holiness. When this came to the knowledge of the holy abbot, he feared that after him all would be overthrown. What does he do? Here is an Order in which there is no superior general; each house is mistress of itself; it does not receive a visitation or correction from any other. He implores neighboring bishops, who see any house in a state of disorder, to come down on it by way of reprimands and suspensions, to restrain troublesome and disorderly monks, and even to appeal to the gentlemen of the neighborhood to fall upon them with arms and force to recall them to their duty.[58] I do not mean to say so much but only that, if at some future time, there were some who would propose to abolish this practice, to give up this hospital, to recall the laborers from Barbary, to remain here, not to go there, to abandon this work, and not to rush to the relief of distant wants, those false brothers should be boldly told: "Gentlemen, leave us in the laws of our fathers and in the state in which we are. God has placed us in it and he wishes us to abide there." Stand fast.

"But the Company," they will say, "is encumbered by such or such a work." Ah, if, in its infancy, the Company sustained it and bore all those other burdens, why will it not succeed in them when it has grown stronger? "Leave us," they must be told, "leave us in the state in which our Lord was when on earth. We do what he did: do not prevent us from imitating him." Warn them, you see, warn them and do not imitate them.

But what sort of men will they be who will strive to turn us away from those good works we have begun? They will be free-thinkers, free-thinkers, free-thinkers,[59] who seek nothing but pleasure and amusement. Provided they have a good dinner, they do not trouble their heads about anything else. Who besides? They will be . . . It is better that I not say it. They will be men who coddle themselves (as he said this he placed his hands under his armpits, imitating the lazy), men who have only a narrow outlook, who confine their views and plans to a fixed circumference within which they shut themselves up as in one spot; they are unwilling to leave it, and if they are shown something outside it and draw near to look at it, at once they withdraw to their center, like snails into their shells.

(Note: As he was saying this, he made certain gestures with his hands, and movements of his head while speaking in a sort of contemptuous tone of voice which expressed even better what he wished to express than what he actually said. He then recollected himself, and said to himself:)

O wretch, you are an old man who resembles them, little things seem great to you, and difficulties overwhelm you. Yes, gentlemen, even such a little thing as getting up in the morning seems a great affair to me, and the slightest little obstacles seem insurmountable. They will, then, be small-minded men, people like myself, who will wish to cut down the practices and the functions of the Company. Let us give ourselves to God, gentlemen, so that he may grant us the grace to stand fast. Let us hold fast, my brothers, let us hold fast, for the love of God: He will be faithful to his promises. God will never abandon us so long as we remain fully obedient to him for the fulfillment of his designs. Let us remain within the bounds of our vocation. Let us labor to become interior men, to conceive great and holy affections for the service of God. Let us do the good that presents itself to be done and let us do it in the ways we have said. I do not say that it is necessary to proceed to infinity and to undertake all things without distinction, but those things which God lets us see, he asks of us. We are his and not our own. If he increases our work, he will also increase our strength. O Savior, what happiness! O Savior, if there were several paradises, to whom could you give them if not to a missionary who shall have reverently persevered in all the works you have marked out for him who shall never fail to carry out all the duties of his state! That is what we hope for, my brothers, and that is what we ask of his Divine Majesty. Now let us all give him infinite thanks for having called and chosen us for such holy functions, sanctified as they have been by our Lord himself who first exercised them. Oh, what graces have we not reason to hope for if we exercise them in his Spirit, for the glory of his Father and the salvation of souls! Amen.

Letters of Vincent de Paul

INTRODUCTION

A s the leader of two growing religious congregations, and with numerous other concerns in France and elsewhere, Vincent de Paul was forced to carry on a vast correspondence. Out of an estimated total of 30,000 letters, about 10 percent remain today. The earliest is a letter written to his patron, Monsieur de Comet, dated Avignon, 24 July 1607. The latest is addressed to Bishop Jean de Maupeou, dated Paris, 25 September 1660, two days before the founder's death.

In Vincent's lifetime, his letters covered a wide range of subjects. In some, he reported ordinary news or made simple notes or requests, as one might do today by telephone. In others he was the spiritual director, the father of his confreres, the confidant of bishops and princes. Especially valuable is his series addressed to Louise de Marillac. The spirit of the man comes through in a special way in these letters, characterized by his devotion to using divine means for divine ends.

His extant letters were published by Pierre Coste, C.M., from 1920 to 1925. In this splendid and careful edition, eight volumes are devoted to Vincent's correspondence. Of those, the last five volumes contain letters from 1650 on, that is, from the last ten years of his life. This is a tribute to the willingness of his correspondents to preserve the letters from this famous priest. However, if one were to read the letters written in his older years as indicative of his entire life, one could certainly arrive at a distorted view of Vincent de Paul. Nevertheless, these letters offer a more direct and powerful witness to his spirituality than any other source. He must have written several a day, and in his maturity employed two brothers as his secretaries. His letters, in other words, were mainly personal and not written for publication. Hence their value as revelatory of his spirituality.

Other works, such as conferences and documents, are less reve-
latory. The reason is that the conferences to his confreres are not
transcripts, but represent what his listeners could reconstruct from
memory after his talks. The texts of those he gave to the Daughters
of Charity were, at least in part, reviewed by him, but they still
present Monsieur Vincent as recorded by others. Other documents,
notarial acts, and saying reported of him are valuable, to be sure,
but do not give the insight into his soul that his letters provide.
Those who look to Monsieur Vincent for guidance are grateful for
this gift of his spirit in his letters.

For this ediction, the editors have selected several letters illustra-
tive of the major facets of Vincent's life. They are given in chronologi-
cal order. The editors have used the modern English translation
prepared under the supervision of Sisters Jacqueline Kilar and Marie
Poole, Daughters of Charity.[1] For those letters which have not yet
appeared in their edition, the translation of Joseph Leonard, C.M.,
served as the base, and was reviewed and corrected as needed.[2]

TO LOUISE DE MARILLAC
30 October 1626[3]

In this letter to Louise, the earliest surviving one, Vincent
explains his reluctance to advise her as to the reasons for his hasty
departure. He reminds her to accept this in a spirit of humble
submission—always to wait patiently for the manifestation of
God's will.

Mademoiselle,[4]

The grace of Our Lord be with you forever!

I received your letter here in Loisy-en-Brie,[5] twenty-eight
leagues from Paris, where we are giving a mission.[6] I did not notify
you of my departure because it was a little sooner than I had expected and I was reluctant to upset you by letting you know about
it. Well now! Our Lord will use this little mortification to advantage
if he wishes, and he himself will act as your director. Yes, he will
surely do so, and in such a way that he will lead you to see that it is
he himself. Be then his dear daughter—quite humble, submissive,
and full of confidence—and always wait patiently for the manifestation of his holy and adorable Will.

152

In this place where we are, one-third of the inhabitants are heretics. Please pray for us; we need it, especially myself.

I am not answering all your letters because I am no longer in a situation where I can do what you request.

TO LOUISE DE MARILLAC

circa 1629[7]

In this fragmentary letter to Louise, Vincent consoles her, assuring her that God loves her tenderly in spite of her interior trials and temptations.

. . . the secret of your heart, which I truly wish may belong entirely to Our Lord. I beg the Blessed Virgin to take it from you so as to carry it off to heaven to place it in her own and in that of her dear Son. But do not think that all is lost because of the little rebellions you experience interiorly. It has just rained very hard and it is thundering dreadfully. Is the weather less beautiful for that? Let the tears of sadness drown your heart and let the demons thunder and growl as much as they please. Be assured, my dear daughter, that you are no less dear to Our Lord for all that. Therefore, live contentedly in his love and be assured that I shall be mindful of you tomorrow at the sacrifice which, unworthy as I am, I shall offer to the supreme Sacrificer. If I were not in such a hurry . . . .

TO FRANÇOIS DU COUDRAY

1631[8]

Vincent insists that the Congregation of the Mission be true to its charism: to serve the poor and the ignorant, and Monsieur du Coudray must stand firm in this commitment.

You must make it understood that the poor are being damned for want of knowing the things necessary for salvation, and for lack of confession. If His Holiness were aware of this necessity, he would have no rest until he had done all he could to set things right.

153

It is the knowledge we had of this situation that brought about the establishment of the Company, so as to remedy it in some way. In order to do this, we must live in a congregation and observe five things as essential for this purpose:

1. leave to the bishops the power of sending the missionaries into the part of the diocese they choose;

2. the above-mentioned priests are to be subject to the pastors where they go to give the mission, for its duration;

3. they are to take nothing from those poor people, but live at their own expense;

4. they are neither to preach, nor catechize, nor hear confessions in cities where there is an archbishopric, a bishopric, or a presidial court, except in the case of ordinands and those who will make retreats in the house;

5. the superior of the Company is to have complete control over it; and these five maxims are to be as it were the basic principles of this Congregation.

Notice that Monsieur Duval's advice is that nothing be changed in the plan for which I am sending you the notes.[9] The words do not matter; but as for the substance, it must remain intact. Otherwise, anything changed or deleted would be greatly detrimental. So, stand firm and make them understand that we have had this in mind for many long years and have had experience with it.

TO FRANÇOIS DU COUDRAY
6 November 1634[10]

This letter reassures François du Coudray that his work in Rome is well regarded but that, because of his absence, some matters of importance had to be taken care of by others for the sake of expediency. Vincent also speaks of his high regard for the virtue of simplicity and his presumption that all those involved in the situation were acting in a spirit of simplicity. Monsieur du Coudray should not be troubled.

Monsieur,

The grace of Our Lord be with you forever!

I received your letter, of October 8 I think, in which you informed me that Monsieur Le Bret told you that Dom Le Bret,[11] his cousin, wrote to him with regard to your return. Now I must tell you, before God, in whose presence I am speaking, that I do not know anything about it. I have not said a word to Dom Le Bret, to my knowledge, to give him any reason to write that or anything approaching it. Perhaps it is the result of someone from there telling him that you had no more to do in Rome and that you had said you were to leave in two weeks. All I know about the affair is what I am surmising here in telling you this, because that good Father did not tell me anything about what he wrote.

As for what you say he told you before, along the same lines, I tell you that, while I was speaking to that good Father about our affairs in Rome—for Monsieur Le Bret writes to him about everything that is done—while I was speaking, I repeat, about our stay in Ferrara, I expressed to him my worry about the situation, not telling him anything else than what I could say in your presence without giving you offense. It is true that that good Father, because of the zeal he has for us—which is such that I doubt strongly whether my own enthusiasm for the mission is as great as his—told me that he wanted to write to his cousin to procure the Bulls in your absence. Now, since he said that to me quite simply, I did not pay much attention to it. But having thought it over, I went to see him expressly for the purpose of asking him not to do anything about it because I was afraid it might upset you and because I realized that it was proper for you to take care of it. Nevertheless, I found out later that he had written something about it and I was extremely annoyed.

That, Monsieur, is all I can say concerning the matter, with all the liberty and simplicity in my power. But do not feel that that good Father has any opinion of you except a very good one, thank God, one full of esteem and affection, and certainly with good reason.

That is why I most humbly entreat you not to give rise to any thought contrary to what I am telling you and to put far from you the thoughts, which I see from your letter, that you have formed with regard to me and that good Father. You know that the goodness of your heart has given me, thank God, the freedom to speak to you with full confidence, without concealing or disguising anything. I think you have been aware of that up to now from my way of acting toward you.

Jésus, mon Dieu! could I be reduced to the misfortune of having to do or say something in your regard against holy simplicity! Oh! may God preserve me from that, Monsieur, with regard to anyone whomsoever! Simplicity is the virtue I love the most and to which, I think, I pay the most attention in my actions; and, if it is permissible for me to say so, I would say that I am practicing it with some progress by the mercy of God.

In the name of God, little Father, reject those thoughts as temptations that the evil spirit is putting into your mind. Believe that my heart is not so much mine as yours, and that you are more a pleasure and consolation to me than I am to myself. That is what makes me hope for your return. But I do not want you to come back in the depth of winter and in danger, but the way I wrote to you in my last letter, that is, around the month of February or March, unless you take passage on the galleys from France which are to bring the cardinal of Lyons to Rome.[12] He is supposed to ask leave around Advent, in which case it would be good either to ask Monsieur Gilioli to come and meet you in Rome or to go and get him and wait for the galleys in Leghorn which is the seaport for Florence.[13]

I am not saying anything to you about the Saint Lazare affair because I have already written asking you to have the petition signed by the pope so as to put matters in a state to be acted upon fifty years from now, as you wrote us. If the matter could be expedited at some small cost, you should attend to it.

Well now, Monsieur, here then is all I shall tell you for the present about myself except that I greet you with all the tenderness of my heart. Please take care of your health. I am, in the love of Our Lord, Monsieur, your most humble and obedient servant.

VINCENT DE PAUL

TO LOUISE DE MARILLAC
1 November 1637[14]

Vincent encourages Louise in an approaching confrontation. He reminds her to be gentle and meek, but if needs be, to borrow from the Lord a "dash of vinegar."

Mademoiselle,
The grace of Our Lord be with you forever!

I am very pleased with what you wrote to me about those good young women from Liancourt, especially about the one who knows how to make lace. She will be able to teach that to the poor people and it will serve to draw them to spiritual things. Send them, therefore, whenever you wish.

I see no need at present for Madame Goussault to be with you when you speak to Madame Mussot or to that poor woman. If neither one profits from what you say to them, you can call her in, unless you are meeting at her house and send for them to come there. But that will cause a great deal of delay, I fear. However, if the gentleness of your spirit needs a dash of vinegar, borrow a little from Our Lord's spirit. O Mademoiselle, how well He knew how to find a bittersweet remark when it was needed!

I am, in his love, Mademoiselle, your most humble servant.

VINCENT DE PAUL

TO JANE FRANCES DE CHANTAL
Troyes, 14 July 1639[15]

This letter summarizes, practically better than any other document, Vincent's views on the Congregation of the Mission. The practices and ideals listed here became part of the Common Rules, which he codified in 1658.

Most dear and most worthy Mother,
The grace of Our Lord be with you forever!

Having come to this city of Troyes with the Commander de Sillery to visit the little family we have here in this diocese, I saw, in the letter he received from you, the answer you gave him concerning his proposal for an endowment fund for two men from our little company to work among the poor country people in your diocese.[16] Now, I shall tell you, most worthy Mother, that I received with inexpressible consolation the commander's proposal to me concerning that foundation. It will give us the means of working in the diocese of the saints and it is under the protection and direction of our worthy Mother. Therefore, we have reason to hope that Our Lord will bless the holy intentions of the good commander and the humble labors of his missionaries.

And because you wish to know what constitutes our humble way of life, I shall tell you then, most worthy Mother, that our little company is established to go from village to village at its own expense, preaching, catechizing, and having the poor people make general confessions of their entire past life. We try to settle the disagreements we find among them and do all we can to see that the sick poor are assisted corporally and spiritually by the Confraternity of the Charity, composed of women, which we set up in the places where we give the mission and which desire it.

To this work, which is our principal one, and in order to perform it better, the providence of God has added that of taking into our houses ten days before ordination those who are to take orders. We feed and support them and during that time teach them practical theology, the ceremonies of the Church, and how to make and practice mental prayer according to the method of our blessed father, the bishop of Geneva.[17] We do this for those who belong to the diocese in which we are established.

We live in the spirit of the servants of the Gospel with regard to the bishops. When they tell us: "Go there," we go; "Come here," we come; "Do that," we do it; and that is how we act in what concerns the functions mentioned above. As for the internal discipline of the Company, that depends on a superior general.

Most of us have made the three vows of poverty, chastity, and obedience, and a fourth to devote ourselves all our life to the assistance of the poor common people. We are seeking to have them approved by His Holiness,[18] and we are asking permission to make a fifth vow, that of obedience to the bishops in whose dioceses we are established, in what concerns the aforesaid functions.[19]

We practice poverty and obedience and try to live in a religious manner, even though we are not religious. We get up at four o'clock in the morning and take half an hour to get dressed and make our bed. We make an hour of mental prayer together in the church and recite Prime, Terce, Sext, and None together. We then celebrate our Masses, each in his own place. When that is done, everyone retires to his room to study. At ten-thirty, we make a particular examen on the virtue we are trying to acquire. We then go to the refectory where we have dinner with individual portions and reading at table. After that, we go to adore the Blessed Sacrament together and say the *Angelus Domini Nuntiavit Mariae*, and so forth.[20]

Next we have an hour of recreation together, after which everyone returns to his room until two o'clock when we recite Vespers and Compline together. We then return to our rooms to study until five o'clock, at which time Matins and Lauds are recited together. Another particular examen is made at that time. We have supper next and then spend an hour in recreation. When that is over, we go to the church to make the general examen, say evening prayers, and read the points for the next morning's prayer. After that, we retire to our rooms and go to bed at nine o'clock.

When we are on mission in the country, we do the same, except that we go to the church at six o'clock in the morning to celebrate holy Mass and to hear confessions after the sermon which a man from the Company has just given following the holy Mass he has said beforehand. We hear confessions until eleven o'clock, then go to eat dinner and return to the church at two o'clock to hear confessions there until five o'clock. Following that, one man teaches catechism and the others go off to say Matins and Lauds so as to have supper at six o'clock.

It is our maxim not to preach, catechize, or hear confessions in cities where there is a bishopric and not to leave a village until all the people have been instructed in the matters necessary for salvation and until everyone has made his general confession. We go to few places where there is anyone left who fails to do so. When we have finished in one village, we go to another where we do the same thing. We work from around the feast of All Saints until that of Saint John; we leave the months of July, August, September, and a part of October to the people so that they can take care of the harvest and the vintage. And when we have worked twenty days or thereabouts, we rest for a week or so and then go back to work. It is not possible to continue such labor for a longer time without that respite and without a day off each week.

We have our days of solitude every year. We hold chapter every Friday morning, during which each one accuses himself of his failings, receives a penance from the superior, and is obliged to carry it out. Two priests and two brothers ask the Company for the charity of being warned of their failings and, after them others do so, each in turn. In the evening of the same day we have a conference on our rules and the practice of the virtues. Everyone there shares the thoughts Our Lord gave him in prayer on the topic being discussed.

LETTERS OF VINCENT DE PAUL

We never go out without permission and always two by two. Upon returning, everyone goes to see the superior and gives him an account of what he has done. We neither write nor receive letters unless the superior has seen and approved them. Everyone is obliged to agree to having his faults charitably reported to his superior and to try to accept from and give to others the admonitions needed. Silence is observed from evening until the end of dinner the next day and from after the morning recreation until the one in the evening.

We spend two years in the seminary, that is, in the novitiate. The training there is rather strict, by the mercy of God, so that for a number of reasons the seminarians do not communicate with the priests without permission.

The said congregation is approved by His Holiness and established in the city and in the faubourg of Saint Denis in Paris, and in the dioceses of Poitiers, Luçon, Toul, Agen, and Troyes.

There you have our humble way of life, most dear and most worthy Mother. Please do us the charity, for the love of Our Lord, of telling us your reactions to it. You may be assured, dear Mother, that I shall accept them as coming from God, from Whose love I request this charity of you. . . .[21]

I shall not say anything to you about your dear daughters in Paris except that I think they are advancing more and more in the love of their Divine Savior. I have a great pardon to ask of you because I have not visited them for a long time. The sisters here[22] also have a good reputation and live fervently, and certainly with good reason. You could not believe, dear Mother, how greatly the spirit of Our Lord is evident in both the Mother[23] and the *déposée*,[24] or how well the rest of the house is doing, considering the difficulties it has had in the past.

Well now, dear Mother, permit me to ask if your unparalleled goodness still reserves for me the happiness of enjoying the place it gave me in your dear and most lovable heart? Certainly, I choose to hope so, even though my miseries render me most unworthy of it. In the name of God, dear [Mother],[25] please continue to grant me that favor. Trusting that you will, I am your most humble and most obedient servant.

VINCENT DE PAUL
Priest of the Mission

TO JULES CARDINAL MAZARIN
24 May 1646[26]

Because of Vincent's holiness and practical insight, he was highly regarded among the clergy. They often sought his advice in naming certain people to assume high positions in the teaching of theology.

My Lord,

The Grand Master of the Collège de Navarre[27] told me that Your Eminence had instructed Monsieur Le Tellier[28] to have me write him to say whether the Sieur de Douay, licentiate in theology, has the requisite qualities to be head of the school of philosophy in the same college. The following, My Lord, is what I have learned about him, both from the deceased principal and from several scholars worthy of credence.

They all say he is very capable, a good man, experienced in the duties of this office in which the late principal had employed him for several years; that he holds the usual orthodox views of the Church and, lastly, that the public opinion of the college is that this young man is indisputably the most capable of those being considered for that position.

What further confirms this is that the late principal, a holy man who worked wonders in his duty, came to see me a few days before his death and asked me to use my good offices with Your Eminence, that you might be pleased to give him as Assistant this young man whom he judged before God to be the one most capable of continuing the good order he had established in his office. And I, My Lord, beg Our Lord to sanctify you and preserve you for the good of this State, and am, My Lord, your most humble and very obedient servant.

VINCENT DE PAUL
Unworthy superior of the Mission

TO THE SISTERS AT VALPUISEAUX
Paris, 23 June 1652[29]

In this tender letter to the Daughters at Valpuiseaux, Vincent exhorts them to take care of themselves. He realizes how hard they are working but reassures them that they will be amply rewarded by God. He gives news of how the poor are being served in Paris and regrets not being able to send them help.

My good Sisters,

The grace of Our Lord be with you forever!

Blessed be God that there you are finally back home again and for keeping you safe in the midst of so many trials and dangers![30]

I thank him for this with all my heart. I was very happy to have news of you, and equally sorry to hear that you have been ill. Nevertheless, I submit to the good pleasure of God, who will draw his glory from your sickness, as he has done from your good health, which I hope he will soon restore to you by his grace and by the change of weather. I cannot tell you how grateful I am for your protection; I feel this as keenly as if you were dead and he has brought you back to life.

It must be acknowledged, Sisters, that you have really had a hard time, but you will also be amply rewarded for it. Not only will your reward be great because of what you have suffered, but also because of the good you have done by serving the sick and the wounded in the hospital, and for the good example you have given there. I ask God to be his own praise and thanks for all this.

I have heard there are many sick persons in Val de Puiseau, and that the poor place has great need of assistance right now. This has made me redouble my prayers to God to restore you to a condition in which you can visit and console them, and I beg you, Sisters, to do your utmost to get well. Mademoiselle Le Gras is sending you syrups and medicines for this purpose, and I am asking the poor widow of the late Pierre Charpentier to supply you with the money you need.

Please spare nothing for your recovery. We would send you a Sister to help you, if we could, but you are aware of the dangers on the roads.[31] Besides, the situation in Paris is so bad that Mademoiselle Le Gras does not have enough sisters to care for the sick and the poor refugees in all the places where people are requesting them. Soup is prepared for them in a large number of parishes; our Sisters at Saint-Paul[32] distribute it daily to almost eight thousand poor persons, both the bashful poor and the refugees, not counting the sixty to eighty patients they have on their hands. Your Company has never worked so hard or so effectively as it is doing at the present moment. I hope that, in consideration of this, God will bless it abundantly.

Your good Mother is well.[33] I come back to you, Sisters, to ask you once again to take great care to recover the strength you have lost. Do not be in any hurry to get back to work until you have fully recovered. Just now you are, as it were, in a desert, because I consider Val de Puiseau as such, but remember that Our Lord himself honored solitude, when he willed to spend some time in the desert, as you know. Now, it is always a blessing for us to be in those states through which our good Lord and Master has passed.

I often recommend you to him. Continue to fear and love him well; offer him your difficulties and your little services, and do only what pleases him. In this way you will continue to grow in grace and virtue. Pray to him for us and for me, who am, in his love, my good Sisters, your affectionate servant,

VINCENT DE PAUL
Unworthy priest of the Mission

TO GUILLAUME DESDAMES
Paris, 25 April 1659[34]

This letter to a missionary in Poland is filled with the saint's wisdom. He instructs his priest to be completely abandoned to God's workings, always allowing God to take the needed time to accomplish good. He concludes by urging the priests in Krakow to pray earnestly for the virtues needed to be at peace while awaiting God's response.

Monsieur,
May the Grace of Our Lord be always with you.

I have not had any letters from you for the past three or four weeks. The last I received is the one in which you tell me what happened on your journey to Krakow, and I have not written to you since I wrote in reply to that. You saw by that letter that we have made up our minds not to send you any more men until Providence gives us an opportunity of employing and maintaining them there. That may occur when we least expect it.

God's works are not regulated by our plans and wishes. We should be content with making the best of the few talents he has placed in our hands, and not distress ourselves about having more or greater ones. If we are faithful in that which is little, he will place us over that which is great. That, however, must come from him, and not be the result of our efforts. Let us leave it to him and curl ourselves up in our shells. The Company began without any plan on our part. It has multiplied by God's guidance alone, and was called to Poland by his supreme command without our having contributed anything save only obedience. Let us continue to act, Monsieur, in the same way. Such abandonment will please God greatly, and we shall be at peace.

The spirit of the world is restless, and wishes to do everything. Let us leave it to itself. Let us have no desire to choose our own paths, but walk in those which God may be pleased to prescribe for us. Let us regard ourselves as unworthy that he should make use of us, or that others should think of us, and then all will be well with us. Let us offer ourselves to him to do and to suffer all things for his glory and the establishment of his Church. He asks for nothing else. If he desires results, they rest with him and not with us.

Let us courageously extend the confines of our heart and will in his presence and let us not decide upon doing this thing or that until God has spoken. Let us implore him to grant us the grace to labor meanwhile to practice those virtues which Our Lord practiced during his hidden life. I beg him to animate both you and dear Monsieur Duperroy with his spirit so that you may possess it in the highest degree.

I am, Monsieur, in the sole pleasure of God, the humble servant of you both,

VINCENT DE PAUL
Unworthy priest of the Mission

TO PHILIPPE PATTE
[November or December 1659][35]

This letter to Brother Philippe Patte offers encouragement and consolation. Vincent urges the practice of virtue in the midst of

*dealing with heretics, cautioning that all people, Catholic or Hugue-
not, must be revered as God's children.*

I am deeply grieved to learn that you will have heretics on
board ship and, consequently, much to endure from them. But,
after all, God is the captain, and has permitted this for reasons we
do not know. Perhaps it is to oblige you to be more reserved in their
presence, more humble and more devoted to God, and more charitable to your neighbor so that they may see the beauty and holiness of
our religion and be thereby moved to return to it. Every sort of
dispute and contention with them should be carefully avoided and
you should show yourself patient and even-tempered when you are
with them, even if they attack you or our faith and its practices.
    Virtue is so beautiful and amiable that they will be compelled
to love it in you, if you practice it well. It is desirable that, in the
services which you may render God on board ship, you should
make no distinction among persons and make no apparent difference in your treatment of Catholics and Huguenots, so that the
latter may know you love them in God. I trust your good example
will prove serviceable to both.
    Please take care of your health and that of our missionaries.

TO SISTER MATHURINE GUERIN
3 March 1660[36]

*Vincent consoles Mathurine on the death of Father Antoine
Portail and on the illness of Louise. He reports on Louise's declin-
ing health and what is being done to preserve her. He reminds
Mathurine that in spite of these setbacks, God will maintain the
Daughters of Charity because it is he himself who called and assem-
bled them.*

My dear Sister,
    The grace of Our Lord be ever with you!
    I have received your letter, and fully share in your grief. It is
true that God has taken good Monsieur Portail from us (he died on
February14), and that Mademoiselle Le Gras was then in great
danger, and has been so ever since. These are two severe blows for

your little Company; but, coming from God's fatherly hand, they are to be received with submission, and we should hope from his charity that the Daughters of Charity will profit from this trial. It is he who has called them and he will maintain them. He never destroys his work; rather, he brings it to perfection; and, provided they be firm in their vocation, and faithful to their exercises, he will always bless them in their persons and activities. I beg you, Sister, for your part, to continue to carry out your duties well, and to remain in peace; if you do so, you will be more pleasing to God than by acting otherwise.

Thanks be to God, Mademoiselle is now improving. Her chief trouble has been a large inflammation on the left arm, for which three incisions were necessary. The last was made the day before yesterday. She is suffering severely, as you may imagine, and, although she is no longer feverish, she is not yet out of danger, both on account of her age and her weakness. Everything is being done to preserve her; but this is the work of God, who, having preserved her for twenty years, contrary to all human appearances, will preserve her as long as it may be proper for his glory.

We shall let you know, Sister, the results of this distressing illness, and also inform our other Sisters who are living at a distance.

I now beg you to be at peace as to what may happen, for uneasiness disturbs the soul, and is displeasing to God, who governs all things with wisdom and love, asking from us a complete and loving resignation to his guidance. Surely the great secret of the spiritual life is to abandon to him all that we love by abandoning ourselves to all that he wishes, in perfect confidence that all will be for the best; and hence it has been said that all things turn to good for those who serve God.

Let us serve him then, Sister, but let us serve him according to his own good pleasure, and let us leave him to act. He will take the place of father and mother for you; he will be your consolation, your strength, and, in the end, the reward of your love. Pray to him for me, who am, in his love. . . .

Rules of the Daughters of Charity, Servants of the Sick Poor

INTRODUCTION

*T*he Common Rules of the Daughters of Charity stem from the experiences of Saints Louise de Marillac and Vincent de Paul. Service of the poor by women living a new form of consecrated life became so powerful a motive for dedication to God that the Common Rules were adopted and adapted by numerous other communities. They continue to nourish the Church.

The early rules governing the lives and activities of the first Daughters of Charity took many forms. The earliest extant rules predate the official foundation of the Company on 29 November 1633. Vincent de Paul commented on them in conferences he gave to the new community, and the earliest surviving text of one of these conferences dates to 1634. The text of the second oldest conference is dated 1640. From that period, he delivered other conferences on the rules, but a full text of the rules followed in this formative period has not survived.

The archbishop of Paris, Jean-François-Paul de Gondi, gave initial approval of the Company in 1655, and Vincent de Paul then gave to the Daughters of Charity a lengthy series of conferences on these rules in forty-three articles. In many cases, the text of the Vincent's conference quoted the rules in their entirety, but in others the text is lacking. Fortunately, at least one manuscript of the complete text of the 1655 rules has survived wars and revolutions. The text of this extraordinary document has been given in this publication, but only in the footnotes, since these are not, strictly speaking, the Common Rules of the Daughters of Charity. (These original *rules from 1655 appear here for the public for the first time in English.) Their interest comes from the illumination they give to the later, official, rules.*

Both Louise de Marillac and Vincent de Paul died before publishing the rules for the Daughters of Charity. That task of revising and publishing, begun by Sister Marguerite Chétif, Louise de Marillac's successor in office, was completed by Sister Mathurine Guérin and René Alméras, C.M., Vincent's successor as superior general. Approved by Clement IX in 1668, this text was published in 1672. [1] As will be noted, the text of the 1672 rules, the official Common Rules, differs in some respects from the 1655 rules that Saint Vincent explained in his conferences. The revisers clarified texts, rearranged some, and occasionally added new materials. These rules of 1672 guided the lives of the Daughters of Charity until 1954. [2] In that year, a revised version of the Common Rules was prepared on the basis of changes in the Church stemming from the Code of Canon Law of 1917, as well as from modern experience.

Besides the Common Rules, to be observed by all, constitutions describing community government, and several other rules existed. Some were particular rules, either governing a specific place, for example the hospital at Angers, or setting down regulations for Sisters working in similar apostolates, such as those who taught school. Besides it constitutions, its common and particular rules, the Company also had rules of office, as well as specific Community customs. Since Vincent de Paul gave conferences on the particular rules for the Sisters living in the parishes, those rules follow the Common Rules in this publication. As with the text of the Common Rules, some differences also exist between the text Vincent commented on in his conferences and the official one, published after his death. Where they occur, these differences have been noted.

Attentive reading of these rules will unveil the theological and spiritual world inhabited by the two founders. It was a world of divine activity, with human actions done in relation to God's work. The rules summoned the Sisters to imitate Jesus in his mysteries, but also to minister to him in others, particularly in the poor. So unified was this world view that to obey superiors was to obey God; to leave scheduled prayers or other activities to serve the poor was, in a memorable phrase, to "leave God for God." The means that to serve others was principally efficient spiritual and physical service, done with a view to one's own perfection in accomplishing the will of God. Though these Common Rules are no longer observed to the letter, their spirit permeates the constitutions and statutes of the post–Vatican II Company of the Daughters of Charity of Saint Vincent de Paul, Servants of the Sick Poor. [3]

CHAPTER I
THE END AND FUNDAMENTAL VIRTUES
OF THEIR INSTITUTE

1. The principal end for which God has called and established the Daughters of Charity is to honor our Lord Jesus Christ as the source and model of all charity, serving him corporally and spiritually in the person of the poor, whether sick, children, prisoners, or others who, through embarrassment, dare not make known their wants. Therefore, that they may worthily correspond to so holy a vocation and imitate so perfect a model, they should strive to live in a holy manner and labor with great care to attain perfection, uniting the exercises of a spiritual life with the exterior duties of Christian charity toward the poor, according to the present rules which they will endeavor to practice with great fidelity as the surest means of attaining this end.[4]

2. They should consider that although they do not belong to a religious order, that state not being compatible with the duties of their vocation, yet as they are much more exposed to the world than nuns—their monastery being generally no other than the abode of the sick; their cell, a hired room; their chapel, the parish church; their cloister, the public streets or the wards of hospitals; their enclosure, obedience; their grate, the fear of God; and their veil, holy modesty—they are obliged on this account to lead as virtuous a life as if they were professed in a religious order; to conduct themselves wherever they mingle with the world with as much recollection, purity of heart and body, detachment from creatures; and to give as much edification as nuns in the seclusion of their monasteries.

3. The first thing they shall endeavor to observe inviolably is to value the salvation of their soul above all earthly things, and to spare nothing in order to be in a state of grace, avoiding with that

intent all mortal sin, more than the demon and death itself, and doing all they can with the help of God not to commit deliberately any venial sin.[5] But to obtain from God the graces necessary for this end, and to gain the reward which our Lord promises to those who devote themselves to the service of the poor, they should, moreover, earnestly endeavor to acquire all Christian virtues, particularly those which are recommended to them in the following rules.

4. They shall perform all their exercises, both spiritual and corporal, in a spirit of humility, simplicity, and charity, and in union with those which Our Lord Jesus Christ performed when he was on earth, forming for this purpose their intention in the morning, and at the beginning of each principal action, particularly when going to serve the sick, and they shall be mindful that these three virtues are like the three faculties of the soul, which should animate the whole body in general and each individual member of their Community, and that in a word they should constitute the peculiar spirit of their Company.

5. They shall abhor the maxims of the world and embrace those of Jesus Christ, among others, those that recommend mortification, both interior and exterior, contempt of self and all earthly things, preferring employments that are humble and repugnant to the inclinations of nature, to those that are honorable and agreeable, always taking the last place and the refuse of others, believing that with all this they are better off than they deserve on account of their sins.[6]

6. They shall not be attached to any created thing, particularly to places, employments, or persons, not even to their relatives and confessors. They shall always be ready to leave everything when obedience requires it, remembering that our Lord says we are not worthy of him if we do not leave father and mother, brothers and sisters, and renounce ourselves and all things of this world to follow him.[7]

7. They shall endure willingly and for the love of God inconveniences, contradictions, mockeries, calumnies, and other mortifications which may befall them, even on account of the good they do, remembering that Our Lord, who was most innocent, suffered much more for us, praying even for those who crucified him, and that all this is but a part of the cross which he wills them to carry

after him on earth, in order that they may deserve to be one day with him in heaven.[8]

8. They should have great confidence in Divine Providence, committing themselves to it without reserve, as an infant to its nurse. They should be well convinced that, provided on their part they try to be faithful to their vocation and to the observance of their rules, God will always keep them under his protection, and will provide them with what they need both for soul and body, even when all appears to be lost.[9]

CHAPTER II
POVERTY

1. They shall honor the poverty of our Lord, being satisfied with having their little wants supplied in the customary simplicity and according to the usage of the Community, reflecting that they are the Servants of the Poor and should therefore live a life of poverty. Accordingly they shall put all in common like the first Christians, so that no one among them shall have anything to keep or use as belonging to herself alone. They shall not give, lend, nor dispose of the property of the Community, or even of that belonging to themselves, nor of anything that may remain to them from their maintenance or still less of the property of the poor which is entrusted to them. Neither shall they borrow, purchase, or receive anything from others, without the consent of the superioress in small and ordinary matters. For those that are extraordinary and of more consequence, they will need the permission of the reverend superior.[10]

2. They shall do their utmost to acquire that holy practice so much recommended by the saints, and so strictly observed in well-regulated communities, namely, that of neither asking nor refusing anything in temporal matters. Nevertheless, should a Sister really stand in need of something, she may mention it simply and with indifference to those who should attend to it, and then rest satisfied whether it be given her or not. But, that no one may have occasion to fail in this holy practice, the officers and Sister Servants should inquire every week into the wants of each, individually, and supply her with everything necessary, retrenching what would be superfluous.[11]

3. As they should not use without permission any article intended for the Community or for some particular Sister, neither should they complain, if by the same permission another be accommodated with something previously appropriated to their use, but rather, be pleased at having an opportunity of practicing holy poverty and mortification. If, however, it be necessary to mention it, as when they have reason to believe or suspect that something has been taken from them without permission, they shall neither speak of it in public nor in private except to the superioress, some officer of the Community, or the Sister Servant, when this happens in one of their distant houses. They shall also beware of leaving off, or altering without permission, the articles given them for their use when they are old or do not suit them, very far from throwing them away or wishing to arrange them according to their own taste.[12]

4. They shall make it a matter of conscience to manage well the money and other things committed to their charge for the use of the Sisters, remembering that not doing so would be a sin against the virtue of poverty which they promised to practice when they assumed the name and habit of Servants of the Poor. And to prevent abuses which might insensibly glide into the use they make of these things, particularly with regard to dress, as would happen if each one had the liberty to buy linen and cloth and make her own clothing, which would cause much disorder in the Company and ruin holy uniformity, so necessary in communities, the Sisters of the houses in villages and cities shall make use of the money which the Ladies and others give them for their nourishment and maintenance, in accordance with the ordinary poor and simple manner of living, observed from the beginning in their principal house of Paris, and those of the hospitals shall try to conform to it as much as possible, even in houses where the common portion of the poor is given to them. None of thse who are supplied with money necessary for their habits and linen shall buy any serge or linen for their clothing, but shall ask the superioress for it, sending her the amount of what it will cost, and giving her an account at least once a year, either verbally or in writing, of the money which has been given them. The Sister Servants in very distant houses shall send the superioress samples of such cloth and linen as they can procure, to see if it be similar to that which is used in the Community, and

follow her decision thereon. If they need anything else, they shall not buy it without asking her permission.[13]

5. They should as much as possible preserve uniformity in all things as the means of maintaining, not only the spirit of poverty, but also union and regularity in the Community. They should shun all singularity as the source of discord and disorder. For this end they shall conform in every point to the common manner of living, where the superioress resides, adopting the maxims and practices there inculcated, for the spiritual and temporal administration, without following others although apparently good or even better, and, with regard to the necessities of the body, they shall be careful not to have anything different from others or better than others have, whether in dress, headdress, shoes, bedding, food, or furniture. If, however, anyone having reflected before God thinks she stands in need of some particular indulgence on account of indisposition, she shall mention it simply and with indifference to the said superioress, who will consult with the reverend superior as to what is best to be done.[14]

6. They shall also observe holy poverty in time of sickness, contenting themselves with the common treatment of the poor with regard to medicine, food, and other similar necessities, without repining or murmuring at not being treated according to their liking. They shall consider, particularly in this case, that the Servants of the Poor ought not to be better attended than their masters, and that it is a great blessing to suffer something for the love of God, who deigns to try their patience in order to increase their merit. Besides, they do not know what is fit for them, as well as the physicians and infirmarians, to whom, therefore, it is just they should give up the care of their health. Accordingly, they shall eat only at the hours appointed, and in no other place than in the infirmary or refectory, and they shall neither receive nor cause anything to be bought for them without the permission of the Sister Servant. The other Sisters who visit them shall give them nothing without the same permission. Should externs wish to supply them more delicately or liberally, they shall humbly thank them for their kind intention, and respectfully entreat that they will not prevent them from observing their rules on this point, which, however, do not forbid them to receive, with the permission of the Sister Servant, some little delicacies when greatly needed.[15]

7. While they remain in the house where the superioress resides, they shall beware of inviting externs either to eat or take lodging there without her permission. The Sisters of the parishes shall act in like manner with the Sister Servant, who should not do it nor permit it to be done without great necessity, and not without a special or general permission of the superioress, and then only with regard to persons of their own sex, were there no other harm in it than the disposal of property which does not belong to them, and the use of which is given for their personal wants alone.[16]

CHAPTER III

CHASTITY

1. They shall do their utmost to preserve perfect purity of heart and body. For this purpose they shall quickly banish all thoughts contrary to this virtue and carefully avoid whatever might in any way wound it, particularly the desire of appearing agreeable, vanity and affectation in their dress, walk, or manner of speaking, also curiosity to hear and see people of the world, either through the windows, or in going through the streets; self-confidence and frequent contact with externs without real necessity. In a word, they shall avoid all that might give their neighbor the least cause to suspect them of being ever so little inclined to the contrary vice, such a suspicion alone, though quite unfounded, being more prejudicial to their Company and its holy employments than all other crimes that might falsely be imputed to them.[17]

2. And, inasmuch as holy modesty is not only necessary that they may edify their neighbor, but also that they may preserve that angelic purity which is easily tarnished by acts of immodesty, they shall be careful to observe it at all times and in all places. They shall therefore be mindful to keep their eyes down, particularly in the streets, churches, houses of seculars, above all in speaking to persons of the other sex, and even when they are together in their rooms, during the time of prayers, conferences, silence, and meals. They shall avoid precipitancy in their walk and actions, and preserve cleanliness in their dress and furniture, without affectation. They shall also refrain even in their recreations from childish levity, excessive laughter, unbecoming gestures and conversations, all for-

bidden plays,[18] or any that might lead to a want of delicacy. They shall never touch one another without necessity even through playfulness or in token of friendship, unless it be to embrace in a spirit of charity those who have just been received into the Company, or those who come back from the country, or to become reconciled with those to whom they have given pain. In these cases they are allowed to kiss each other, but always kneeling, and on the cheek only, not on the mouth, neither shall they do so in the streets, nor in churches.[19]

3. They shall carefully avoid idleness as the mother of all vices and especially of impurity. Therefore, when the duties of their office and the exercises appointed in the order of the day afford them some moments of relaxation, they shall employ them faithfully in sewing, spinning, or other similar work. If they have nothing to do, they shall ask the superioress or her assistant to give them some employment, and those in distant places shall ask the Sister Servant. They shall nowhere keep birds, lap dogs. or other animals, merely for the sake of amusement, as this might cause them to misspend that time of which they should make it a matter of conscience to lose even a single moment, remembering that God will demand a strict account of it. Neither shall they employ their time on weekdays in saying other prayers than those prescribed in the order of the day, nor shall they remain to hear more than one Mass, unless some particular circumstance oblige them to do so.[20]

4. Whereas ill-regulated contact with externs may be as prejudicial to their purity, as it is advantageous and meritorious when directed by obedience and for the purpose of discharging their duty towards the poor, they shall not leave the house without the permission of the superioress, to whom they shall mention where they are going and for what purpose. On their return they shall give her an account of what took place during their absence. Those of the parishes and other houses will act in like manner with the Sister Servant, who shall also inform her companion before going out.[21] All shall be mindful on this occasion to take holy water and kneel down in their chapel or oratory, to offer to Our Lord on going out the action they are going to perform, and beg his blessing and grace not to offend him. They will do the same on their return, to thank him for the favors he has granted them, or to ask pardon for the faults they may have committed.[22]

5. They shall pay no visits but such as are necessary, and these, with the permission of the superioress or Sister Servant. If they are obliged to see magistrates, administrators, or such like persons, they shall always go two together, so that the companion never lose sight of her Sister. If they cannot be accompanied by one of their Sisters, they shall take some girl of the school or a woman of the neighborhood, whom they shall request not to leave them.[23]

6. They shall always be accompanied in the same manner when they take food to any poor sick ecclesiastic, or persons in colleges, prisons, and other places where they might have reason to be more carefully on their guard. They should even, if possible, contrive to have the remedies administered to such persons by others, and never give any to those who are in suspected places. Neither shall they take them the ordinary allowance of charity, nor have anything to do with persons defamed for the vice of impurity, or attacked with the disease proceeding therefrom. As for other poor sick people, particularly those of the other sex, they should always be very cautious in administering remedies to them or in serving them, and they should not go too near them, even during their agony, or while preparing them for death.

7. If externs come to visit them, they shall not speak to them or permit them to speak to any Sister, until they obtain permission from the superioress or the Sister Servant, and then they may speak to them at the door or in some place close by if there be one destined for strangers, but they shall not bring them any farther into the house, still less into their rooms, without an order from the reverend superior, though they be persons of their own sex wishing to see the house. They should not even allow priests or their confessors to enter therein unless in case of sickness, when one Sister, at least, should be present in some place near enough to see them. They should observe the same precaution with regard to the physician, apothecary, surgeon, or others who may have permission to visit them in their illness. Much less should they visit their confessors or other priests at their houses, in their rooms, unless they be very sick. For then they may do so, but always two together, without leaving each other. If besides this it be necessary to speak to them, they should do so in the church or at the entrance of the house, in presence of witnesses, and never at an undue hour.

Should they happen to be alone with any man, they must not remain a moment with him unless the doors be open.

8. Whenever they meet with persons of the other sex, they should observe great modesty and reserve in their words and demeanor, being careful not to manifest too much cordiality or courtesy, being brief with them, even though their conversation be on matters of piety, the relief of the poor, or other useful subjects. For the same reason they shall not be taught to write by men, and especially they shall never allow them to touch them, or suffer any other familiarity from them under any pretext whatsoever.

9. When they go through the streets and to houses where the service of the poor demands their presence, they shall not stop with externs without great necessity, and then they must endeavor to reply to their questions in few words, prudently evading by some pious remarks any worldly news that might be related to them. They shall studiously refrain from inquiring curiously into such things, not only of externs, but even of their Sisters, also into private family affairs, though under pretext of consoling the poor, such inquiries being very contrary to the spirit of devotion and the good example they owe their neighbor.

10. Sobriety and good order at meals greatly contributing to the health of both soul and body, and particularly to the preservation of purity, they shall do their utmost to conform in this respect to the regulations observed in the house of the superioress, as well with regard to the quality and quantity of their food and drink, as to the time and place of taking them. If however, any one stands in need of eating between meals, or out of the house, or of taking some extraordinary nourishment, she shall ask permission of the said superioress, or of the Sister Servant of the place where she resides, but the use of wine shall not be granted to anyone without special permission from the reverend superior of their Company.[24]

11. Although the incessant labors of the Daughters of Charity do not allow them to undertake many penances and bodily austerities, they may, however, sometimes make use of them with the permission of the superioress in ordinary matters, and with that of the reverend superior in extraordinary things. They shall, moreover, fast on the vigils of the feasts of obligation of Our Lord, and the Blessed Virgin, and on all Fridays of the year except Easter to Pentecost, or when the feast of the patron or of the

dedication of the parish falls on that day, or when there is any other fast in the same week. They shall also abstain on all the Wednesdays of Advent, and on Monday and Tuesday after Quinquagesima. But on all these days, the infirm and those who go to attend the sick, or who are employed at other laborious work, may take in the morning a piece of bread or some other little thing by way of medicine, even on fast days, that is on those appointed by the rule, with the permission of the superioress, or in her absence, of her assistant, or the Sister Servants in distant places, and on those of the Church, with the approbation of the superior or the director. However, they shall bear in mind that exterior mortification avails but little if not accompanied by that of the interior, which consists in submitting their judgment and will to the orders of superiors, in combating and overcoming their passions and evil inclinations, and in refusing the senses any satisfaction out of the case of necessity.[25]

CHAPTER IV
OBEDIENCE

1. They shall render honor and obedience according to their institute to the bishops in whose dioceses they are established. They shall also obey the superior general of the Congregation of the Mission as the superior of their Company, and those whom he shall appoint to direct or visit them, the superioress, and, in her absence, her Sister assistant, and the other officers of the house in whatever concerns their offices, also the Sister Servants who are given them in the parishes and other places where they are established, the Sister officers of the hospitals, and those Sisters who have charge of them during their journeys. They shall even obey the sound of the bell, without the least delay, as the voice of Our Lord calling them to the exercises of the Community.[26]

2. They shall especially endeavor to practice punctual obedience, with submission of the judgment and will, in all things in which there is no sin, and to all sorts of superiors and officers, as well those who are imperfect and disagreeable as those who are perfect and agreeable, remembering that it is not so much persons whom they obey, as Our Lord, Jesus Christ, who commands by their mouth, and who says himself, speaking to those who have

charge of others, "He who hears you, hears me, and he who despises you, despises me."[27]

3. When they are sent to a parish to reside there and to serve the sick poor, the Sister Servant, accompanied by one of her Sisters, shall go to receive kneeling the blessing of the pastor. As long as they remain in the parish they shall pay him all honor and respect and even obedience in the assistance of the sick, particularly with regard to the spiritual help they may afford them. They shall also show great respect toward all other priests, but particularly to those who hear their confessions, and to the confessors of the poor, always regarding them with nearly the same veneration as when they are at the holy altar and submitting to their orders and advice in everything that is not sinful or contrary to the rules and customs of their Company, nor against the intentions of their superiors. If any one of them should not discharge his duty toward the sick in a proper manner, they shall not take the liberty of reproving him, but request the pastor to remind him of what he should do.[28]

4. They shall also pay honor and obedience in all that concerns the service of the poor, to the administrators of hospitals where they are established, and to the Ladies belonging to the parish, who are in office, that is, to each one according to her office, conformably to the regulations of the place and the rules of their Company. They shall likewise obey the physicians, accomplishing punctually their orders as well with regard to the poor as to their sick Sisters, who shall also obey the physician and infirmarian in all that relates to their office and is not contrary to their rules.[29]

5. They shall not open the letters or notes addressed to them without the permission of the superioress, who should previously read them herself. Neither shall they write any without the same permission, and they shall give her those they write that she may see them, and send or detain them, as she may think proper. The Sister companions who are distant from the house of the superioress, shall act in like manner with the Sister Servant, whose duty it is to open and read the letters addressed either to herself or to her Sisters, or any that they may write to others.[30]

6. Each one should know, however, that the preceding rule does not oblige them to show the letters that they write to the reverend superior, the director, or the superioress, any more than those which they may receive from them. These should not be

shown to externs or even to their Sisters, it being sufficient to tell them verbally such things as it would be well for them to know. They should also know that all letters which the Sister Servant or their companions write, either to externs or to private Sisters of their Company, should be addressed to the superioress, without any seal but that of the envelope, when they are sent to the place where she resides, or are to pass that way.

7. The Sister Servants who are out of Paris shall be careful to write at least two or three times a year to the superioress, to give her an account of their employments and of the state of their Sisters. Moreover, they as well as their Sister companions shall write to her or to the reverend superior whenever they have anything of consequence to propose, and the Sister Servants shall always give full liberty to their companions to write to superiors, without evincing any desire to see their letters or those which they receive from them. The Sisters who do not know how to write can ask one of their Sisters, the pastor, or some other trustworthy person to do them this favor which, however, they should use with great prudence, dictating nothing that could not be made known to them without wounding charity.

CHAPTER V

THE CHARITY AND UNION WHICH SHOULD

EXIST AMONG THEMSELVES

1. They shall often think of the name of Daughters of Charity which they have the honor to bear, and endeavor to become worthy of it by a true and sincere love of God and their neighbor. Above all they shall cherish and respect one another as Sisters whom Our Lord has united together for his service by the special profession of works of charity, and they shall do their utmost to maintain perfect union among themselves. For this purpose they shall quickly banish from their heart every feeling of aversion and envy, and be on their guard not to make use of any unkind expression in speaking to one another, but behave together with Christian meekness and respectful cordiality, which should always appear on their countenance and in their words.[31]

2. They shall willingly bear with their companions in their imperfections as they would wish to be borne with by them, and

shall condescend, as much as possible, to their feelings and opinions in everything that is not sinful or against the rules, being particularly careful to show great charity toward those whose disposition agrees least with their own, for this holy condescension, joined with mutual support, is an excellent means to maintain union and peace in the Community. [32]

3. Should it happen through human frailty that a Sister gives cause of offense to another, she shall not fail to ask pardon immediately on her knees or at least at night, before going to bed. The other shall receive humbly and cordially the humiliation of her Sister, and shall also go on her knees; this holy practice being a sovereign remedy for healing the bitterness of heart and the resentment that might remain on account of the fault committed. But not to prevent the salutary effect of this holy practice, she who has received the offense shall beware of taking advantage of her Sister's humiliation in order to satisfy the inclination of her nature by exaggerating her fault or making use of rude and reproachful words, although the Sister may have often fallen into the same fault. [33]

4. They shall take great care of their sick Sisters, particularly out of the house of the superioress. For this end they shall look upon them as servants of Jesus Christ as they are servants of his members, the poor, and, as their own Sisters, because they are all in a special manner daughters of the same Father, who is God, and of the same mother, their Company. On this account they shall wait upon them with all possible affection and exactness. They shall, above all, be mindful to give timely notice to the confessor when a Sister is sick and procure for her all the sacraments and other spiritual assistance she may need. As to the treatment of the body, they shall observe what is prescribed above in the sixth rule on Poverty, Chapter II.

5. And whereas too much tenderness for self which is very contrary to well-regulated charity and to a moderate care of health might often lead the Sisters, particularly those of the parishes, to mention their slight indispositions to the physician of the poor, and who, by being too ready to give them remedies, might expose them to the danger of ruining their health instead of improving it. They shall not take any medicine, be bled, or consult a physician or any other person of similar profession for this purpose, without the permission of the superioress, that is, those who are near her or in

the parishes of the city where she resides, unless the case be urgent, such as apoplexy, hemorrhage, and so forth. Whatever the ailment may be, they shall always make it known to the superioress, the second or third day at least. Those who are at a distance should ask this permission of the Sister Servant, who must not grant it unless she sees it is necessary. She herself should endeavor to give example to the others in practicing this rule, and all, after their recovery, shall cheerfully resume the common way, without pretending to a longer use of the particular dispensations granted them during their illness.[34]

6. They shall assist at the funeral of their Sisters who die at or near their place of residence, if they are informed of it in time. They shall offer for each their first three Communions on ordinary days, and the nine chaplets[35] which they say on the following days. They shall also have one high Mass and three low Masses celebrated for each, and shall observe for the rest the custom in use in their Community as followed in the house where the superioress resides. They shall also assist at the burial of the poor whom they have served, if their employments allow them, and pray to God for the repose of their soul.

CHAPTER VI

SOME MEANS OF PRESERVING CHARITY
AND UNION AMONG THEMSELVES

1. Although they should entertain much love for one another, they should carefully avoid particular friendships, which are the more dangerous as they appear less so, because they are ordinarily concealed under the mantle of charity, though they are in reality but disorderly affections of flesh and blood. They shall therefore avoid them with as much or even more care than aversions—these two vicious extremes being capable of ruining in a short time a whole Company.[36]

2. In order to remove all cause for murmuring, which is no less prejudicial to the peace and union of a Community than the two above-mentioned vices, and which generally proceeds from curiosity to know all that is going on under pretext of zeal for the common good, they shall not inquire into, nor speak about, the government of the Company, nor of the reasons why this one is sent, and

another recalled, nor about the offices of others, which they should not enter or interfere with, without permission, or finally, about the rules of the Company, to find fault with them, and still less to complain of them. But if anything appears to them of some consequence, they shall humbly and simply disclose their thoughts to the reverend superior, the director, or the superioress without giving themselves any further trouble, being careful never to murmur at their conduct, or the proceedings of the Sister Servant, all such murmurs being a source of scandal and dissension, which draw down the malediction of God not only on those who are guilty of them, but on those also who listen to them with pleasure and even on the whole Community.[37]

3. They shall beware in their conversation of speaking of the faults of their neighbor, particularly those of their Sisters. Neither shall they relate at home what they may have heard about them abroad, unless it be to superiors. But if any one among them should so far forget her duy as to hold discourse contrary to charity in presence of her Sisters, these, far from listening to her, shall do all in their power to prevent her from continuing, and if necessary beg her on their knees to desist. If even that does not deter her, they shall speedily withdraw as if they heard the hissing of a serpent.[38]

4. And inasmuch as silence is the most efficacious means to remedy, not only a great many faults contrary to charity committed by the tongue, but also many other sins which are always to be found in excessive talkativeness, according to the testimony of Holy Writ, they shall be careful to observe this silence faithfully at the times pointed out in their employment of the day, among others, from evening prayers until after Mass the next day which they shall hear about seven o'clock, and from two in the afternoon until three, so that they should always remember, even while going through the streets, that this is the time of strict silence. If it then be necessary to speak together, they shall do so in few words and in a low tone. They shall also observe the same silence at all times, in churches, sacristies of hospitals of which they have charge, in domestic oratories, and in the refectory, especially during meals. They shall also take care not to make a noise in the rooms or when going through the house, nor in opening and closing doors, particularly during the night. Even at those times when they are permitted to converse

together, they shall be on their guard not to raise their voice too much, but endeavor to speak in that moderate tone befitting their state, and the edification they owe their neighbor.[39]

CHAPTER VII
CHARITY TOWARDS THE SICK POOR

1. Their principal employment being to serve the sick poor, they shall acquit themselves of it with all possible care and attention, considering that it is not so much to them as to Jesus Christ that they render service. On this account they themselves shall carry their food and remedies to them, treating with compassion, mildness, cordiality, respect, and devotion, even the most troublesome, and those for whom they may feel some repugnance or less inclination. They shall consider it a matter of conscience to let them suffer by omitting to give them at the right time and in the proper manner the assistance they need, whether this happen through negligence, blamable forgetfulness, or some inordinate attachment to their spiritual exercises, which they should postpone for the necessary relief of the sick poor.[40]

2. They shall not forget, from time to time, to say a few kind words to them, to dispose them to patience, or to make a good general confession, to die or live well. They shall be particularly careful to teach them the things necessary for salvation, and see that they receive the sacraments in due time, and even more than once if they relapse after convalescence, all this in the manner, and according to the regulation given them in the particular rules concerning their duties toward the sick.

3. And as ill-directed charity is not only displeasing to God but prejudicial to the souls of those who practice it, they shall never undertake to give either food or medicine to any sick person against the will of those on whom they depend, nor against the order given them, without heeding the complaints which the discontented poor are accustomed to make. They shall, nevertheless, try to console and satisfy them the best they can, showing compassion for their sufferings and regret at not being able to relieve them according to their desire, and urging as much as possible the Ladies of Charity and others to do them all the good they can.[41]

4. If any charitable persons give them alms for the sick poor of the parish where they live, or for other needy persons, they shall be very exact in distributing them in the manner prescribed by the benefactors, by no means to other poor people, as it is not lawful for them to dispose of these alms except according to the intention of the persons who have placed them in their hands. If they have poor relatives, they shall be more careful not to fail in this respect to the prejudice of their conscience. For fear that natural love might deceive them under pretext of charity, they shall not ask any assistance for them, even from externs, without the permission of the superioress.

5. They shall not undertake to sit up with the sick out of the house or hospital where they reside, and much less with rich persons, whose service they should not undertake either in sickness or in health, nor even the care of their sick domestics, unless they be admitted on the list of charity, it not being conformable to their institute, the sole end of which is the assistance of the poor. If, however, in pressing need, a physician or surgeon cannot be found in the place, they may bestow even on rich persons the usual relief which they give to others, provided however, the poor be first served.

6. They shall not associate with them in their employments any servant or other extern, without an express permission of the superior of their Company; neither shall they admit boarders into any of their houses, not other persons of their sex, for a spiritual retreat, for more than eight days; and this only in the house where the superioress resides and not in the others, without the express permission of the said superioress.[42]

CHAPTER VIII
SPIRITUAL PRACTICES

1. They shall always endeavor to acquit themselves faithfully of their spiritual exercises, having particular need of them to preserve themselves in a state of grace and in the fervor necessary to persevere constantly in the labors of their vocation, although they should make no scruple of sometimes changing the hour of these exercises, or even of omitting some when the urgent necessities of

the poor require it. Still they shall take care never to fail in them through negligence, indevotion, or too great an inclination for exterior things which is sometimes cloaked under the pretext of charity.

2. They shall go to confession every Saturday and the vigils of feasts, to the confessors designated by the reverend superior, and not to others without his permission. Those in Paris shall also make every month a review of the principal faults committed during that time to the director or to another deputed by the reverend superior. By the same opportunity they shall present themselves to the superioress to give her an account of their employments and to propose to her their difficulties, or if they cannot do so then, they shall return for that purpose another day.[43]

3. Every year they shall make at the time appointed, a spiritual retreat and their annual confession of the faults committed since their last retreat.[44] Whenever they are informed that there will be a conference held by the reverend superior or any other appointed by him, in the house of the superioress, they shall be punctual in attending, at least, each one in turn, so that it may not in any way be prejudicial to the service of the poor or to any other employment of stricter obligation.[45] Those at a distance of one or two days' journey from the house of the superioress shall try to go there at least once a year, one after the other, to make their retreat, having previously asked permission of the superioress or of the director, and arranged with the Sister Servant concerning the day most convenient for their departure. She on her part shall do all in her power to afford them this consolation. Those who live in much more distant establishments shall apply for the aforesaid exercises and other spiritual aid which they may need, to those whom the reverend superior of their Company shall designate for that purpose in the places where they are established, and to the visitors whom he may occasionally send them, but neither those who are at a distance, nor those who are near, shall join any confraternity without an express permission from the same reverend superior.[46]

4. They will give evidence of so great purity of soul and so ardent a spiritual fervor, as to be considered worthy of receiving the most holy sacrament more frequently, or even every day, according to the decision of their confessor.[47]

5. Every Friday, except Good Friday or when some feast of obligation falls on that day, they shall assemble at half past seven

o'clock to say prayers and assist at the little conference held by the superioress, or by the one who represents her, concerning the faults committed against the rules in order that they may be corrected. For this end each one shall make her accusation in presence of the others in the usual manner, receiving cheerfully the admonitions and penance which may be given her, and ask pardon of those to whom she may have given cause of mortification or bad example. Every one shall be mindful to ask, once a month, to be publicly admonished of the faults which have been remarked in her. The others shall do this in a spirit of humility and charity, never mentioning any fault committed against themselves in particular. The Sisters who are admonished of their faults shall receive this favor with humility and a desire to correct, without justifying themselves or manifesting any displeasure at the admonitions they have received. Those who reside in the parishes and other establishments shall practice the same in presence of the Sister Servant.[48]

6. To prevent many serious evils which would finally cause the ruin of the Company if each one had the liberty of unburdening her heart to whomsoever she pleased, they will not communicate their temptations or other trials to their Sisters, and still less to externs, but they shall have recourse to the reverend superior, or to the director appointed by him, or to the superioress, and in case of need, the Sister Servant, God having destined them for that purpose and no others. If, however, anyone thinks before God that she stands in need of conferring with or of asking the advice of any extern, she may do so, but not without permission from the aforesaid superior, director, or superioress, lest in acting otherwise God might permit her to receive bad advice in punishment of her disobedience.[49]

7. They shall be particularly careful to keep silence with regard to things which bind to secrecy, and among others, what is said or done at conferences, communications, and confessions, it being certain that, besides the offense committed against God by revealing a secret, they cause all these practices to become in the end odious, useless, and even sometimes hurtful to many. It is not, however, forbidden to speak of some useful remark which the reverend superior, the director, or one of the Sisters may have made there, provided they do so to edify others and without saying where it was heard, particularly if in confession. but it is never permitted

to speak of such things by way of recreation, and still less in order to complain or murmur. Neither shall they make known their rules to externs, unless they have express permission from the reverend superior or the director of their Company. The Sister Servant shall keep them locked up in the room, never taking them out of the house, nor leaving them exposed to the view of externs, nor taking any copy of them.[50]

8. As neither the reverend superior nor the superioress can remedy the faults which may be committed in the Community, if those who know them do not give information, and that for want of this, the Company might in time degenerate, each one shall be careful to inform humbly and charitably the reverend superior, director, or the superioress, and even in pressing necessity, the Sister Servant, of the serious faults or dangerous temptations she may have noticed in her Sisters. She shall also be pleased that her own faults be in like manner made known to the aforesaid superiors, receiving cheerfully and without excuse the admonitions given her both in public and private. All shall beware of reproaching any one, or of showing any displeasure toward those whom they may suspect of having made known the faults for which they have been reproved.[51]

CHAPTER IX

THE EMPLOYMENT OF THE DAY[52]

1. At four o'clock they shall rise at the first sound of the bell making the Sign of the Cross and giving their first thoughts to God. They shall dress with diligence and modesty. Before drawing their bed curtains, they will put on at least the first articles of their clothing. As soon as they shall have them on, they shall take holy water and kneel down to adore God, to thank him, and to offer themselves to him with all the actions of the day. Then they shall make their beds promptly and finish dressing.[53]

2. At half past four they shall say prayers in common, beginning with the *Veni Sancte Spiritus*,[54] and the five customary acts of morning exercise. Then they shall listen to the points of meditation which they shall make until a quarter past five, and conclude with the *Angelus*, the Litany of the Holy Name of Jesus, and other customary prayers. After this they will begin their chaplet of which

they shall say one decade, and then make repetition of meditation until six o'clock.[55]

3. At six o'clock they shall attend in silence to whatever is most pressing, each one according to her office, as shall be prescribed, and, at half past six those who have permission to learn to read shall do so until seven o'clock.[56]

4. At seven o'clock, or about that time, they shall go together to Mass, two and two, if they can do so then, if not, at some other more convenient hour, as the superioress or Sister Servant may think proper. While waiting for Mass to begin, or from the beginning until the Gospel, they may say some decades of their chaplet.[57]

5. After Mass they shall go together to the refectory for breakfast, where they shall take nothing but a piece of bread, unless the superioress, another officer, or the Sister Servant thinks it proper to give something else on account of infirmity, old age, or hard work, but all shall keep silence at this time. Those who are not able to hear Mass until late shall make no difficulty on working-days, to breakfast before they go, but after half past nine no one shall breakfast without permission of the superior or Sister Servant.[58]

6. After breakfast each one shall resume her occupations. If they work together, they may converse on some pious subject in a serious manner, but not by way of recreation.

7. At half past eleven they shall make the particular examen for about the time of a *Miserere* or two,[59] stopping on the resolutions they made in the morning, and particularly on the acts of the virtue which they have for practice, then having said the *Benedicite*, which the superioress begins and the others continue, they shall dine, each one having her separate portion. Meanwhile they shall listen attentively to the spiritual reading which shall be made by one of them, concluding with the reading of the Martyrology for the following day. They shall say the *Angelus* at the time it rings, although they may not have finished dinner. Having risen from the table they shall say grace in the same manner as the *Benedicite*. Then they shall say a decade of their chaplet. In parishes where there are only two Sisters and they cannot have their reading at dinner, they shall do so immediately before that meal, during which they shall occupy themselves interiorly and in silence on what has been read.[60]

8. After dinner they shall apply, if necessary, each one to her office. If not, they shall work together at spinning or sewing, and

meanwhile they may converse during an hour on something edifying by way of cheerful and modest recreation, being mindful often to raise their hearts to God. Should anyone forget herself so far as to hold conversations that are contrary to modesty or decorum, a Sister appointed for the purpose shall say, "Let us remember the presence of God."[61]

9. At two o'clock, after the *Veni Sancte Spiritus* is said, one of the Sisters shall read aloud during a quarter of an hour on some spiritual subject, concluding by these words, *Deus charitas est, et qui manet in charitate, in Deo manet, et Deus in eo.*[62] The others shall listen to this reading and continue their work in profound silence until three o'clock, occupying themselves meanwhile with some good thought, or attending to the instruction which is given in the same place at this time, to the Sisters who are in the house where the superioress resides, to teach them the duties of good Christians, and of true Daughters of Charity, at which instruction they shall endeavor to assist when their occupations permit.[63]

10. At three o'clock they shall kneel down and a Sister shall say aloud, *Christus factus est pro nobis obediens usque ad mortem, mortem autem crucis, propter quod et Deus exaltavit illum.*[64] And all shall together adore the Son of God dying for the salvation of souls, and offer him to the Eternal Father at this moment, when he gave up the ghost, beseeching him to apply the merit of his death to those especially who are in their agony, or in a state of sin, and to all the souls detained in Purgatory. Having made this act for the space of three *Paters* and *Aves*,[65] they shall kiss the floor and then rise. Those who keep school should make this act before going to class. They who find themselves with externs at this hour, or in the streets, will make this act in spirit only, without kneeling. Such as are entirely prevented from making it at that time should do so as soon as possible.

11. After the act of adoration, if they are to continue their work together, they can converse on some edifying subject, but more seriously and piously, and in a lower tone than after dinner, the time of recreation being past. Those who have permission to learn to write may devote to this purpose half an hour, at most, of the afternoon, at the time the superioress or Sister Servant shall think proper, and when they are entirely free from all necessary occupation. Every one shall apply to this duty in such a way that

she may be always disposed to interrupt or omit it entirely on days when the same superioress or Sister Servant thinks it should give place to another of stricter obligation, in order that it may not be in the least prejudicial to the service of the poor, nor to any of the duties of their Company.[66]

12. At half past five they shall make meditation until six, if they have not made it some time previous, as is customary in hospitals. They shall make the particular examen, as before dinner, then go to supper, saying the *Benedicite*[67] and grace, having reading at table without the Martyrology, then saying the *Angelus* with one decade of their chaplet, and observing everything else that was said concerning dinner.[68]

13. After supper they shall attend, if necessary, to the duties of their office. Otherwise they shall work together, and observe what has been prescribed as recreation after dinner.[69]

14. At eight o'clock, at the sound of the bell, they shall assemble for the evening exercise in the same place where they usually have the two o'clock reading. The superioress or the Sister Servant having said the *Veni Sancte Spiritus*, each one shall resume her work and listen to the first two points of meditation, which are read aloud by the Sister whose week it is to do so. Then, while waiting for the clock to strike, the superioress or Sister Servant shall call on some of them to repeat what they have remarked, or say a word herself on the subject proposed, in order to facilitate meditation for the young Sisters. But on Saturdays and eves of feasts the reading of the meditation will be deferred until after prayers, and the Gospel of the following day will be read in its place. To this all shall listen kneeling, and then resume their work. If a feast fall on a Sunday, only the Gospel of the feast which the Church celebrates that day shall be read.

15. At a quarter after eight they shall go to the chapel or oratory to make the general examen, and say the usual prayers, after which the first point only of the meditation shall be read again, if two have already been read before prayers. They shall then retire in silence, and after taking holy water and saying some prayers during the space of two or three *Paters* at most. They shall go to bed modestly, each one undressing out of sight of the others and keeping her bed-curtains drawn during the night. They shall try to go to sleep with some good thought, particularly on the subject of the

next day's meditation, and manage to be in bed and have the lights extinguished by nine o'clock.[70]

16. On Sundays and festivals they shall observe the same order as on other days, except in the following particulars: 1. They shall spend the time above specified for manual labor in spiritual exercises, such as frequenting the sacraments, assiting at divine service, sermons, catechism, or in pious conversation; reading books of devotion selected by the reverend superior or others appointed by him; the practice of catechism among themselves in order to be capable of instructing the poor and children in things necessary for salvation; and other similar employments suitable to their state.[71] 2. Those who have permission to learn to read or write shall take for that purpose half an hour in the morning at the most convenient time, and the same after dinner, provided it does not prevent them for attending to the service of the poor or to some other duty of obligation.[72] 3. They shall not refrain on these days from taking their usual moderate recreation after meals, according to the time remaining, but they shall never amuse themselves with forbidden plays,[73] or with any unbecoming their state.[74]

17. Besides the aforesaid exercises which are common to all, the young Sisters shall observe the following, appointed for them during the time of their probation in the house of the superioress: 1. Every day at eight in the morning they shall attend spiritual reading during a quarter of an hour, and then an instruction until half past eight. 2. At two o'clock, after reading, they shall assist attentively at the instruction which is given until three. 3. Every Wednesday they shall attend a conference like that held on Friday evening for the whole Community. Even the young Sisters in the parishes of Paris shall come to the house of the superioress, if their duty toward the poor will permit. They shall not come, however, for the two other exercises, which take place every day at eight and two o'clock, but the Sister Servants with whom they live shall try to supply for them, when they are able, by instructions like those given at the house of the superioress. The elder Sisters who are there shall assist at them if their occupations permit, as well for the spiritual benefit they may derive therefrom, as for the good example they owe their Sisters.

18. They shall all set a high value on their rules and on the holy practices and praiseworthy customs which they have hitherto

observed, considering them as means which God has given them to advance in the perfection suitable to their state, and to enable them more easily to work out their salvation. They shall therefore read them or hear them read, with those of their offices, once a month as far as this can be done conveniently, and ask pardon of God for the faults they have committed against them, endeavoring at the same time to conceive a renewed desire of observing them entirely until death.[75] Should there be any which are repugnant to their judgment or private opinion, they shall strive to overcome and mortify themselves in those very things, considering that Our Lord has declared that "The kingdom of heaven suffereth violence, and the violent bear it away."[76]

Signed: René Alméras, and sealed with his seal.[77]

Particular Rules for the Sisters of the Parishes

1. They shall consider that as their employments oblige them to spend the greater part of their time out of the house, in the midst of the world, and being often alone, they have need of greater perfection than those who are employed in hospitals and other similar places, which they seldom have occasion to leave. They shall therefore strive in a particular manner to advance in the virtues recommended to them by their Common Rules, but especially in profound humility, punctual obedience, perfect union among themselves, detachment from creatures, and constant vigilance in preserving entire purity of body and mind.[78]

2. They shall often think of the end for which God sent them to the parish in which they reside, namely, to serve the sick poor not only corporally, by giving then food and medicine, but spiritually also, in causing them to receive the Sacraments worthily and in due time, so that those who are near death may leave this world well prepared, and those who recover may firmly resolve to lead a better life.[79]

3. The spiritual assistance which they shall endeavor to give them, according to their humble ability and the dispositions of the sick, shall consist principally in consolinig and encouraging salvation, teaching them to make acts of Faith, Hope, and Charity toward God and their neighbor, of contrition for their sins or reconciliation with their enemies, asking pardon of those whom they have offended; teaching them to resign themselves to the holy will of God, either to suffer or to recover, to die or to live, and to make other such acts, which should be suggested to them, not all at a time, but some each day and very briefly, for fear of fatiguing them.[80]

4. They shall endeavor especially to prepare them to make a good general confession of their whole life, particularly if their

illness be dangerous, making them understand the importance of this action, and teaching them the manner of performing it well. If they are not able to make this confession of their whole life, the Sisters shall excite them, at least, to conceive general contrition for all their sins and to make a firm resolution, with the help of God's grace, rather to die than ever to commit them in future.

5. If the sick become convalescent and afterward relapse once or several times, they shall exhort them to receive the Sacraments again, even that of Extreme Unction, and shall be careful to procure them this great blessing. If they happen to be with them during their last moments, they shall assist them to die well, making them recite briefly some of the aforesaid acts, praying for them, giving them holy water, and reminding them to gain the plenary indulgence by means of a crucifix, pronouncing at the same moment, either with the lips or in the heart, the Holy Name of Jesus. After their death, they may help to lay them out.[81]

6. If the sick be restored to health, they must redouble their attention and excite them to profit by their illness and their recovery, telling them that God permitted them to suffer sickness of the body in order to heal their soul, and that he restores them to health that they may henceforward do penance and lead a good life, for which they should make firm resolutions, and renew those which they made while sick, advising them to adopt some little pious practices according to their ability: such as to pray kneeling, both morning and evening, to go to confession and Communion frequently during the year, and to avoid occasions of sin, but they should tell them these things briefly and with humility.[82]

7. For fear that these spiritual services might become prejudicial to the corporal assistance they owe the sick, as would be the case if they were to loiter and spend too much time with one, and thus let others suffer by not bringing them their food and medicine at the right time, they shall try to take measures on this point, regulating their time and exercises according to the number and wants of the sick.[83]

8. If the instruction they give to a sick person can be extended to others who are in the same room, they shall endeavor to do this with discretion. This can easily be done where there are children, because in questioning them on the principal mysteries of our faith,

or pointing out their duties to them, the parents, being present, will be able to profit by what is said, without perceiving that it is intended likewise for their instruction.[84]

9. They shall make it a matter of conscience to fail in the least service which they ought to render the sick, especially with regard to remedies, which they should give in the manner and at the time prescribed by the physician, unless some great necessity obliges them to act otherwise; as for example, if the sick suddenly become much worse, or are suffering from the effects of chill or perspiration, or if any similar obstacle should occur.[85]

10. In serving the sick, they should have God alone in view, and pay no more attention to the praise they receive than to the insults they may meet with, only endeavoring to make good use of both, declining all praise interiorly at the thought of their own nothingness, and willingly accepting contempt in honor of the insults which the Son of God received on the cross from the very people whom he had overwhelmed with benefits.[86]

11. Although they should not be too lenient and condescending when the sick refuse to take the remedies or become too insolent, yet they must beware of showing either resentment or contempt in their demeanor toward them; on the contrary, they shall treat them with respect and humility, remembering that all harshness and disdain, as well as the services and the honor they render them, are directed to Our Lord himself.[87]

12. They shall receive no present, however trifling, from the poor whom they relieve; and they shall beware of thinking that the sick are under any obligation to them for the services they render to them; but, on the contrary, the Sisters should be well convinced that they are greatly indebted to the poor, since, for the slightest alms they bestow upon them, not of any part of their property, but merely of a little solicitude and care, they acquire friends who have the right of one day opening to them the gates of heaven; and that, even in this life, they receive on their account more honor and satisfaction than they would ever have presumed to expect in the world; and they should not make an ill use of this, but be confused at the sight of their unworthiness.[88]

13. In order to prevent many serious evils that might happen, they shall not undertake to sit up with the sick. If they are requested to do so by the Ladies of Charity, by the poor, by their

neighbors or others, they shall humbly refuse, saying that it is forbidden by their rules. Though certain cases of very urgent necessity may seem to oblige them, they must not undertake to do so without the permission of the Sister Servant.[89]

14. If they meet with sick persons so totally destitute as to have no one to make their bed, or render them other services more humble still, they may do this if they have time and the Sister Servant judges proper. However, they should try to get someone else to continue this charitable office, for fear of being delayed in assisting other poor people.[90]

15. When any Sister is sick and obliged to keep her bed, the superioress should be informed of it on the second or third day at the very latest.[91]

16. They shall be careful of the money entrusted to their management; for that purpose the Sister Servant shall keep separately, and carefully locked up, that which is for the Sisters; and they shall take particular care not to use for themselves anything appropriated to the poor, whether food, clothing, or money, bearing in mind that by doing so they would commit a theft, of which they would be guilty and responsible before God. They are only allowed to make use at all times of the furniture and coarse linen, such as sheets, tablecloths, napkins, and so forth; and during their sickness, the common portion of the sick poor will be given them, and all necessary remedies.[92]

17. As to the money given them for their support, the Sister Servant may leave a certain amount in the hands of a Sister who will attend to their little expenses, but who will purchase nothing, however, without the consent of the Sister Servant, unless it be in pressing necessity and in ordinary things; but no one shall dispose of what may remain of the money given them for their support, except with the permission, and according to the intentions of the superioress.

18. They shall also pay particular attention to the other points of their Common Rules which particularly concern them, especially the following:

1. To prefer the service of the sick poor to any other employment, whether corporal or spiritual, and make no scruple either to advance or postpone anything else, provided it really be the urgent necessity of the sick, and not sloth or dissipation, which leads them

to act thus, and that they be always punctual in going to bed at nine and rising at four.[93]

2. To show great respect to the Ladies of Charity, physicians, and especially the pastors, confessors of the poor, and other priests, always acting with proper reserve, avoiding all familiarity and above all never becoming attached to them.[94]

3. Never to loiter or to hold conversations while walking through the streets, or when in houses where their duty calls them, unless there is great necessity; and even then they should despatch their business promptly and in few words, particularly with persons of the other sex.[95]

4. Not to undertake to attend the sick or give anything to the poor in cases contrary to their regulations, or against the will of the Sister Servant.[96]

5. Not to make use of any remedies or drugs for themselves nor consult the physician for this purpose, without the permission of the superioress, of the Visitatrix, or of the Sister Servant.

6. When sick, they shall be satisified to be treated as the poor whom they assist, since servants should not expect to be better attended than their masters. If, however, they stand in great need of some little delicacy and the Ladies or their Sister Servant give them any, they can make use of it.[98]

7. To buy no clothing, nor furniture, nor food, nor medicines for themselves, but remain satisfied with whatever the Sister Servant may give for their personal necessities and if they need anything they should make known their needs to her.[99]

8. To beware of indulging any disorderly affection for the parish in which they reside, on account of the gratification they experience in being with some particular Sister, or in holding conversations with the Ladies or their confessors; and should they perceive that such is the case, they must strive to break off the attachment by making known promptly to superiors their weakness in this respect, and the need they have of immediate assistance.[100]

9. Neither to eat nor drink in the houses of others, not even in those of the Ladies of Charity, but always in their own.[101]

10. Not to admit anyone into their rooms; still less should they allow anyone to eat or take lodging in their houses, not even their relatives, especially those of the other sex.[102]

11. Not to visit priests, unless under those circumstances men-

tioned in the Common Rules; even then, never to go alone, but two together; and should only one be able to go, she should take as her companion some trustworthy person.[103]

12. Not to absent themselves from their parish without necessity, not even to hear a sermon, gain indulgences, or join in a procession.[104]

13. To be expeditious in all they have to do, and when they have any spare time, to employ it in sewing or knitting; if they have no work, they can ask it of the Sister Servant.[105]

14. To be very submissive and to have great respect for their Sister Servant, even if younger in years and vocation than themselves; undertaking nothing without her permission or order; not even giving an egg or a larger portion nor any remedy; nor visiting the Ladies. If they are obliged to do so, they should exercise great prudence and discretion.[106]

15. Not to fail, once a month, to give an exact account of their employments to the Sister Servant as is prescribed for them in the Common Rules.[107]

16. With regard to the order of the day, they should conform as much as possible to that of the Community, adapting it to the service of the sick, but without dispensing themselves from the exercises prescribed by the Common Rules except in case of necessity.[108]

Signed: René Alméras, and sealed with his seal.[109]

Conferences of Vincent de Paul to the Daughters of Charity

INTRODUCTION

*T*here exist today 120 Conferences to the Daughters of Charity given by Saint Vincent de Paul from 1633 to 1660. The conferences were faithfully written down by the first Daughters of Charity and preserved, particularly through the efforts of Sister Marguerite Chétif, superioress general of the Daughters of Charity after Louise de Marillac. The conferences selected for this publication are given in chronological order. They include: (1) Vincent de Paul's thoughts on the rules of the Daughters of Charity (1634), which stress reliance on Divine Providence and the way of life conducive to the first Daughters of Charity; (2) "Virtues of Marguerite Naseau" (1642), the first Daughter of Charity whose life and death showed her intense love of the poor; and (3) "Virtues of Louise de Marillac" (1660), given six months after her death and shortly before Vincent de Paul himself died. In that conference, he and the assembled Daughters of Charity reflected together on Louise's life and her thirty-eight year collaborative relationship with Vincent.[1]

EXPLANATION OF THE RULE[2]

Louise de Marillac copied this first conference in her own hand. It is clear from the text that, one year after the "little company" was founded in 1633, twelve Daughters of Charity attended it. In this earliest surviving explanation of the rules, Vincent de Paul employed his so-called Little Method: nature (what the rules *were), motives (why follow them), and means (how to do so). He discussed reliance on Divine Providence, and leaving Mass to serve God in the poor.*

On the last day of July 1634, Monsieur Vincent, in a third and final conference, gave the rules and an explanation of how they were to be practiced to the little Congregation of the Daughters of Charity. The following account has been compiled from notes.

He knelt down, as did all who were present, and after reciting the *Veni, Sancte* ["Come, Holy (Spirit)"], began as follows: My dear daughters, I said to you the other day, when I was speaking to you, that you have now been living together for some time with one object in view and that, nevertheless, you have not had so far any regulations for your mode of life. In this, Divine Providence has led you, as it guided the people of God who were without a code of laws for more than a thousand years after the Creation. Our Lord acted in the same way in regard to the early Church for, while he was on earth, the New Law was not set down in writing and it was his apostles who, after he had gone, collected his teachings and commandments.

Providence has brought the twelve of you together here with the intention, as it would seem, that you should honor his human life on earth. Oh, what a favor to be a member of a community, for each member shares in the good that is done by all. By this means you will have more abundant grace. Our Lord has promised this to us, when he said: "When two or three are gathered together, I will be in the midst of them."[3] With all the more reason, then, when there are several who have the same intention of serving God: "My Father and I will come and abide among them, if they love us."[4] It is for persons who have the same spirit and in this same spirit help one another to love God that his Son prayed, in the last prayer he uttered before his Passion when he said: "Father, keep them in your name that you have given me, so that they may be one just as we are."[5] And so let us see, my dear daughters, how you should spend the twenty-four hours that make up the day, just as the days make up the months and the months the years that will bring you to eternity.

You should, as far as you can, observe the prescribed times, for it will be a great consolation to you, on rising, to think: All my other Sisters, wherever they may be, are now rising for the service of God.

You shall rise then at five o'clock, whenever your work in connection with the Confraternity of Charity has permitted your going to bed at ten, for you must take care of yourselves so as to serve the poor and give your bodies what is justly their due.

Your first thought should be of God: Thank him for having preserved you during the night, and consider briefly whether you have offended him. Thank him, or beg forgiveness. Offer him all your thoughts, the movement of your heart, your words and actions. Resolve never to do anything to offend him, and all that you will do during the day will derive its strength from this first offering made to God; for you see, my daughters, if you neglect to offer everything to God, you will lose the reward of your actions.

Saint Paul tells us how much we lose when the first thoughts of our minds are occupied with anything else but God. The devil does his best, when you waken, to inspire you with other thoughts. That is why you should drink deep of this holy practice, like good Christian women and true Daughters of Charity.

The first thing you should do when you have risen and put on some clothes is to kneel down and adore God. What do you think it means to adore God? It is to offer him the homage that belongs to him alone, and to acknowledge him as your creator and sovereign lord. You shall then ask for his holy blessing, bowing down slightly to receive it with devotion and with the intention that it make all your thoughts, words, and actions pleasing to his divine Majesty, and of its granting you the will to do them all for the glory of his most holy love.

After you have dressed and made your bed, you will set about praying. My daughters, this is the center of devotion, and you should eagerly desire to acquire thoroughly the habit of prayer. No, don't be afraid that poor village girls, ignorant as you think you are, should not aspire to this holy exercise. God is so good and has already been so good to you as to call you to practice charity. Why then should you think he would deny you the grace you need to pray well? Don't let such an idea enter into your mind.

I was very much edified today when conversing with a good village girl who is now one of the greatest souls I know.

Always begin all your prayers with an act of the presence of

God because, sometimes, for want of doing so, an action will cease to be pleasing to him. Just consider, my daughters, that although we do not yet see God, faith teaches us that his holy presence is everywhere, and this is one of the means which we should propose to ourselves. I mean, this presence in all places, penetrating all things and even our hearts to their very depths. This is even more true than the thought that we are all here present, because our eyes may deceive us, but the truth that God is in all places will never deceive. Another means of placing ourselves in the presence of God is to imagine ourselves before the most blessed sacrament of the altar. It is there, my dear daughters, that we receive the dearest proofs of his love. Let us love him dearly and remember that he said when on earth: "Whoever loves me, we will come to him,"[6] where he speaks of the Father and the Holy Spirit, and souls will be guided by his holy providence as a ship by its pilot. Take care to give an account of your prayer [to one another] as soon as possible after making it. You cannot imagine how useful this will be. Tell one another quite simply the thoughts which God has given you and, above all, carefully remember the resolutions you made at prayer. Blessed Sister Marie of the Incarnation made use of this means to advance very far in perfection. She gave a careful account of her prayer to her maidservant. Oh, yes, my daughters, you cannot imagine how greatly this practice will profit you and the pleasure you will give God by acting in this way. Just think, dear Saint Mary Magdalene hid in her heart the good thoughts which she gathered from the words of Our Lord, and the same thing is even said of the Blessed Virgin. The good thoughts which God gives you in prayer are relics. Gather them carefully together in order to translate them into acts and you will gladden the heart of God. You will then be the joy of God and all the saints will hold high festival.

Go to Holy Mass daily but do so with great devotion, and conduct yourselves in church with great modesty and be an example of virtue to all who may see you. And I shall give as an example a dear lady named Madame Pavillon who for many long years was a source of admiration to her parish.[7] It seems that she walked and carried herself as if she were visibly in the presence of God. She seemed almost insensible to everything, sin excepted. She would let herself be trampled on rather than be diverted from the presence of

God. That, my daughters, is the way to behave reverently in church and, principally, during Holy Mass. What do you think you should do during Mass? It is not only the priest who offers up the holy sacrifice but also those who are present, and I feel quite sure that when you have been well instructed, you will have great devotion to the Mass, for it is the center of devotion.

My daughters, remember that when you leave prayer and Holy Mass to serve the poor, you are losing nothing, because serving the poor is going to God and you should see God in them. So then be very careful in attending to all their needs and be particularly watchful in respect to the help you may be able to render them for their salvation, so that they may not die without the sacraments. You are not to attend to their bodies solely, you are also to help them to save their souls. Above all, urge them to make general confessions, bear patiently with their little fits of bad temper, encourage them to suffer patiently for the love of God. Never get angry with them nor speak to them harshly. They have enough to do to put up with their illnesses. Reflect that you are their visible guardian angel, their father and mother, and do not oppose them except in such things as are bad for them for, in that case, it would be cruelty to yield to their demands. Weep with them; God has made you their consolers.

You see, my daughters, the fidelity which you owe to God. The exercise of your vocation consists in the frequent remembrance of the presence of God and, to make this easy, make use of the sounds given by the clock when it strikes, and then make an act of adoration. Make this act, that is, say in your heart: My God, I adore you, or simply: My God, you are my God. My God, I love you with my whole heart, I wish, O my God, that all the world should know and honor you in honor of the contempt which you endured on earth. When you begin these acts, you might close your eyes to recollect yourselves.

You shall make an examination of conscience before dinner for the space of one or two *Misereres*[8] on the resolutions you took at prayer. Let these resolutions be, as far as possible, on the practice of some specific virtue. As a rule, they should tend toward combating the imperfection to which you are most inclined, for, you see, my daughters, even the holiest person falls seven times a day. Some are subject to vanity, others to a certain want of modesty. That is what you have to work at: the conquest of your bad habits. It is essential to be very modest and reserved and to guard one's eyes. A glance destroyed David, and he had been a good man. It is almost impossible for a person who is exteriorly immodest to be really interiorly modest. And if you ask me how long you should keep to the same resolution my answer is: just as long as you have an inclination to the vice which you wish to combat. Be very much on your guard against unchaste and frivolous language. The best means of being reserved is to think frequently that God sees you.

You should make good use of whatever free time you have after attending the sick. Never be idle. Study how to read, not for your own particular advantage but so as to be ready to be sent to places where you can teach. How do you know what Divine Providence wishes to make of you? Always strive to be prepared to go wherever holy obedience may send you.

You shall keep silence from after the evening examination of conscience until after prayer the next day in order that this state of recollection, which will appear on the exterior, may foster the conversation of your hearts with God. Above all, observe it after the act of adoration which you offer to God before going to bed and after having received his holy blessing.

Go to bed modestly and sleep with a good thought in your mind. This will be a useful means of remembering God when you waken and, in the morning, your mind will be better prepared for prayer.

You shall go to Communion on Sundays and feast-days and some other festivals, but always with your confessor's permission.

As obedience perfects all our works, there shall always be one among you who will hold the office of superior. Sometimes, it will be one person; sometimes, another. This is what we do when we give missions. Don't you think it's necessary? May God be pleased with your submission to her, in honor of his Son's submission to Saint Joseph and the Blessed Virgin. Take care, my daughters, always to look on her who holds the place of superior as the Blessed Virgin, or even see God in her and you will in this way profit more in a month than you would otherwise do in a year. By practicing obedience, you will learn holy humility, and by commanding out of obedience you will instruct others usefully. I should like to tell you, in order to stir you up to the practice of holy obedience, that when

God placed me in the home of the wife of the General [of the Galleys],[9] I resolved to obey her as I would the Blessed Virgin and God knows all the good it did me.

Honor the Ladies of Charity and always treat them with great respect; also, honor the sick and look on them as your masters.

So now, Sister Marie of Saint-Savior,[10] you shall be the superior of your Sister for the whole month, and Sister Michelle,[11] [you shall be] the superior of Sister Barbe,[12] at Saint-Nicholas; Marguerite, of her Sisters at Saint-Paul's, and you, Sister at Saint-Benedict's, your guardian angel shall be your guide. Mademoiselle Le Gras will be superior at the Hôtel Dieu. Be very friendly with one another, and let those who belong to other parishes come here from time to time to be assisted in the observance of your rule.

It now remains to say what fruits you will gather from this mode of life. The first is that you should believe that if there is any creature who should hope for Paradise, it is those who are faithful to it. And why so? Because God has promised this reward. You may rest assured that, by observing it, you are doing God's most holy will. That was Saint Clement's idea.[13] He used to say that whoever lived in a community and observed the rule had nothing to fear.

In the second place, it is the beginning of a great good which will last perhaps forever. Yes, my daughters, if you begin to observe your rule with the intention of doing God's most holy will, there is great reason to hope that your little Community will continue and increase. But you should also fear that, if you neglect it and do not carry it out, the Community may be destroyed. Oh, take great care of that. What disorder! It is nothing less than the abandonment of a good work which perhaps God has decided on from all eternity and for which he has chosen you. Your Community will last, not only for a time, but after you are dead it will be the source of an increase of your glory in heaven.

In the third place, the lives of 10,000 persons depend perhaps on your fidelity. How many husbands restored to their wives, and fathers and mothers to their children! You may perhaps be the cause of the salvation of many who would otherwise be lost.

But how is it that God has chosen you for such greatness? It is God's will to choose poor folk. He chose the apostles to overthrow idolatry and to convert the whole world. Remember, my daughters, that God began the Church with poor people, and say: Because I am nothing, God has chosen me to offer him great service. God has so willed it. I will never forget my lowliness and will always adore his great mercy to me.

Fourth, consider what a misfortune it would be if, God having chosen you for this holy work, you should ever fail him through your own fault. At the hour of death, God would reproach you and would say: Depart, O wretched creature, because you did not obey your rule nor comfort the sick poor, you have been the cause of the premature death of many persons, and of the failure of your little company.

Now, since it is good and reasonable that it should last, here are the means. The first is to beg God to give you the grace to live conformably to the little rule of life that has been proposed to you.

The second is that you must make a good effort and also resolve to observe it, saying in your hearts: Yes, my God, I am resolved to begin the observance of those good things you have taught us. I know I am weak, but with your grace I can do all things, and I feel confident you will help me. By that love which led you to teach us your holy will, I beg you to give us strength and courage to carry it out.

The third means for observing your rule of life is to live together in a spirit of great friendliness and charity. Persons chosen to do the same sort of things ought to be united in everything. You have been chosen to carry out a design, but the building will not last if you do not love one another, and this bond of charity will prevent its destruction. Our Lord said to his apostles: "You, my apostles, if you are willing to carry out the design I have had from all eternity, love one another."[14] My daughters, it is true you are weak, but bear one another's imperfections. If you do not, the building will collapse and others will be sent to take your place. And as there may be personal conflicts, it would be well if you changed houses, with the permission of your superiors and the consent of the lady superiors.[15] Saint Peter, Saint Paul, and Saint Barnabas certainly had differences among themselves, and hence it should not be surprising if poor, weak girls should have them. It is essential that you should be ready to go anywhere you may be ordered, and even to ask and say: I do not belong to this parish or that, but to wherever God is pleased I should be. Do not act like the sons of Zebedee for whom places were asked surreptitiously, which God, for their own good, did not grant them. You have been chosen to be at the disposition of Divine Providence and, if you do not fully submit to it, you will lose much.

Another means is perfect detachment from father, mother, relatives, and friends so that you belong to God alone. Now, to possess this great blessing, you must strip yourselves of everything and possess nothing of your own. The apostles had such detachment. For one écu, you shall have a hundred; and as many mothers as there are Ladies of Charity so that, my daughters, Providence will never fail you. Will you not have sufficient courage to give yourselves to God who thinks so much of you? Do not put in a claim for anything apart from your subsistence, and always rely on Providence. Rich people may become poor, owing to accidents which frequently occur, but those who are resolved to depend utterly on God shall never be poor. Is it not a good thing to live like that, my daughters? What is there to fear? God has promised that those who will take care of the poor will never want for anything. My daughters, do you not love God's promises better than the deceitfulness of the world? God has bound himself to look after all your needs.

The [fifth][16] means is that you should make a retreat every year in order to renew your good resolutions, and each one shall make it at the time and in the place which shall be judged most fitting and wherever obedience may send her. It may be that it would be good to hold it here.

Another means to preserve the Company in an exact observance of the rule of life is that each of you should give an account every month to her who has general charge of you, and that a little discourse should be given in this house dealing with the excellence of your way of life in order to encourage you. I myself will do so, as far as I can, or else one of our confreres.

My daughters, for the coming week, let the subject of your mental prayer be considerations on the graces you have received from God since the days of your childhood, and the dangers from which you have heard your parents say you have been delivered by the providence of God. For this, you should divide your life into a number of periods; your baptism, the other sacraments, and especially your vocation, and you should say: "When I was not even thinking of it, God was thinking of bringing me into a community which would be a means of my salvation."

How many graces does he not wish to bestow on you in carrying out your responsibilities! I know a person who was profoundly moved by the love of God by noting a grace which she received at her birth, and without which she might never perhaps have been baptized. You cannot imagine how much she has benefited by this. My daughters, say: "From all eternity God has thought of doing good to me even when I had not begun to feel any sentiments of gratitude and thanks." And think over in your hearts the resolution you should select, and resolve to observe for the whole course of your life your rule to serve the sick. Continue to do this for a week, after which you may, for the rest of the month, make use of the meditations in the Introduction;[17] I beg you not to grow weary of them.

But, my daughters, all our resolutions are of no avail without grace. Hence you must pray to God to strengthen you and you must work courageously. Give yourself to God for that end, and to the Blessed Virgin. Also, invoke Saint Louis,[18] and the other saints who were so happy serving God in the way you do.

Well now, my daughters, consider what mercy God has granted you by choosing you to be the first members of this foundation. When Solomon determined to build God's temple, he used precious stones as a foundation to show the excellence of the work he had decided on. May God's goodness grant you the grace that you who are the foundation of this little company may be eminent in virtue. For, if you were not very virtuous, you would do wrong to those who will come after you, if God be pleased to bless this beginning. As trees bear fruit only according to their nature, it is likely that those who will come after you will not aim at greater virtues than those you have practiced.

All the Sisters then declared that they desired to follow the advice that had been given them and to practice the mode of life prescribed. All knelt down, and Monsieur Vincent added: May the goodness of God be pleased so to imprint on your hearts and mine what I, a wretched sinner, have just said to you on his behalf, that you may be enabled to remember it well so as to practice it, and that you may be true Daughters of Charity. In the name of the Father and of the Son and of the Holy Spirit. Amen.

CONFERENCES TO THE DAUGHTERS OF CHARITY

Although Marguerite Naseau came to serve the poor before the official foundation of the Company, she is known as the first Daughter of Charity. She served in the Confraternity of Charity in the parish of Saint Savior. Vincent de Paul remarked on the strategies she used to learn how to read, and on how she helped other village girls to read and to instruct others in their turn. In her charity to the poor, she died from sharing her bed with a plague victim and contracting the disease.

A memorandum of what was said at the conference held by Monsieur Vincent in presence of the Daughters of Charity on the virtues of the first eight deceased Sisters. The first point will be found in the original. The second point consists in considering the virtues which each of us remarked in our Sisters who have gone to God.

Sister Marguerite Naseau was the first who came to serve the sick poor in the parish of Saint Savior, where the Confraternity of Charity was established in 1630. Marguerite Naseau, from Suresnes,[20] was the first Sister who had the happiness of pointing out the road to our other Sisters, both in the education of young girls and in nursing the sick, although she had no other teacher than God. She was a poor, uneducated cowherd. Moved by a powerful inspiration from heaven, the idea occurred to her that she would instruct children and so she bought an alphabet book, but, as she could not go to school for instruction, she went and asked the parish priest or curate to tell her what were the first four letters of the alphabet. On another occasion, she asked what were the next four, and so on for the rest. Afterward, while she minded her cows, she studied her lesson. If she saw anyone passing by who seemed to know how to read, she would say: Sir, how is this word pronounced? And so little by little she learned to read, and she then taught the other girls of her village. She afterward made up her mind to go from village to village instructing the young, accompanied by two or three other girls whom she had taught. One girl went to one village, another to another. It was remarkable that she undertook all this without money or any other help save that of Divine Providence. She often fasted for whole days, and dwelt in places of which nothing remained but the walls. She spent day and night in teaching not only young girls but also older ones and did so without vanity or any motive of self-interest, having no other design than that of glorifying God, who provided for all her needs without her ever thinking of them. She even told Mademoiselle Le Gras that on one occasion, when she had been without food for several days and yet had not told anybody of the state of distress in which she was, on her return from Mass, she found sufficient food to last her for quite a long time. The harder she worked at teaching the children, the more the village folk laughed at and maligned her. Her zeal only burned the brighter. She was so completely detached that she gave away all she possessed, depriving herself even of necessities. She provided for the education of some young men who had not the means of doing so, frequently supplied them with food and encouraged them to serve God. These young men are now good priests.

Finally, when she learned that there was a Confraternity of Charity in Paris for the sick poor, she went there moved by a desire to be employed in this work, and although she greatly desired to continue instructing the young, nevertheless she laid aside this charitable work to take up that of nursing the sick poor, which she believed to be more perfect and necessary. This was, indeed, the will of God, for he intended her to be the first Daughter of Charity and servant of the sick poor in the city of Paris. She attracted to the work other girls whom she had helped to detach from all earthly vanities and to embrace a devout life.

She was most humble and submissive. She was so little attached to anything that she gladly changed parishes three times in a short period and never left a parish save to the great regret of all.

She showed herself just as charitable in the parishes as she had been in the country, giving away all that she could, whenever an opportunity arose of doing so; she could never refuse anything, and would have liked to bring everybody home with her. It should be noted that at this time the community had not yet been formed, and there was no rule commanding her to do otherwise.

She was most patient and never complained. Everyone loved her because there was nothing in her that was not lovable. Her charity was so great that she died from sharing her bed with a poor plague-stricken girl. When she was attacked by the fever, she bade good-bye to the Sister who was with her, as if she had foreseen she was about to die, and went to the hospital of Saint Louis, her heart filled with joy and conformity to God's will.[21]

ON THE VIRTUES OF LOUISE DE MARILLAC[22]

Louise de Marillac died 15 March 1660. Vincent de Paul did not hold this conference until 3 July because of his own ill health. He opened the conference by inviting the Sisters to speak about the virtues of Louise de Marillac that touched them most. He reflected on her awareness of the presence of God, love of the poor, prudence, and tender-heartedness. The Sisters commented on her spirit of poverty, love of the interior life, and humble spirit of reconciliation. At the end of the conference, one Sister spoke about the charity of Antoine Portail, who had died a month before Louise.

Our Most Honored Father, having arrived at the place where the conference was held, invoked the help of the Holy Spirit in his usual manner, and said:

My dear Sisters, I give thanks to God for having preserved me up to the present and for having enabled me to see you all assembled together. I would have liked very much indeed to have brought you together during the crisis of the illness of dear Mademoiselle, as you may well imagine, but I too was suffering from an illness which weakened me considerably. It was God's good pleasure that all this should have happened in this way and, in my opinion, it was for the greater perfection of the person of whom we are now going to speak, I mean Mademoiselle Le Gras.[23] And dear Father Portail,[24] who was always so zealous for the sanctification of the Company, although he is not the subject of this conference, nevertheless if any of you say anything about him incidentally, that will be all right. The conference then is on Mademoiselle Le Gras, the virtues you have observed in her and which of those virtues you would wish to imitate. My God, may you be blessed forever.

Then, beginning to question the Sisters, he said: The first point of this conference is the reasons that Daughters of Charity have for discussing the virtues of their Sisters who have gone to God, and especially of those of their dearest mother, the late Mademoiselle Le Gras; the second point, the virtues they remarked in her; the third point, the virtues that touched them most and which, with the help of God's grace, they propose to imitate.

Well, now, Sisters, what are your reasons for conversing about your late Sisters and especially your dearest mother?

Father, the first reason that occurred to me is that we can thereby give thanks to God, and the second is that it will encourage us to imitate her virtues and, if we do not, we should feel greatly ashamed before God, because he gave her to us for that purpose.

The virtues I remarked were, first that during her illnesses and when in pain she had her mind constantly raised to God and always looked to his good pleasure in these circumstances. No one ever heard her complain of her infirmities; on the contrary, she was always joyful and content. She loved the poor greatly and took great pleasure in serving them. I have seen her gathering poor people around her who were coming out of prison; she washed their feet, dressed their sores, and clothed them from her son's wardrobe. She was also very kind to Sisters who were ill and often went to visit them in the infirmary; she was always most pleased to offer them any little service, was careful to assist them at the hour of death, and, if they died during the night, she always got up, unless she were very ill. If she was unable to visit them, because of her illness, she sent her assistant every day to see them for her, bidding them good-day and sending them a few words of consolation. She also strove to go and see those who died in parishes in Paris, and she was so tender-hearted that it was most necessary to use precaution when telling her of the death of a Sister. She was so touched that she sometimes shed many tears. She had also great natural affection and love for her son and his family. She was the first to confess her faults and to ask pardon of all the Sisters. I have seen her lie down on the floor and express a wish to be walked on. She also washed the dishes and would have greatly desired to do all the menial work of the house, if she had been strong enough. She sometimes served in the refectory, and often asked pardon there and did acts of penance such as holding her arms stretched out or lying on the floor.

Ah, my Savior! And you, Sister, what did you remark?

Father, Mademoiselle was most prudent in all things and it seemed as if she knew the failings of everyone, because she told us about them before they were mentioned to her. But she used the greatest discretion when giving admonitions. She always urged us not to seek our own interests in our actions. She was also most recollected.

Sisters, our Sister has pointed out one of the principal virtues, which is prudence. It is true that I do not know if I have ever seen anyone as prudent as she was. She had this virtue in a high degree and I wish with all my heart that the Company had it. Prudence consists in seeing the means, the times, and the places when we should give admonitions and also how we should comport ourselves in all circumstances. O Savior, her prudence was not indeed a prudence like yours, yet she had this virtue in a high degree. And so, Sisters, I beseech God to give you this virtue for he knows you need it because, Sisters, you have to deal with all sorts of people, with people of rank and condition and with the poor. It is necessary to know how to behave in all circumstances. And how can that be done? By prudence. There is a false prudence which causes people not to consider either the circumstances of time or place, and which causes them to do everything without consideration. Therefore, Sisters, remember the time when God brought you together and how dearly it cost those who were wanting in prudence. They allowed themselves to be carried away by things which ultimately caused the ruin of their vocation. It is very difficult not to fall into this fault. Ah, my God, in all religious orders there are some who are wanting in this virtue. What harm, Sisters, will not imprudence cause among you? The result of imprudence will be that people in some places will speak well of you and, in others, criticize you harshly. How highly spoken of are our Sisters in Narbonne! They are Daughters who are wonderfully modest and give great edification. Elsewhere people will say: Those Sisters are not prudent, and don't think of what they are doing.

Prudence, then, Sisters, is a virtue which causes us to strive to do everything in the way it should be done. Prudence, Sisters, prudence in all things. And what shall we do, my dear Sisters? You will resolve to practice this virtue earnestly all your life, and ask our good God for his assistance. And who will help you to be prudent? Your dear mother who is in heaven. She has no less love of you now than she used to have and her charity now is even much more perfect, because the elect love in the way that God wishes. Prudence, therefore, Sisters. God will give it to you if you ask him for it for love of her, because, although we should not pray in public to the dead who are not canonized, one may pray to them in private. You may therefore ask prudence from God by her intercession. Be prudent in everything you do and you will have peace and tranquility wherever you go; on the other hand, there is nothing but disorder without it. Well now, blessed be God! You know its value. Blessed be God! Yes, Mademoiselle Le Gras had this virtue in a higher degree than anyone I knew.

Then our Most Honored Father asked another Sister: And you, Sister?

Father, I noticed that she was most careful and ardently desired that the Company should preserve the spirit of poverty and humility. She often used to say: "We are the servants of the poor; therefore, we should be poorer than they."

Your remark about her, Sister, is, in my opinion, most true, when you tell us that she loved poverty greatly. You saw how she was dressed, clad in the poorest fashion. And she loved this virtue so much that she asked me long ago that she might live as a poor woman. She always urged that the Company preserve this spirit and it is certainly a sovereign means for its preservation. Poverty is a virtue which Our Lord practiced when he was on earth and which he desired his apostles to practice. That is why he said: "Woe to the rich!"[25] And the contrary vice manifests the beauty of this virtue. Moreover, you are the servants of the poor; that is the only title given to you in all the letters coming from both the Holy Father and the parlement.

It was also the spirit of Our Lord, who was poor in every respect, poor in his clothing, in his mode of life, in his Spirit. And he tells us, speaking of himself: "Foxes have dens and birds of the sky have nests, but the Son of Man has nowhere to rest his head."[26] You see, then, Sisters, that the Son of God had this spirit of poverty, and that it was he who gave you this title of servants of the poor, which Mademoiselle Le Gras has always had used for twenty-five years; poverty in your dress, in your food, in all things necessary for your maintenance; and she always believed that the happiness of your Company lay in the poverty of your refectory. If what you are given does not suffice for you, well then, you have not the spirit of poverty. How does it happen that people asked for you in so many places? Because they say: These Sisters are satisfied with a hundred livres apiece for their food and maintenance. They admire that and say: Just look at those Sisters who come from Paris and are satisfied with bread and cheese, or something like that. On the other hand, if some Sisters begin to grow lax in cultivating this spirit of poverty, then little by little they will think that what is given to them is not enough, as was seen in the case of some Sisters who were quite pleased to go and dine with the Ladies of Charity. Ah, Sisters, I have always believed that the happiness of your Company depended on its frugality. As long as you are frugal, people will give you control of the purse, as they do now. It is a characteristic mark of true virtue that all those who give themselves to God to obey another become, in some fashion, mistresses. If a servant obeys her master or mistress as if she were obeying God or the Blessed Virgin, she soon becomes a mistress herself, because her masters, who observe this spirit of obedience in her, yield to her will, which they see is very good and then they obey her. And so she becomes a mistress. I feel sure you have noticed this in your parishes.

Accordingly, this beautiful virtue will cause you to be esteemed by persons of rank and condition. If anyone happened to say: We are not well enough fed; how can we manage like this?—it would be necessary to drive out such a spirit as being the spirit of the demon, which must be rooted out from the beginning. If that were to happen, it would be necessary to stand fast and cry out: Wolf! Wolf! if people wish to clothe us in rags, all right. Sisters, cherish dearly the love of holy poverty and it will preserve you. O Lord, imprint this on our hearts so that whoever sees a Daughter of Charity will see this spirit of poverty. Blessed be God who gave this spirit to Mademoiselle Le Gras. Remember how she held fast to it. Let us follow her example, Sisters, in the way she loved this virtue of poverty.

The Sister began to speak again and said: Father, she showed just as much affection for one Sister as for another so that she strove to please everybody.

I will say this, Sisters: Her tenderness of heart was not apparent to all and yet I know well that she loved you all.

Father, she was greatly interested in the salvation of souls. She was of a most interior spirit and her mind was much occupied with God.

Ah, Sister, what is the meaning of being interior and how does one become interior? Her soul was raised up to God, and this was because she had for a very long time created a deep fund of devotion in her heart. An interior spirit then consists in withdrawing one's affections from the world, from parents, country, and all earthly things. Ask God for it, Sisters, and frequently say: Destroy in me, O Lord, all that displeases you and grant that I may no longer be so full of myself. Mademoiselle Le Gras had this gift of blessing God in all things.

If, by human weakness she sometimes fell into a little act of hastiness, there is no reason to be astonished at that. The saints point out that there is no one without imperfections. We see this in what happened to Saint Paul and Saint Peter. God allows such things to happen that he may be glorified by them. And also it often happens that what is a fault in our eyes is not so in reality, as we may see in Our Lord himself. It is said that he was angry, when he drove the money-changers out of the temple. Instead of his anger being a fault, it was an act of piety and of zeal for the glory of God. So there are things which appear to be faults and are really virtues. And so little acts of hastiness were sometimes to be observed in Mademoiselle Le Gras. This was nothing, and I am far from thinking there was anything sinful in them. She was always firm. And so, Sisters, if you ever feel any angry impulses you should at once humble yourselves, as she used to do. Oh, that is the sign of a person who fears God. Sisters, ask God fervently to give you the grace, by the prayers of Mademoiselle Le Gras, to make a good act of virtue.

I often reflected before God and said to myself: O Lord, it is your will that we should speak of your servant, since she is the work of his hands; and I wondered: What have you observed during the thirty-eight years you have known her? What did you see in her? I remembered some tiny mite of imperfection but, as for mortal sin, oh! never! The slightest stirring of the flesh was unbearable to her. She was a pure soul in all things, pure in her youth, in her married life, in her widowhood. She sifted her conscience in order to tell her sins and all her imaginations. She confessed her sins most clearly. I have never seen any who accused themselves of their sins with so much purity. She wept so that one had great difficulty in calming her. Well now, you must believe that your mother had a great fund of interior spirit to regulate her memory in such a manner that she only used it for God, and only used her will to love him.

Sisters, an interior Daughter of Charity is one who devotes herself only to God. For what is the meaning of being interior if not to be occupied with God? That is perfectly obvious. On the other hand, go over in your memory and consider a Sister who has no interior spirit. You have observed it in those who left. Alas! What were they like? They had no interior peace and were a source of trouble to everyone. Well now, my dear Sisters, let us strive to do our best to become wholly interior. Those of you who can read will read a book which will be given to you and which treats of the interior life. How is it to be acquired? If any member of your Company were tempted to yield to unruly movements, she ought to say to herself: What! I am a Daughter of Charity and therefore a daughter of Mademoiselle Le Gras who was such an interior woman, although by nature she had a bent in the opposite direction. I resolve to overcome myself by her example. My dear Sisters, that is the key of perfection. Often say: Oh! I no longer desire to live according to my own inclinations; I renounce them entirely for the love of God. Sisters, if you only knew the happiness of doing that! As long as you study to be interior, you will be on the road to perfection.

Oh! there are some of you who, by the grace of God, are walking in the path of good Daughters of Charity. I shall not name them. I scarcely ever see any lady of rank who does not tell me of the good done by the servants of the poor. There are plenty of them. Don't be afraid, Sisters. You have no reason to worry. God will never fail you. Therefore, let those to whom God has given the grace to strive after this virtue take firm resolutions to advance in it more and more. And let those who, unfortunately, have yielded to self-esteem and sensuality, let those Sisters . . . . Courage! You have a mother who enjoys a great deal of credit in heaven and who will obtain for you from God the grace to rid yourselves of these defects. Hold fast; don't relax, because when a person steps backward once, twice, three times, all is lost. O Savior! Ask God fervently for this virtue; frequently desire it. Ah! my God! What! a Daughter of Charity should say, if anything goes wrong: That is my fault. Ah! Sisters, that is what Judas said: *Numquid ego sum?*[27] Is it not I who am this wicked person? And you may say with Judas: Is it not I who am preventing the Company from advancing? Sisters, only one person is needed to prevent the Company from advancing in virtue. Do you know what prevents a ship from advancing? Nothing but a little wind; it stops everything.

Sisters, is it not hateful that so many holy souls, who most of the time have worked so earnestly for their advancement in perfection, are yet stopped by some little thing, and that a single person can ruin many? Courage then, my daughters, courage! God will preserve your Company, he who has already blessed it in so many places. Our confreres in Poland tell me that the queen has just made a long journey,[28] during which our poor Sisters devoted so much attention to the management of their works that they attracted a large number of good girls. They acted with such prudence that this good queen was so pleased that, on her return, she spent a whole day in their House with them, and showed a great joy and gave evidence of a marvelous affection for them.

Observe what a good reputation your Company has. Take away this luster, you take away everything. Ah! what harm a Daughter does who robs a Company of its luster! She will cause a whole city to gossip, what am I saying, a whole province and more. Priests and even princes will hear of it. Yes, Sisters, the harm done by one person is capable of ruining a whole Company. And that, Sisters, should inspire you with great zeal for the sanctification of the whole Company in general and for each of its members in particular; and you will see that the Company will multiply.

And you, Sister, what did you notice?

Father, I can say nothing else than that the life of Mademoiselle Le Gras is a mirror in which we have only to gaze. I always observed that she had great charity and forbearance in our regard, so that she was quite consumed with it.

Another Sister: Father, she had such great charity for me that sometimes, when she saw my mind was troubled, she treated me with the greatest sweetness.

A Sister who had been questioned in the beginning and who could not reply because her tears prevented her from speaking, now rose up and said: Father, if you allow me to speak, I will do so.

Our Most Honored Father said: My daughter, it will give me great pleasure. And he could not restrain his tears, when listening to this Sister, so deeply was he moved.

The Sister began by saying: Father, the first reason we have for talking about our dear mother is that God may be thereby glorified; the second is that we may remember for the rest of our lives to follow the examples she gave us, because we are bound to do so, seeing that God willed us to make use of her to teach the Company the way in which he wished it to serve him in order to be pleasing to him. As for the virtues she practiced, a whole book would be necessary if they were to be written down, and persons of far greater intellect than ours to report them. However, as obedience obliges me, it must be done. But when I have said all I remember, a great deal more will remain to be said.

First, she had wonderful humility which was apparent in so many ways that it is impossible to relate them all. This led her to show such great respect to all our Sisters, always speaking to them by way of entreaty and supplication, and thanking them so affectionately either for the services they gave her, or for the extraordinary difficulties which some Sisters encountered in their employments, that occasionally I felt quite ashamed. I have seen her humble herself to the point of begging me with great humility to admonish her of her faults, which I found it very hard to do, because I had not observed any, although I paid attention to her request in order to obey her.

You are right, Sister; I have already said so. It would have been very, very difficult indeed to be able to remark a fault in Mademoiselle Le Gras; not that she had no faults, oh, no, but they were so slight that no one could notice them. Continue, my daughter.

Father, occasionally, when some Sisters did not take the admonitions well which she had given them and had shown, in my presence, that they were annoyed, she afterward asked me if she had not been the cause of their annoyance, if she had not spoken too sharply or otherwise than she should have done. I told her that it seemed to me one could not have acted otherwise. She always made excuses for those she had annoyed and so, when informed of the faults of others, she excused them by saying: "We should suffer; God has chosen us for that; we should give an example to others; we should be very courageous in bearing with our Sisters." She sometimes sent expressly for me to ask my forgiveness, when she thought she had given me any pain, although it was I who should have asked her forgiveness, and she anticipated me over and over again when I should have been the first to ask for pardon.

She always accused herself of her faults with great humility at conferences, on Fridays, and declared that it was she who was guilty and responsible for all the faults of the Company. She frequently made public acts of humility in the refectory, asking forgiveness there, holding her arms outstretched, or lying on the floor, and serving at table. She also helped to wash the dishes and would have greatly desired to do all the other household duties.

She had also great charity for the poor and was always very glad when she was able to serve them. She had a great love and charity for all the Sisters, always bearing with them and excusing them, although she would admonish them severely whenever it was necessary. But she did this from a principle of charity and was compassionate for all those in any pain of body or mind, for many years bearing with Sisters who might justly have been sent away on account of their imperfections. She always wanted to see whether they would change.

She had such a great love of holy poverty that she could not be induced to consent to have anything new for her own use although she gave most willingly to others all that they needed. She kept for five or six years some serge which had been given to her for a cloak, without ever consenting to have it made. The serge was not used, although her cloak was full of patches, quite worn out and of different colors, so that on several occasions attempts were made to get her to lay it aside.

We had to make her believe that her coifs were bought at an old-clothes shop, and we sometimes succeeded in getting her to wear something new without her perceiving it. As soon as she became aware of the fact, she quickly got rid of it, and showed her annoyance that it had been given her. It was necessary to beg her earnestly to put it on a long time afterward.

She also had a great desire that the whole Company should preserve this spirit of poverty and frugality in all things, and she strongly urged that it should be observed after her death as a means for the preservation of the Company.

She was greatly upset when, on account of her infirmities, she had to take different food from that of the Community. This filled her with shame, and she also grieved that she was not able to observe all the rules, for which she often begged pardon.

She had a wonderful confidence in the providence of God in all things and especially in all that concerned the Company, often urging us to put our trust in it at every conference she gave.

Her submission to the will of God was very great, as was apparent in her last illness. She bore all her pains and sufferings, which were very violent, with the utmost possible submission. Moreover, she bore the loss of those who were dearest to her in all the world, without manifesting any pain, although she felt it most deeply. She was most gracious and easily approached. She had a wonderful gift for the guidance and government of the Company, as is apparent, seeing that she left it in such a good state, both spiritually and temporally, owing to her prudence. She referred it all to God without whose grace, as she used to say, nothing whatsoever would be done.

I resolved, by the grace of God, after she died, to strive to imitate her as far as I possibly could, and especially her humility, charity, and love of poverty. Father, I have also written something about her last illness, but I think it would be too long.

Our Most Honored Father resumed by saying: My dear Sisters, those were words which clearly showed you what she was like. Nothing now remains but to provide a new mother, and where shall we find one? Because it would be desirable to have somebody like her. The question has been raised whether one should be sought outside the Community or selected from your own Company. After many prayers for guidance, God has permitted a resolution to be taken that one should be chosen from among yourselves. Consider which of you is most like her whom you had. But, in order that God may be pleased to give you a good mother, whom he himself has formed in Heaven, as he once formed yours, and that he may give all that is necessary for that purpose, Sisters, you should do two things.

In the first place, Sisters, you must pray fervently to God. Let all the prayers you say be offered up to ask him for that grace. The apostles, wishing to elect someone in the place of Judas, prayed and said: "Lord, show which of these two you have chosen."[29] Well now, my dear Sisters, pray then fervently to God that he may give you a good superioress. In the second place, the Company should strive, both in general and in particular, that God may be pleased to form it by his hand in heaven, yes, to form the Company by his own hand. Therefore, each one should cut off all selfishness, as it were by the stroke of a razor, and study herself so that she may clearly perceive the graces she has received from God and also recognize her faults and failings. Yes, Sisters, you must cut off from yourselves everything that is displeasing to God. The result of this will be that you will obtain from God the graces needed for her whom he will give you.

Another thing, Sisters, which I recommend is not to speak at all of your affairs to externs. Be secret, Sisters. Our Lord always recommended his apostles not to spread abroad what he had done. He said: "Beware of the leaven of the Pharisees."[30] You know how you have always been recommended to be secret in all things.

You may say: But is there any harm in talking about it? We are not talking about anything bad, but of something good. No, Sisters, you are not talking about anything bad in itself. But, because it is a mystery and because God's affairs are in question, you should keep it secret. As long as a matter is kept secret in the Company, the devil does not interfere with it, but as soon as the world learns it, the prince of the world will overthrow it. And so, my dear Sisters, keep your affairs secret and say, like the Spouse in the Canticle: "My secret is mine."[31] Oh, Sisters, what a great thing a secret is!

People may say to you: Well, well, Sister, you have been to Saint Lazare; what were you doing there? You may simply reply: We were talking about the virtues of the late Mademoiselle Le Gras, as we are accustomed to do about our deceased Sisters. But they may go further and say: Were you not talking about appointing a superioress? You may reply: We do not trouble ourselves about that.

Sisters, if you keep your secrets carefully, all will go well. You will reflect on this tomorrow morning at prayer. And as several conferences were held on some Sisters, one not sufficing, so, Sisters, we shall have another on the same subject and you shall be informed about it. In the meantime, I beseech you to pray fervently to God and to have prayers said—without saying why—but just simply for a matter of importance. And that, Sisters, is what I had to say to you about your dear mother, and now pray to God that he may give you a good one who shall be like her.

A Sister said: Father, we thought something might have been said about the late Father Portail, and as you told us we might say something about him I may say that I remarked he had great charity for all our Sisters. He was not afraid to go even as far as La Cha-pelle[32] to hear a Sister's confession in the depth of winter and through the mud. He used to say that Our Lord had gone to great trouble for only one Samaritan woman. He was also very humble and most zealous for the salvation of souls and even went so far as to shed tears when he saw a Sister lose her vocation.

May God bless you, Sister, and may he be forever blessed. Well now, we must leave. Though I am an unworthy and wretched sinner, I beseech Our Lord to give you his holy blessing, by the merits of the blessing he gave his apostles, on leaving them, that he may detach you from all things of earth and attach you to those of heaven. *Benedictio Domini nostri . . . Sub tuum praesidium.*[33]

Writings of
Louise de Marillac

INTRODUCTION

*T*hose who look to Louise de Marillac as foundress and spiritual guide are blessed with the large number of her writings: letters, reflections, rules, and other notes. Her letters alone number about 740, published in a careful edition of 900 pages.[1] Her main correspondents were Vincent de Paul, and her Sisters in Community; there also remains one letter written to her son, Michel. Other documents, including letters sent to her, notably by Vincent de Paul, run to 1,000 pages.[2] The publication of those two volumes of letters and documents was occasioned by the call of the Second Vatican Council to religious congregations to return to the sources of the whole Christian life and to the primitive inspiration of their institutes.

The words and spirit of Louise de Marillac can be found in other sources besides her own writings. One such collection is the minutes of the council meetings at which Vincent de Paul presided. Her thoughts were regularly recorded there.[3] Another source is the collection of 120 conferences given by Monsieur Vincent to the Daughters of Charity. He often called on the Sisters to share their own thoughts, and gave pride of place to the thoughts of Mademoiselle, as he called her on those occasions.[4] The notes she prepared for her contributions to those conferences are also valuable indications of her thinking.

In comparison with the 2,800 or more extant letters of Vincent de Paul, the correspondence and writings of Louise are less extensive. Nevertheless, what remains shows well the spiritual traits that led the Church to recognize her sanctity. To facilitate reading the writings of Louise de Marillac, four main themes, which summarize many of the main points of her thinking, have been chosen for this

*publication: theology and spiritual experience, community life, ad-
ministrative and organizational skills, and gentleness and sensitivity. The selections conclude with her spiritual testament. Within
these subject areas, the writings are presented in chronological order. The translations given here are those of Louise Sullivan, D.C.,
based on the critical French edition mentioned above.*

THEOLOGY AND SPIRITUAL EXPERIENCE

LIGHT[5]

*This text is the key to understanding Louise's journey of
faith. Louise treasured it, keeping it on her person throughout her
life. This document relates her conversion experience on Pentecost, 1623, and her insight into the mission God would be entrust-
ing to her.*

In the year 1623, on the feast of Saint Monica, God gave me the
grace to make a vow of widowhood should he call my husband to
himself. On the following feast of the Ascension, I was very disturbed because of the doubt I had as to whether I should leave my
husband, as I greatly wanted to do, in order to make good my first
vow,[6] and to have greater liberty to serve God and my neighbor.

I also doubted my capacity to break the attachment I had for
my director,[7] which might prevent me from accepting another during his long absence, as I feared I might be obliged to do.

I also suffered greatly because of the doubt I experienced concerning the immortality of the soul. All these things caused me
incredible anguish which lasted from Ascension until Pentecost.

On the feast of Pentecost,[8] during holy Mass or while I was
praying in the church,[9] my mind was instantly freed of all doubt. I
was advised that I should remain with my husband and that a time
would come when I would be in a position to make vows of poverty,
chastity, and obedience and that I would be in a small community
where others would do the same. I then understood that I would be
in a place where I could help my neighbor but I did not understand
how this would be possible since there was to be much coming and
going.

I was also assured that I should remain at peace concerning my director; that God would give me one whom he seemed to show me.[10] It was repugnant to me to accept him; nevertheless, I acquiesced. It seemed to me that I did not yet have to make this change.

My third doubt was removed by the inner assurance I felt that it was God who was teaching me these things and that, believing there is a God, I should not doubt the rest.

I have always believed that I received this grace from the blessed bishop of Geneva,[11] because before his death I had greatly desired to communicate these trials to him, and because since that time I have had great devotion to him and have received many graces through him. On that occasion, I had a reason for believing this to be so, although I cannot now remember it.

Account of the pilgrimage to chartres[12]

Louise had a great devotion to the Blessed Mother, as did other French women of her day. She would freqently make a pilgrimage to the shrine of Our Lady of Chartres. This account from 1644 tells of the importance of the Mother of God in Louise's life and of how on the feast of the dedication of the cathedral church of Chartres she offered to God the designs of his providence on the Company of the Daughters of Charity.

We arrived in Chartres on Friday, 14 October. My devotion for Saturday was to render to God, in the chapel of the Blessed Virgin, the thanks I owe him for the many graces that I have received from his goodness.

Sunday's devotions were for the needs of my son. On Monday, Feast of the Dedication of the Church of Chartres, I offered to God the designs of his providence on the Company of the Daughters of Charity. I offered the said Company entirely to him, asking him to destroy it rather than let it be established contrary to his holy will. I asked for it, through the prayers of the Holy Virgin, Mother and Guardian of the said Company, the purity of which it stands in need. Looking upon the Blessed Virgin as the fulfillment of the promises of God to mankind, and seeing the fulfillment of the vow of the Blessed Virgin in the accomplishment of the mystery of the Incarnation, I asked him for the grace of fidelity for the Company through the merits of the Blood of the Son of God and of Mary. I prayed also that he might be the strong and loving bond that unites the hearts of all the Sisters in imitation of the union of the three Divine Persons.

In my prayers for myself, I placed in the hands of the Blessed Virgin the decision to be made concerning the outlines which I have given to my Most Honored Spiritual Father, as well as my desire for practices to help me to prepare for death while awaiting the plan of God in my daily life through the practice of holy obedience.

THOUGHTS ON THE IMMACULATE CONCEPTION OF THE VIRGIN MARY[13]

In this document, Louise illustrates her understanding of the dogma of the Immaculate Conception more than two hundred years before its official proclamation by the Church. She also demonstrates her incarnational spirituality and highlights Mary as model, intercessor, and mediatrix of graces. Louise also refers to her devotion to the Trinitarian life.

Would to God that I could fully express the thoughts that, in his goodness, he has granted to me on the subject of the Immaculate Conception of the Blessed Virgin, so that the true understanding that I possess of her merits and the desire that I have to render her fitting homage may remain always in my heart.

Thus, reflecting on this Holy Conception, I saw, at one and the same time, the design of God in the Incarnation and its application to the matter that was to form the virginal body of Mary so that, although she was a true daughter of Adam, there was to be no stain of sin in her. This was because in her was to take form the sacred body of the Son of God who could not have satisfied the divine justice by his death had he participated in original sin. The most pure body of the Blessed Virgin is a worthy dwelling place for the soul that God created for her. Both are agreeable to God because, from the moment of her pure conception, both have been enriched by the merits of the death of her Son.

As into a very precious vessel, more and more graces have been poured into her soul and she has never failed to make good use of them. Therefore, with every good reason, she should be honored by all creatures and served in a particular way by Christians since she is the only pure creature who has always found favor in the eyes of God. This makes her the astonishment of the heavenly court and the admiration of all humanity.

The Immaculate Conception of the Blessed Virgin leads us to realize and to adore the omnipotence of God because grace totally vanquished nature in her. She was saved without ever having been lost, not only through mercy but also through justice, since this was essential for the Incarnation of the Son of God in the eternal plan for the Redemption of mankind. We must, therefore, honor this Holy Conception that made her so precious in the eyes of God and believe that it depends only on us to receive the assistance of the Blessed Virgin in all our needs. This is so because it seems to me that it would be impossible for God to refuse her anything. His divine and loving glance never left her since she always lived according to his will. Therefore, we must be convinced that he is always ready to grant whatever she requests because she asks for nothing that is not for his glory and our good.

We must carefully consider the advantages that the Blessed Virgin has enjoyed over all other creatures as a consequence of her Immaculate Conception. The first is that she never harbored tendencies that could push her to sin. She never knew this evil that dwells in all the children of Adam. Oh, what peace, gentleness, charity, and humility there were in the soul of the Virgin since it is this instinct that causes us so much trouble by leading us into sin.

The knowledge that God gives us of the Immaculate Conception of the Blessed Virgin should cause us to glorify him eternally for this masterpiece of his omnipotence in a nature that is purely human. We are also led to admire the beauty of the purity of Our Lady's thoughts. Her mind never indulged in useless thoughts nor was it occupied with sin.

May the frailty of human beings, conceived in sin that leads them to revolt against God, bring to light the honor that the Blessed Virgin rendered to him by remaining immersed in justice and truth. May souls devoted to the holy and most pure Virgin attentively consider her actions, which were never in the least disagreeable to God since they were always accomplished according to his will.

The Immaculate Conception of the Blessed Virgin, therefore, completely enlightened her mind and strengthened her will so that she continually acted in such a way that she never omitted anything that God asked of her. Consequently, she was filled with virtue both in the matter and in the form of the being which God gave to her.

This is why, throughout my life, in time and in eternity, I desire to love and to honor her to the best of my ability by my gratitude to the Blessed Trinity for the choice made of the Holy Virgin to be so closely united to the Divinity. I wish to honor the three Persons separately and also together in the unity of the divine essence.

ON HOLY COMMUNION[14]

On the feast of Saint Genevieve, the patron saint of Paris, 3 January 1660, Louise gives an account of her own mystical experience after receiving Holy Communion. She received an extraordinary thirst and this image reflected her love of the Eucharist. Her asceticism and tranquility in the last year of her life is captured well in her thought: "No desires, no resolutions. The grace of my God will accomplish in me whatever he wills."

On the Feast of Saint Genevieve, in 1660, as I was receiving Holy Communion, I felt, upon seeing the Sacred Host, an extraordinary thirst which had its origin in the belief that Jesus wanted to give himself to me in the simplicity of his divine infancy. When I was receiving him and for a long time afterward, my mind was filled by an interior communication which led me to understand that Jesus was bringing not only himself to me but also all the merits of his mysteries. This communication lasted all day. It was not a forced, interior preoccupation. It was rather a presence or a recurrent recollection, as sometimes happens when something is troubling me.

I felt that I was being warned that, since Jesus had given himself entirely to me, laden with the merits of all these mysteries, I must make use of this occasion to participate in his submission to humiliations.

One means to attain this end is to be found in the fact that, without any cause in me, I appear to others as having received some graces from God. This both humbles me and gives me courage.

No desires, no resolutions. The grace of my God will accomplish in me whatever he wills.

LETTER TO SISTER FRANÇOISE CARCIREUX[15]

Louise addressed in this letter to Sister Françoise a variety of subjects, including spiritual direction. Monsieur Vincent was anxious that the Sisters seek spiritual direction, not from their confessors but from their superioress. This letter addresses interior examination of one's spiritual life by avoiding excessive analysis.

My very dear Sister,

I received one of your letters, dated some time back. Since I am inclined to believe that you are no longer suffering from the little trials you mentioned to me, I am not going to respond concerning them. I believe that they are the same ones I spoke about previously. Only allow me, my very dear Sister, to say that I praised God many times for the graces he has granted you. I begged him to help you to forget yourself and to mortify your desire for self-satisfaction which, in you, hides under the beautiful appearance of striving for great perfection. We are greatly deceiving ourselves if we think that we are capable of it, and even more so if we believe that we can attain this perfection by our own efforts and by constantly and closely watching over all the movements and dispositions of our souls. It is a good thing, once a year, to apply ourselves seriously to this kind of examination while being duly distrustful of ourselves and recognizing our weaknesses. But to put ourselves through a continual purgatory to analyze our souls and to give an account of all our thoughts is useless, even dangerous. I am repeating to you what I was told long ago.

I beg you, my dear Sister, to help me by your prayers, as I will help you by mine, so that we may obtain from God the grace to walk simply and confidently along the path of his holy love without too much introspection, lest we resemble those persons who, instead of growing rich, become bankrupt while striving to find the philosopher's stone.

Believe your Reverend Director,[16] although you speak with

him only once a month, and very briefly even then. Rest assured that that is sufficient for you. Succinct confessions are always the best. What are we looking for in this sacrament? Grace alone, and we can be certain that the divine goodness will not withhold it from us if we approach the sacrament with the necessary dispositions of simplicity, heartfelt sorrow, and submission. I beg Our Lord to grant us these dispositions and I am in his holy love, my very dear Sister, your very humble Sister and servant.

LETTER TO SISTER MARGUERITE CHÉTIF[17]

Written to her eventual successor two months before the foundress's death in 1660, this letter manifests Louise's concerns. It illustrates the significance of the relationship with Vincent de Paul and her convictions about Divine Providence. Louise raises issues about service and the relationship of the Daughters of Charity with the Ladies of Charity. She refers to new vocations and the qualities of candidates, as well as to her devotion to the Incarnation.

10 January 1660

My very dear Sister,

I believe that you have probably just received the letter I wrote at the end of December in which I blamed myself for letting so much time go by without allowing myself the consolation of writing to you. I gather from your dear letter that you hold my illness to blame rather than me. I must tell you that, although I have been confined to bed for only a short time, nevertheless my little ailments often make me lazy and prevent me from performing my duties. Moreover, my dear Sisters, the business of the Company increases daily. This past summer, as I told you, three or four more works were established. Blessed be God for everything! May he grant the Company the strength and generosity to maintain within itself the primitive spirit that Jesus instilled in it through his Spirit and by his holy maxims. Let us often give ourselves to God so as to obtain from his goodness the generosity needed to advance his glory by fulfilling his designs on the Company.

Please let me know, my dear Sister, if you received a book, written by our pastor, entitled *The Charitable Lady of the Parish*, along with the quarter pound of *gamboge* that you requested.[18] I am also conveying to you our Most Honored Father's acknowledgment of something you asked me to tell him. I urge you, my dear Sisters, to redouble your prayers asking God to preserve his health. He has been confined to his room for a month because of his bad leg so we never see him anymore. He has so many visitors and his business responsibilities have greatly increased so it is quite difficult to obtain a response when we write to him. So you can see the state in which it has pleased Divine Providence to place us. May his holy will be done now and forever!

Please send me news of yourself and let me know about your Confraternity of Charity. Do the Ladies run it there as they do in Paris? Are there officers? Do they replace one another in office on a regular basis? This is essential, otherwise it will be very difficult for the Company of the Ladies of Charity and their work to continue. Also, please let me know if they prepare the soup, if they collect alms, and if they fulfill the requirements of the Ladies of Charity of that region. In the book I sent you, you will find the Rule for the Confraternity of Charity of Saint-Laurent.

I urge you, my dear Sister, to let me know when you need money. I do not intend you to be deprived of the food and clothing you would received here at the House.

So you have not found any girls who want to give themselves to the service of Our Lord in the poor as members of the Company? You surely know that some of our Sisters have come from farther away than Arras. However, this requires strong characters who desire to reach the holiness of true Christians and who want to die to themselves by mortification and a veritable act of renunciation, which they already made at the time of their holy Baptism, so that the Spirit of Jesus Christ may abide in them and grant them the strength to persevere in this way of life which is totally spiritual, although they will be employed in exterior works which appear lowly and despicable in the eyes of the world but which are glorious in the sight of God and his angels.

My dear Sister, please greet Mademoiselle des Lions for me and assure her of our most respectful affection and readiness to be of service.[19] We took the liberty of selecting one of our holy pictures and maxims for her. Please give it to her with our apologies that it is not as beautiful as we would wish. I also ask you, my dear Sister, to accept the ones that Divine Providence allowed to be selected for you. Believe that my heart is filled with renewed affection for you and that I am in the love of the Infant Jesus who began to shed his precious blood in the crib, my very dear Sister, your very humble Sister and very loving servant. . . .

P.S. All our Sisters send greetings in the love of the Infant Jesus. Our Most Honored Father and Monsieur Portail are both well, thank God. They often remember you with affectionate esteem.

Addressed: To my very dear Sister Marguerite Chétif, Daughter of Charity, Servant of the Sick Poor, at Arras.

LETTER TO VINCENT DE PAUL[20]

In one of her last letters, Louise describes the relationship of the Ladies of Charity with the Daughters of Charity, as it is characterized by the poverty of accepting nothing, except for the poor. Her reflections came from some concern that there be fidelity to the rules and that the Sisters live poorly, simply, and humbly. She expresses concern for Vincent's illness.

My Most Honored Father,

From time to time, I feel strongly the pain of the state to which your charity has reduced you as well as the suffering of being deprived of the honor of speaking to you. Since I am still the same, I am afraid that my cowardice, self-love, and the other threats to my salvation may profit from this situation. As I reflect upon the present condition of the Company, I also worry about no longer being able to discuss matters with you. I am afraid that reading my letters imposes a burden upon you; nevertheless it seems to me, my Most Honored Father, that I must speak to you about the Company and tell you that I think that there is reason to fear that it may fail in several ways. Firstly, I have noticed that in several parishes the Ladies are beginning to distrust them.[21] I believe that I can assure you that I know of no Sister who gives them any real reason to do so unless it may perhaps be those who, in their zeal to relieve the poor, accept alms from the Ladies but who do not submit to the requirement of rendering an account of them to the officers. The latter are offended by this.

In addition, it appears that our Sisters are no longer as esteemed or loved. They are treated more rudely and there are places where they are much more carefully watched because they are mistrusted. There are a few places where orders were given at a public assembly to give them nothing. Even the butcher who furnishes the meat for the poor was forbidden to do so. It is not as if they had a considerable amount of anything, but however little there was helped them.

All this, my Most Honored Father, leads me to realize how necessary it is for the rules to continue to oblige the Sisters to live poorly, simply, and humbly because I fear that if they settle into a way of life that requires great expenditures, is ostentatious and partially enclosed, they would thereby be obliged to find ways to maintain it, and so they would become a very withdrawn and inactive group, living apart from passers-by and poorly clothed people, leading some to say that this wearer-of-a-rough-headdress, this Sister in name only, has no authority, rather she elicits contempt. I know that not only the Sisters but others, who are obliged to honor the designs of God for the spiritual and corporal service of the sick poor, will have a strong inclination toward this way of life which is so dangerous for the continuation of the work of God, which, my Most Honored Father, your charity has so firmly sustained against all opposition.

I am truly distressed to cause you this trouble. If your charity sees that God wills something other than what has been done until now, then, in the name of Our Lord, be the one to declare and order it. I will always remain the same, offering no argument once I have taken the liberty, as I do now, of representing the reasons that occur to me. Because of my infidelities, I dare not say that they are the thoughts given me by God. If I am not expressing myself clearly and your charity is willing to have my views put forth by Monsieur Alméras or someone else whom you consider more appropriate, that will perhaps make me better understood.

Permit me, my Most Honored Father, to inquire about your ailments, which I believe could be relieved if you would allow yourself to be treated as your charity would command someone else to be treated.

I think that I have already spoken to you about the contents of this letter except for a few details. I very humbly ask your pardon for any repetitions there may be. I hope to obtain forgiveness from your goodness because I am, Most Honored Father, your very humble, most obedient and most grateful daughter and servant.

L. DE MARILLAC

Addressed: To Monsieur Vincent.

COMMUNITY LIFE

LETTER TO SISTERS BARBE ANGIBOUST AND LOUISE GANSET,[22] AT RICHELIEU[23]

Louise writes to both Sisters to point out that their community life could be a haven for them. She mentions some points to enable them to get along better. Throughout the letter, Louise speaks of her own shortcomings. Her humility would go far in influencing the Sisters to change their attitudes and behavior.

26 October 1639

My dear Sisters,

I have no doubt that you have been greatly moved by the death of Madame Goussault, widow of the president.[24] The debt we owe her should lead us to imitate her so that God may be glorified. I hope that you will do so with the help of his grace. You have already felt the effects of this grace, my Daughters, in the good which his loving kindness has willed you to accomplish in the place where you now are. However, I have learned what I have always greatly feared. Your work, which has been succeeding so well for the relief of the sick and the instruction of girls, has done nothing for your advancement in perfection. On the contrary, it seems to have hindered it since the good odor of virtue which you were spreading is beginning to dissipate.

Reflect, my dear Sisters, on what you are doing. You frequently cause God to be offended. God is not glorified and your neighbor is scandalized. On account of you, the holy exercise of charity is held in less esteem. How will you dare one day to appear before God to render him an account of the use you have made of the great grace which he gave you when he called you to the state in which he has placed you? He had expected to derive glory from your works but you have usurped it. You, Sister Barbe, do so by your lack of cordiality toward the Sister whom God has given you, by your haughty attitude and by the little forbearance you show for her infirmities. How could you forget that when you were placed with her as her superior you were obliged to become like a mother with even greater responsibilities than a natural mother since you must help your Sister to work out her salvation and grow in perfection? This obliges you to act with great gentleness and charity as the Son of God recommended when he was on earth. When you accepted this duty, were you not immediately aware of the degree of humility which it required of you since it furnishes you with so many occasions to recognize your weaknesses? Should you not always keep before your eyes the awareness that when you command something you are doing so by obedience, and that of yourself you have no right to order anything?

Courage, my dear Sister! I hope that the harm is not so great that it is without remedy. Place your faults clearly before your eyes without making excuses because in reality nothing outside of ourselves is the cause of the evil we commit. Admit this truth before God. Stir up in your heart a great love for our dear Sister Louise. In the sight of the merciful justice of God, throw yourself at her feet and ask her pardon for your coldness toward her and for all the pain that you have caused her. Promise her that, with the grace of God, you will love her as Jesus Christ himself wills you to and show her the concern that you must have for her. Then embrace her with these true sentiments in your heart.

And here you are, my dear Sister Louise, fallen once again into your bad habits! What do you think of the state you are in? Is it a life without restraint? Far from it. It must be one of continual submission and obedience. Is it possible that you have never reflected upon this, or if you do so that you have so little love for God and so little fear for your salvation that you fail to do what you are obliged to do? My Daughter, practice a little mortification. What do you gain by making visits or going on pilgrimages without permission? Do you want to live according to your own will in everything? Have you forgotten that you must not do anything or go anywhere without the permission of Sister Barbe, whom you accepted as your superior before your departure, and whom you must love as much or more than if she were your mother? I think that you never reflect on your state in life because you do so many things that are incompatible with it. Would you not regret losing your vocation for such trifling satisfactions? I believe that the cause of most of the faults that you commit—and this has just occurred to me—is that you have money and have always liked possessing it. Take my word for this and rid yourself of this affection. Place everything in the hands of Sister Barbe and be satisfied with what she considers appropriate. Cultivate a love for poverty in imitation of the Son of God. By so doing, you will obtain the graces necessary to be a true Daughter of Charity. Otherwise, I doubt very strongly that you will persevere. I say this to you with the fear that you will not heed my word, but I could not refrain from speaking. Accept it graciously because it is the love that God gives me for each of you that causes me to speak in this way. Courage, my dear Sister! I am confident that you will not disregard my little corrections. Recognizing how much God merits to be loved and served, repent for having so badly acquitted yourself of this responsibility from the time he gave you the grace of calling you to this way of life, and particularly to this place where he has bestowed his blessings upon your holy employment. Take a much firmer resolution than you have made in the past. Throw yourself at Sister Barbe's feet with . . . [*letter torn*].

Do you not see that your souls are not at rest, and therefore, that you are not sharing in the holy peace which the Son of God brought to those who are of good will, nor are you partaking in that peace which he left to his holy Apostles when he ascended into heaven?

Admonishing you of your faults has brought my own before my eyes. This causes me, my Daughters, to tell you that the one that troubles me most at this time is the bad example I have given you in the practice of the virtues which I recommend to you. I beg you, my dear Sisters, to overlook this, to ask pardon of God for me and the grace to amend my life, which I desire with all my heart.

I have also been very negligent about writing to you. I hope and pray that you pardon me. I offer to our good God the act of reconciliation which I am convinced you will make with hearts filled with good will. I unite my heart to yours so that together we may obtain the mercy of which we stand in need and the grace to live henceforth in the love of Jesus Crucified, in whom I remain, my very dear Sisters, your very humble Sister and servant.

P.S. Do you know, my very dear Sisters, what I expect of your reconciliation after a renewal of affection? It is that you will open your hearts to one another; that you will rarely be seen one without the other; that you will make your visits to the city together; that you will avoid particular friendships with the Ladies, refraining from visiting them at all and preferring to remain at home with one another. I do not mean that you should refuse the visits that good women will have the charity to make to you. True humility will regulate everything.

NOTE ON THE SUBJECTS WHICH NEED TO BE TREATED DURING THE CONFERENCES[25]

Louise prepared this brief outline in incomplete sentences and forwarded it to Vincent. It illustrates her vision of the important points affecting the lives of the Sisters. Fundamental principles should guide their service of the poor. A community life supporting the Sisters in their service needed to be reinforced by mutual care and affection, forgiveness, and confidentiality, with each Sister calling her companions to grow in the life to which they had committed themselves.

To help us to understand the nature of the calling of the Daughters of Charity and the dispositions that this vocation requires. To this end, to point out the esteem they must have for their state in life and for the poor since they are paid and nourished from the funds provided for them. What the Sisters are to do to avoid receiving in this world their recompense for the service they render to the poor. This could happen because of the slight effort they put into a service which they no longer perform but for which they receive great honor.

If the Sisters do not sometimes deceive themselves in their overeagerness to serve the poor of the parishes or in the Hotel-Dieu, which can cause them to be less satisfied to remain in the House.

If those Sisters who remain in the House do not have the same merit as those engaged in the direct service of the poor. What care and affection the Sisters should have for the Rule of the House and how faithful they should be in observing it.

How the Sisters must esteem and love one another and be willing to have their faults reported to the one who holds the place of superioress.

How each one in turn should warn the same superioress of the faults which they have seen her commit.

How each Sister should spontaneously remind her companions of their faults and how they should accept these admonitions.

On the danger to be found in complaining to one another of the faults they find in their Sisters, and particularly in murmuring and in unburdening themselves to others about the admonitions they have received.

INSTRUCTIONS TO THE SISTERS SENT TO MONTREUIL[26]

In these instructions Louise reviews the attitudes and behaviors that characterize their lives in community, and their comportment with the poor and with those who direct their work. To be effective servants of the poor and evangelizers in Montreuil, the Sisters should conduct themselves so as to present a unified, committed, and genuine witness to God's presence in this community. Louise touches on many aspects of life to present clearly to the Sisters what was expected of them.

Our Sisters Anne Hardemont[27] and Marie Lullen[28] are going to Montreuil in order to discover what Divine Providence wishes them to do there.

First and foremost, they must remember to keep in mind God and his glory. Then they must consider the welfare of the people with whom they will be associated in order to serve them better according to their aptitudes. Thirdly, they shall remember that none of their actions among themselves or with externs should be prejudicial to the Company of the Daughters of Charity because we must honor God in the interest of the Company. Above all, they shall beware of crediting to themselves the least portion of the works in which God does us the honor of employing us. This can come about through vain complacency, satisfaction, or self-serving plans; all things which we must renounce often.

En route, they shall be as exact as possible in the practice of their rule. If they cannot make their morning meditation before leaving, they shall make it without fail while in the coach. Before leaving their bedroom they shall make an act of adoration. In the evening they shall make their examen while kneeling. They shall take a book along with them in order to read in the coach. They shall try to keep their exercises private and shall avoid bothering others in the coach.

They shall guard against uttering improper, careless, or idle words, and against any unbecoming action. In order to prevent this, they shall watch over one another in order to give a charitable warning if a Sister accidentally forgets herself. The Sister given the warning shall willingly accept it even if she is not aware of her fault.

If they have the opportunity to say a few good words to some poor person or to the servants at the inns, they should do so with humility, never mocking the person's ignorance. After leaving the coach, before thinking about eating, they shall go to the nearest church to adore God in the Blessed Sacrament. They shall make the same act of adoration in every village through which they pass. They shall acknowledge the guardian angel of each town and the guardian angel of each soul living there in order to commend them to their protection for the glory of God. If they are able to do so before the coach departs in the afternoon, they shall visit some of the sick or the hospital, if there is one in the village. Arriving at Montreuil, they shall go directly to the church and then to the Chateau to pay their respects to the governor [the Count de Lannoy], telling him that they are there to receive his orders.

They shall remember that true Daughters of Charity must be united in order to fulfill God's expectations. Because our corrupted nature has deprived us of this perfection, and since sin separates us from our unity which is God, following the example of the Blessed Trinity, we must have but one heart and act with one mind as do the three divine Persons. We must do this in such a way that, when the Sister in charge of the sick requests the help of her Sister, the Sister who instructs the children shall readily comply. And, if the Sister in charge of the children requests assistance from the Sister in charge of the poor, she shall do likewise since both tasks are equally the business of God. Considering themselves both chosen by Divine Providence in order to act in unison, we hope never to hear the words, "That is your business, not mine."

If they are housed outside of the hospital, they shall not go to the hospital unless the count orders them to do so. If they are housed at the hospital and their only task seems to be the service of the poor of the city, and, nonetheless, the count wishes them to take charge of the school for girls and the care of the sick of the hospital as well, then they shall comply and shall not involve themselves in other things. Should the count request that they tell him all that happens at the hospital, then they shall do so with great prudence and charity.

Prudence consists in speaking about important matters only and not relating a lot of trifles that are not worth saying. That which you feel obliged to say should be expressed in as gentle a manner as possible, remembering that what seems evil is often so only in our feelings and opinions. In order to avoid conflict with the women and girls who have run the hospital for a long time, our Sisters must have great respect for them and manifest great love and cordiality toward them. The Sisters shall do nothing without their permission, not even take a pot, a frying pan, or anything else for their own needs.

In this matter, they shall remember the instruction and example of our Most Honored Father: that they shall enter this house prepared to suffer and to humble themselves beyond all their expectations. This they can do by apologizing to persons apparently angry with them even if they did not provoke this anger.

If some of these good women and girls get the idea that you are there to dismiss them and send them away, in the name of God, my Sisters, bear with such little suspicions, but prevent them as much as you can from arising by showing submission and cordiality in your words and actions. Consider that, in reality, you must respect these good persons as your mothers and as persons chosen by God to begin this work and to administer it so well during all these years.

Never respond to any complaints or reproaches that they may address to you. Although you are assured that the count will provide for all your needs, do not take advantage of this, and bear in mind that you are there on a trial basis. If these good girls do fairly well and you, on the contrary, are at odds among yourselves and exhibit discord, you shall most certainly be sent back. This fact shall oblige you to act always with purity of intention, only looking upon God with more humility, mistrusting yourselves and trusting in God so that, if we are sent back, we shall be able to believe that it is the will of God; that it will not harm the Company or give bad example to anyone.

Consequently, you must go there with the intention of accomplishing the will of God manifested through the will of the count; and in order to obey the count more perfectly, you shall consider him in God and God in him. Remember that such is the teaching of our Most Honored Father and that, perhaps, he owes the great blessings he has received from God to this holy practice.

In his goodness, the count will often speak freely with you; be careful to show respect always and to be reserved in your speech. Above all, my dear Sisters, if God should allow some small disputes between you, never mention the matter to him or to anyone else. And, if you have grounds to complain about one another, never allow it to appear on the outside.

It is most necessary that you never say anything rude to one another, especially in front of externs. With the help of God, your charity will prevent your being unpleasant with one another.

The close union that should exist between you shall be maintained by mutual forbearance with one another's failings and by the account you give of what you have done, where you have gone, or where you are going during the day. When some difficulty arises in your exercises, for example when the Sister in charge of the sick, or she who is in charge of the children, experiences some doubt, you shall talk it over together. As soon as you have found a solution, both of you, if possible, shall discuss it with the count or with the superioress [of the hospital], if there is one.

You are to conduct yourselves simply, according to the practice common to Paris and other places. However, if someone wishes you to act otherwise, you shall follow their orders so long as they are not offensive to God. Recall the same practice of our Most Honored Father who believes that the advice of others is always worth more than his own.

One of the great needs of our Sisters is that they satisfy the people, and in this way God will bless their work and it will result in his Glory. This need is encountered everywhere, but especially there where the people are extremely fond of the hospital. Great gentleness and cordiality are necessary in order to win over these people. That is why it would be well if every morning each Sister would individually pray (so as not to multiply the prayers said under the rule) for the blessing of our good God in order that they might act in the manner of his son while he was on earth as they carry out the works of charity to which they have been called. Better yet, they should pray that the same Spirit that acted in him should act through them. They should begin their day by reflecting that they are accompanied by Jesus Christ, the Blessed Virgin, and their guardian angel. It would also be well to have devotion to the guardian angels of all the souls in the city.

Our Sisters shall be mindful to show great respect to priests, particularly to the chaplain of the hospital, to whom they should show no familiarity. If necessity requires them to speak to him, they shall always do so together or in the company of another person. They shall take the parish priest as their confessor, believing that they will always find a blessing in remaining obedient.

As for your conduct toward the sick, may you never take the attitude of merely getting the task done. You must show them affection; serving them from the heart—inquiring of them what they might need; speaking to them gently and compassionately; procuring necessary help for them without being too bothersome or too eager. Above all, you must have great care for their salvation, never leaving a poor person or a patient without having uttered some good word. When you meet someone who appears quite ignorant, have them make acts of faith, contrition, and love; for example, "I believe all that the Holy Church believes, and I wish to live and to die in this faith." At other times, it would be well to have such persons recite separately the principal articles of our faith.

They shall not forget to give a report of the expenditures for their trip and any money remaining to the count. If they are housed separately, either in or outside the hospital, their expenditures are to be taken care of by the count and kept separate from other accounts. If they are also required to spend money for the poor, one of them should handle these funds and the other, the money for the maintenance of the Sisters.

If, as is the custom in the parishes of Paris, you were to receive an annual sum, it would not be necessary to give an account of your expenditures to the count. However, since he sets no limits and money is requested as needed, you must furnish him with separate accounts for yourselves and for the poor. As for your food, you may not change it even if you are offered better than that which you receive where you are housed. Our Sisters shall remember to be as recollected as possible in all places, visiting no one and allowing no one to enter their quarters, whether to visit or to engage in useless conversation. When they are requested to do something the propriety of which they doubt, they shall defer the matter as long as they can in order to have the time to seek the advice of the superioress.

Our dear Sisters are most humbly requested, at the beginning, to send us news every two weeks, and to pray for us and for the entire Company. On our part, we shall often implore God to grant them the blessings they need for the fulfillment of his will. May He be eternally blessed.

LETTER TO THE SISTERS AT RICHELIEU[29]

Louise uses this letter to guide the Sisters in considering the use of their time. They seemed to have tended to overextend themselves, thereby depriving one another of the time they needed for their life in common. She reminds them of the value of their vocation and, to encourage them, asks them several questions on specific aspects of their community life. In the last paragraph she tells her Sisters the latest community news as well as other considerations, both marks of her practical care for them.

My very dear Sisters,

I beg God, in his goodness, to continue to bestow his holy graces upon you, especially love for your vocation, which you will know that you possess if you are faithful to the observance of your rules, insofar as the service of the poor permits. Above all, my dear Sisters, be exact in retiring at nine o'clock so that you will be able to rise at four. Thus, you will have time to accomplish everything. If you have developed the habit of allowing outsiders, even the sick, to come when they please, rid yourselves of it little by little and have the poor come for what they need at the appointed hours, because I believe that only this can interfere with your obligations.

As for visits, I do not think that you permit any that could turn you away from your duty. Above all, I am certain that you do not receive men, of any social class, unless it is for a very serious matter, which must then be handled in a few words. Our Most Honored Father recommends this to us in recent conferences. He went so far as to say that we should not receive even him in any of the parishes or at this House where he comes only in case of illness, for serious matters, or to give a conference. I beg you to consider what must be done in other cases.

I also urge you, my dear Sisters, to remember very well that you are to make no visits except to the poor or the sick; that you are never to eat anywhere other than in your own House; and that you are not to relate what happens in the House to anyone except the director, and then only what he needs to know. If your infirmities sometimes require you to take a little wine, oh, let it be done rarely, in small amounts and for a clearly recognized need.

Gentleness, cordiality, and forbearance must be the practices of the Daughters of Charity just as humility, simplicity, and the love of the holy humanity of Jesus Christ, who is perfect charity, is their spirit. That, my dear Sisters, is a summary of what I think I should tell you about our rules until such time as Divine Providence permits you to have the entire text.

How happy I am when you send me detailed news of yourselves. Once and for all, I would like to know all about your manner of acting in the areas I have asked you about. Do you love your way of life? Do you esteem it as more excellent for you than all the hermitages and religious convents because God has called you to it? Do you believe that you have assembled together for your sanctification by a secret action of Divine Providence? Does the stronger support the weaker lovingly and cordially as the need arises? Do you often recall the counsel our Most Honored Father gave us in a conference when he said that we, as well as religious, have a cloister, and that it is as difficult for faithful souls to leave it as it is for religious to leave theirs, although it is not a cloister made of stones but rather one constituted by holy obedience which must govern all our actions and desires? I beg Our Lord, whose example has enclosed us in this holy cloister, to grant us the grace never to violate it.

Our newest arrivals got here safely and are in very good health, thank God. It was a bit tiring for Sister Françoise but she is over that now. I beg you to give news of them to their relatives and to send us news of their families. Also please send the forty pounds I already mentioned to you. Sister Jeanne, to whom the money belongs, met, here in Paris, the man who had donated this sum and he assured her that it had been received. Please have this man speak to Monsieur du Chesne,[30] if he is still in Richelieu. Greet Monsieur du Chesne for me with all the respect I owe him and assure him that I have written to him two or three times. I also send my very humble greetings to Monsieur Cuissot,[31] and the other priests. All our Sisters greet you in the love of Jesus Crucified, in which I am, my very dear Sisters, your very humble Sister.

P.S. I sent your letters to be held in Beauvais. Sister Charlotte's parents are well, thank God, and ask for her prayers, particularly her mother.

Addressed: To my very dear Sisters Daughters of Charity at Richelieu.

LETTER TO SISTER LAURENCE[32]

Louise points out the practical ways that unity of spirit can be exercised by Sisters who live together. They should be sensitive to each other's needs and feelings. Good communication will preserve unity and eliminate the need to seek consolation elsewhere.

19 February

My very dear Sister,

Thank you for sending me news of yourself. Let me know if you wrote the letter yourself. If not, do not ask anyone to write for you except Sister Barbe,[33] who will do so willingly. However, if I am not mistaken you are learning to write. However limited your ability to write may be, if you have a private matter to share with me, write the letter yourself. Although you are under no obligation to show your letter to Sister Barbe, nevertheless courtesy requires you to tell her that you are going to write to us. Fear not; she will not ask what you want to tell us nor will she look at it since she knows that would offend God.

I have the impression that the two of you are living together in great peace and with the desire of animating one another to strive for union and cordiality. This creates a climate in which you communicate with one another, telling one another what you did while you were apart and letting one another know where you are going when you leave the house. In this instance one of you acts from an obligation of submission while the other has the duty of support and courtesy. The same applies to your community exercises. If one of you is sad, let her overcome herself so as to recreate with her Sister. At the same time, let the one who is cheerful moderate her exuberance so as to accommodate herself to the mood of her Sister and, little by little, draw her out of her melancholy. All this should be done for the love of God and to avoid listening to the temptation that might cause you to want to go elsewhere to unburden your soul and to seek satisfaction. This would bring about the total ruin of the holy friendship that should exist between two Sisters. I beg Our Lord to preserve you from this by his holy love in which I am, my dear Sister, your very humble Sister and servant.

Addressed: To Sister Laurence, Daughter of Charity, Servant of the Sick Poor at Bernay.

INSTRUCTION ON RECREATION[34]

Louise explains the importance of common recreation to support the Sisters in their community life. She motivates the Sisters by reminding them of the presence of God in their midst as well as their obligation of honoring the union existing in the Blessed Trinity. Louise elaborates on various aspects of recreation and its value for those participating in it. Communication, cordiality, and mutual support as well as a positive attitude toward each Sister would make this act life-giving.

Recreation must always begin with a reminder of the presence of God and of the equality of all reasonable beings in his eyes, reflecting that the least esteemed by men are perhaps the best loved by God.

Recreation should be regarded as a time allowed by the goodness of God to unite ourselves by means of a sincere communication of thoughts, words, and actions. This time should be used to honor the true union of the three distinct Persons of the Blessed Trinity and the admirable union of the blessed in heaven.

During recreation, conversation should be truly lighthearted and cordial. We should converse with those who are agreeable to us as well as with those we favor less, replying graciously without arguing and without taking offense at what is said, bearing in mind the meekness with which Jesus Christ received the blame for his holy words and actions.

Never make fun of a Sister who does not speak well unless you are certain that she does not mind it and that your heart is free from uncharitable feelings. Should you be the target of others' amusement, accept the situation graciously and consider your Sisters as better than yourself and, therefore, as better loved by God. Look upon yourself as blessed in the occasion offered you of serving them.

From time to time during recreation, raise your mind to God and recall that you are strengthening your mind and body in their weakness during this period of rest. Because of this, they can be better employed in the service of God, according to your obligations, and they are once again given courage for the work at hand.

During this time of recreation, reflect on the eternal joy that you will have in heaven if, on earth, you love God and your neighbor as he has commanded you. To help you practice the love you owe your neighbor, remember when you are together that the bond of union among you is the Blood shed by the Sacred Heart of Jesus Christ.

Conversation during the time allowed must be in a spirit of great charity, following the example set for us by the Son of God while on earth. You must try to associate with those Sisters who bring you the closest to virtue, or with those whom you can help in the same way. Keep yourself interested in others. Do not get angry over the actions of the others, especially over their intentions. Avoid exclusive friendships since you are obliged to a mutual communication with one another in order to maintain the union which must be preserved in your religious family.

Be amiable with all your Sisters. Always respect your superior whom you must look upon as Jesus Christ on earth. Never criticize her manner of governing even when her orders sometimes appear to be contrary to your views or perhaps far from reasonable. Certainly, with a little patience, you will discover that it is the spirit of God more than the spirit of the superior that is governing.

Be zealous in defending the Sisters who are absent. Let your charity be such that you do not easily give in to rash judgments. Always put yourself in the place of those who are blamed either by reflecting on your own faults or by taking into consideration the power of natural inclinations on a person's way of thinking and the near impossibility of getting rid of a habit. Finally, remind yourself and those with you of your mutual obligations to God if you are all exempt from the fault in question. However, be careful that what you say about others proceeds from a truly Christian heart and not from pretended virtue.

Your conversation should center mainly on subjects which help you to fulfill the obligations of your rules. You should bear in mind that all other acts are more prejudicial than helpful to you.

OBLIGATIONS OF THE SERVANT OF THE POOR[35]

Louise presents both the motives and the means that should guide the Sisters in their community and apostolic lives. Not content with generalities, she specifies commonsense reasons for the need of direction. The means she outlines provided the Sisters with realistic, time-tested, and effective means of living their lives fruitfully.

The first reason that should cause us to desire to be instructed on the manner in which the Sisters of Charity should act, in all the places where they are employed for the service of the poor, is the danger they are in of doing just the opposite if they do not know how to behave.

The second is the danger that, by acting otherwise, they will go against the will of God.

The third is the danger that God will not derive glory from our employments if we do not act as we should.

1. Great faults can be committed if they are not well informed concerning their responsibilities. It takes great temerity for a Sister to act without knowing how she should conduct herself.

2. There is always the danger of offending God when one is uncertain how to behave.

3. This lack of instruction could lead to discord rather than to

the union which should exist among them. This is the most damaging thing that could happen to the Company and the most opposed to what God is asking of it.

4. The fourth evil is that a Sister who does not know how she should act would be in great danger of becoming a source of disedification to persons of the world. Moreover, she would not serve the poor in the spirit of Jesus Christ, and she could draw down upon herself the indignation of God by her repeated faults. Little by little, she would become lax, thereby rendering herself unworthy of the graces of God. This might even cause his goodness to withdraw from her the grace of her vocation. Such great faults might finally lead to the total destruction of the Company.

It seems to me that the first means to help us to act as true Daughters of Charity is always to be disposed to respond to holy obedience with the view of accomplishing the will of God.

To be available to go anywhere; to be disposed to be submissive to the Sister who will be given to us as Sister Servant; and to do nothing without communicating with her. Before leaving for a new mission, to take the firm resolution to do nothing contrary to the rules and maxims of the motherhouse or of the Company.

To be faithful neither to give nor to receive news, except when told to do so by the Sister Servant, who shall not fail to send it to the superiors in Paris.

To be very respectful to the Ladies of Charity and to others employed in the service of the poor.

Neither to meddle nor to speak with them without the advice of the Sister Servant.

To be very circumspect in speaking with externs, especially concerning private community matters.

To be supportive, cordial, and submissive to one another. To preserve the spirit of gentleness and charity.

This could be done easily if the Sisters are as faithful as they should be to the practice of their rule, which should be repeated frequently so that they can learn it by heart. It should be read in places where this can be done.

In order to accomplish these things, they must have great mistrust of themselves and great confidence in God.

A practice to be remembered is the thought that if Jesus Christ had not been. . . .[36]

ADMINISTRATIVE AND ORGANIZATIONAL SKILLS

LETTER TO VINCENT DE PAUL[37]

Louise organized systems to help the Confraternities of Charity to run well. In this letter she discusses with Vincent de Paul the role of the procurator or business manager. She gives detailed instruction for beginning documentation and encloses a report of each of the assemblies of Beauvais.

4 September

Monsieur,

I am returning the Rule of Saint-Savior to you. I had not seen it. It appears that the first part makes the confraternity completely dependent upon the pastor. I do not know if this is wise. It is certainly true that the pastors in Beauvais would be delighted to have it that way. However, this would immediately lead them to want no one else to know what was happening within each confraternity. On the other hand, I believe, Monsieur, that the officers must keep them informed about the reception of the sick, at least telling them whom they will accept. A provision must be made in the rule stating that the pastor records the votes during an election and that the treasurer gives the financial report in his presence. No mention should be made, however, of the vicar general. The number of Ladies should be indicated as is the case in the present rule. It should also state that vacancies will be filled by those upon whom the Company has agreed, and subsequently they will be presented to the pastor to be incorporated and receive his blessing.

As for the question of a procurator, I do not know if we can easily find one for every confraternity. The Ladies would never turn over the records of the collections to him. As for keeping the accounts, I think that the women can take care of this themselves. There would be nothing else for him to do except perhaps to see to it that any legacies there might be would be administered for the benefit of the confraternity. In that case, one procurator for all the confraternities would appear to be sufficient. These suggestions are only for Beauvais. The ordinary rule is good for Liancourt, especially the provisions which recommend friendship among the members and give the greatest [details] concerning the morning and evening exercises and the practice of recalling the presence of God during the day. Also, Monsieur, I recommend that vacant places be filled as provided here. Good procurators can be found everywhere.

Please let me know, Monsieur, if you will now add a particular article for this officer who is seeking so earnestly to be admitted as procurator for the goods of the confraternity. Let me know also if the rule will provide for two girls to be named by Madame de Liancourt as nurses for the sick.[38] They would reside in the housing which the duchess would furnish for this purpose and would be obliged to bring medicine to the sick of La Bruyère, Cauffry, and Rantigny, as well as Liancourt. They would be expected to visit the sick at least twice a week and to carry out all that is required by and provided for by the foundation set up for this purpose. In this area, collections are taken up in the homes on Sundays and in the churches on major feasts. The procurators keep a book in which they record the receipts from each collection. The treasurer does the same. Only strong boxes with two locks are to be used. I think that it should be added that the two guardians are to be members of the confraternity.

I believe, Monsieur, that it would be appropriate to have a register in each strong box similar to the one which I left with you so that all the happenings of the confraternity could be recorded in it. I think that the Act of Establishment should be written at the beginning, followed by the rule, the names of the Ladies, and the results of the election of the procurator and of the officers. Place could be left after this for subsequent elections.

Toward the middle of the book, a place should be indicated where a record is to be kept of the names of the Ladies who have died and of those who have replaced them. Another section should be reserved for pious legacies and for extraordinary gifts, while a list of furniture belonging to the poor should be kept in another section. The book that I brought you is from La Bruyère because the Act of Establishment contains all the necessary signatures.

I believe that the superioress[39] must also keep a register in which she writes the names of the sick poor, the date on which they were received, and the date on which they died or were discharged by the confraternity.

If you had not told me to draw up this report, Monsieur, I would not have dared to do so. I do not know why I have delayed so long in writing except that I realize that my mind is very slow both to do good for others and for my own practices.

Good Sister Jeanne from the parish of Saint-Benoît[40] has just brought me three girls from Colombe[41] who seem very promising and who desire to serve the poor anywhere that they are sent. I believe that they will go to see you one of these days. I am sorry that I missed the day that your charity was willing to give me. I think it was my fault. I have great need of a few days to think about myself and be renewed. I believe, Monsieur, when the time comes for me to take charge of the Confraternity of Charity of the parish of Saint-Laurent, if you wish to honor me by employing me for this, that I should spend a few days there. I could use this occasion, if you judge it appropriate. But for the love of God, Monsieur, ask the divine mercy to let you know my needs; otherwise, I will believe that he wishes to abandon me completely because he allows you to feel this way.

I am enclosing a report of each of the Assemblies of Beauvais. I believe that it would be well for the rule that you are drawing up to be for Saint-Savior. When you send it, you could ask that it be sent to the other charities to be copied. If you would be so good as to take the trouble to reread the letter I sent you from Liancourt, you will perhaps find something more that I am not telling you at this time. Please excuse the disorder of my presentation. I almost want to blame my poor memory, but you know me as I am and as I always shall be, Monsieur, your very humble daughter and most grateful servant.

P.S. Collections are made every Monday in Beauvais, but I think it would be well to take them up also on major feasts in the church. I believe that with the imminent establishment of the Mission at Beauvais, as the Bishop wishes, it will be easy to obtain all that could be desired for the good of the confraternity. I did not undertake to suggest this collection.

Addressed: To Monsieur Father Vincent.

LETTER TO VINCENT DE PAUL[42]

Having arrived in Bicêtre,[43] the residence of the foundlings, Louise requests that a Vincentian brother, who was a baker, be sent to consult about a new oven. She foresees that there would be a large market to sell wine as a fund-raising project for the Ladies of Charity, but advises against mixing in cheap wine. She recommends the hard-working Sisters in the foundling residence to Vincent's prayers.

Wednesday morning

Monsieur,

We arrived at Bicêtre in good health, thank God. However, we are not going to stay here long. I beg your charity most humbly to send us tomorrow the brother baker, to whom I have already spoken, so that he can advise us, help us to have a good oven built, and find someone for us who is suitable for the job.

I also find it essential to start selling the wine. There is a large market here for it in casks and large bottles because of the soldiers billeted in the area. I fear if we wait much longer our sales will not be as good. Sister Genevieve[44] says she believes that the Ladies want to wait until cheaper wine is available so that it can be mixed in with it. I do not think that would be a saving because we would need a boy to do the mixing and he quite possibly could make off with all the profits. Besides that, it would be a great burden for our Sisters who would have to watch so that nearly unavoidable mistakes would not be made.

I beg your charity most humbly to remember that you promised us a conference for a week from today. Yesterday I saw Monsieur Vacherot's sister.[45] She is quite ill and asked me to recommend her to your holy prayers. If she dared do so, she would beg you to show her the charity of coming to see her. If she gets worse, I will certainly beg you to do so; I am asking Sister Julienne to keep you informed, if you do not mind.[46]

I think much good would be done for our Sisters if you took the trouble to visit them at the House. Sister Hellot could be told of the benefits to the Company when the Sisters become accustomed to being submissive to one another, and it could be made known that those who seem to have some authority should serve as an example.[47]

The work of our poor Sisters here is almost unbelievable; not so much because of the great effort involved as on account of the natural repugnance one has for this type of work. For that reason it is most fitting to help them, to encourage them, and to make known what they are accomplishing and its value in the sight of God. It is also fitting to help them by our prayers. I am more in need of prayers than anyone else since I am the weakest in body and spirit, although I have the happiness of being, Monsieur, your very humble servant and most grateful daughter.

Addressed: To Monsieur Vincent, Superior General of the Mission

LETTER TO SISTER JULIENNE LORET[48]

Louise expresses concern for Sister Julienne's health and advises her to exercise. She encourages the Sisters to seek opportunities to serve the sick poor in the surrounding villages. Her interest lies in making white honey, which could be used in syrups and preserves, as sugar was expensive. She is specific about the supplies that she is sending to the Sisters.

6 October

My dear Sister,

I thank God for all the help his goodness gave our deceased Sister. I believe that, in a short time, she worked diligently to acquire the degree of holiness to which God had called her. You are blessed to have been able to assist her. May Our Lord be your eternal recompense!

Now I beg you to slow down a bit and to look after your health. For this, I think that you need exercise. If we are to believe Sister Philippe,[49] she would willingly undertake anything without taking time out to be sick. This is why I beg you, my dear Sister, to take turns teaching school, looking after the house, and nursing the sick in the villages. Our Sisters do this everywhere else. One of my worries about Chars is that our Sisters are not in the habit of looking for opportunities to serve the sick poor of the surrounding villages. This causes me to fear that our stay there will lead to our humiliation.

I thank you with all my heart for the beautiful, delicious apples you sent us. It seems to me that you once mentioned that you were going to make honey. Please find out if that white honey is natural, or if it can be made some way because sugar is becoming very expensive, and it could be used to make syrups and even preserves.

We are sending you a half-pound of catholicon, a pound of senna, a pound of cassia, and two and a quarter pounds of licorice.[50] If you need anything else, let me know. Sister Marguerite will draw up an account of what you are to pay the nurses.[51] Please let us know how the child is doing. Be sure that he is brought back to us at the time indicated. I am the love of Our Lord, my very dear Sister, your very humble Sister and servant.

P.S. Thank you for your kindness toward my son. He is better, thank God. Help me to thank Him for this.

Addressed: To My Very Dear Sister Julienne Loret, Daughter of Charity, Servant of the Sick Poor at Chars.

GENTLENESS AND SENSITIVITY

LETTER TO THE SISTER SERVANT AT SAINT-DENIS[52]

Louise expresses frustration at the inability of the Sister Servant to see how her love of cats, particularly surrounding her at meditation, could disturb the other Sisters. She speaks directly about getting rid of the animals. She discusses various supplies for the Sisters, and ends on a positive note regarding recognition of faults and their correction.

My very dear Sister,

Well now, here you are failing seriously once again! And you interpret our Sister's fault other than it really is. This Sister became impatient at seeing the two of you surrounded by so many cats during times of meditation. You even admit that another Sister dislikes them. My God, Sister, how amiable the truth is! I have told you over and over to get rid of these animals and you pay no attention to me and then you complain that a Sister does not obey you promptly!

You still owe us 20 sols.[53] We will send you the peas. We are sending ten pounds of prunes at six francs per hundredweight.

My dear Sister, please do not be discouraged at the sight of your faults. Unless we are aware of them, we can neither acknowledge nor correct them.

I think that you would be wise to use salted butter. The best quality costs eight sols here. Let us know if you think that it is more expensive at Saint-Denis and if you want us to send you some from here. You need fresh butter only on certain occasions and these are rare.

Be consoled by the hope that the retreat will do you good. I'm astonished that you still have our two Sisters without our authorization. Beg God to grant me humility and believe that I am in his most holy love, my very dear Sister, your very humble Sister and servant.

LETTER TO VINCENT DE PAUL[54]

A Sister is about to leave the Company after being a member for a year, and Louise seeks Monsieur Guérin as a confessor for her. Another Sister is critically ill and Louise admits being over-whelmed by the spiritual and emotional problems faced by so many Sisters. She seeks advice from Vincent as to how to remedy the situations.

Friday, 4 July 1642[55]

Monsieur,

Madame de Traversay[56] forgot to ask you if we should seek another decree since that one deals only with the foundlings and not with the proposal of the duchess.[57] Although I told her that you had examined it, she wants me to ask you and to let her know tomorrow morning. I beg you most humbly to allow me to speak to you a while before you leave, otherwise I will be very handicapped. We have a Sister here who has nearly made up her mind to leave. She has been with us for more than a year. I met her this evening when she got back from the Foundling Hospital, and I advised her to go to confession tomorrow. If possible, could Monsieur Guérin[58] hear her confession since Monsieur Portail is still ill? Also, could it be in the morning since I have no one but her to send to help the Sisters at Saint-Sulpice where, from what I have heard, a Sister is critically ill. I am a bit overwhelmed by all the spiritual and emotional problems faced by the greater number of our Sisters. I assure you, Monsieur, that my inability to help these good girls reach perfection is a subject of humiliation for me before God and the world. I beg the goodness of God to reveal this to you along with the means to remedy it. I remain, Monsieur, your humble and most grateful daughter and servant.

CONCLUSION

SPIRITUAL TESTAMENT[59]

In 1660, while dying, Louise gave her spiritual testament to her Sisters. She stressed community in union and cordiality above all else, including service of the poor.

My dear Sisters, I continue to ask God for his blessings for you and pray that he will grant you the grace to persevere in your vocation in order to serve him in the manner he asks of you.

Take good care of the service of the poor. Above all, live together in great union and cordiality, loving one another in imitation of the union and life of Our Lord.

Pray earnestly to the Blessed Virgin, that she may be your only Mother.[60]

Notes

INTRODUCTION: SEVENTEENTH-CENTURY FRANCE

1. In 1589, in yet another chapter of France's long civil and religious wars, the last of the Valois kings of France, Henry III, was assassinated by a deranged Dominican monk. Henry of Navarre was immediately proclaimed by his supporters Henry IV. The Catholic League proclaimed Henry of Navarre's uncle, the Cardinal de Bourbon, Charles X. It would take several more years of fierce fighting for the succession to be definitively settled in favor of Henry IV.

2. "Paris vaut bien une messe."

3. For a discussion of Henry's "Grand Design" see Michael Wolfe, *The Conversion of Henry IV. Politics, Power, and Religious Belief in Early Modern France.* (Cambridge: Harvard University Press, 1993), pp. 189–90.

4. Within the context of this era in French history, those who were referred to as the "politique" were those who put the pragmatic interests of Bourbon absolutism above all other considerations in the determination of foreign and domestic policy. In contrast, the party of the *dévots* were those who supported putting the interests of French and European Catholicism as the primary factor in the forming French and European Catholicism as the primary factor in forming French foreign and domestic policies. For more information see, Louis Chatellier, *L'Europe des Dévots* (Paris: Flammarion, 1987).

5. The power of Hapsburg Austria had been declining since the time of the Reformation. The power of Hapsburg Spain, which reached its height in the second half of the sixteenth century under Philip II, was still great even though it too was declining. Yet, even in decline, the Hapsburg encirclement of French territory remained a powerful threat.

6. For more information on the economic realities of this era,

see Catharina Lis and Hugo Soly, *Poverty and Capitalism in Pre-Industrial Europe*, trans. James Coonan (Sussex: Harvester, 1979).

7. In 1664, Louis Abelly included a classic description of the sad state of the Church in France at the end of the sixteenth century in the first chapter of his pioneering biography of Vincent de Paul. See his *Life*, Vol. 1, pp. 1–34.

8. To be "received" into the kingdom, and become the law of the land, papal documents had to be accepted by the king, who, in turn, would order the Parlement of Paris to register them. Although Henry IV had promised to receive the Tridentine decrees as one of the conditions for the acceptance of his abjuration by the papacy, he never did so. The opposition of the magistrates of the parlement was so strong that finally, in 1615, the Assembly of the French Clergy unilaterally legislated the de facto reception of the Tridentine decrees throughout the kingdom's dioceses.

9. For a brief survey of the history of Gallicanism in seventeenth century France, see *The Church in the Age of Absolutism and Enlightenment*, ed. Hubert Jedin and Jay Dolan, chap. 4, "Gallicanism and Protestantism" (New York: Crossroad, 1981), pp. 57–70 (hereinafter referred to as Jedin, *Church*).

10. Briefly stated, these Gallican "liberties" included: (1) that permission of the crown was needed before a papal bull could be published in France; (2) that decisions of the Roman Congregations had no legal force in France; (3) that no French subject could be summoned to appear before a Roman tribunal; and (4) that French courts could take jurisdiction of ecclesiastical matters in all cases where the law of the land was involved. See W. H. Lewis, *The Splendid Century: Life in the France of Louis XIV* (New York: Doubleday, 1957), p. 97.

11. See Georges Aimé Martimort, *Le Gallicanisme* (Paris: Presses universitaires de France, 1973).

12. On the Catholic Reform in France, see the excellent survey in *Histoire de la France Religieuse*, vol. 2, "Du christianisme flamboyant à l'aube des Lumières" (Paris: Éditions du Seuil, 1988). See especially chapters entitled "L'offensive catholique et l'invasion mystique," "La reforme pastorale: le clergé séculier, les réguliers," and "La reforme pastorale: les fidèles" pp. 324–443. (hereinafter referred to as *France Religieuse*.).

13. See *France Religieuse*, pp. 342–67. See also Antonino Orcajo,

C.M., "Las Grandes Corrientes Espirituales del siglo XVII," *Vincentiana* 31 (1987): 507–19.

14. Henri Brémond first popularized the term "French School" to refer to the seventeenth-century spirituality that was heavily influenced by Pierre de Bérulle. According to the strict terms of this definition, many of the major spiritual figures of the seventeenth-century, including Vincent de Paul and Louise de Marillac, would have to be seen as standing outside the French School. It would seem, however, more appropriate to refer to the "French schools of spirituality" as a more inclusive term that would allow all the contemporary spiritualities of the "age of gold" and the *milieu dévot* in France to be compared and contrasted more fruitfully. See Raymond Deville, S.S., *L'École française de spiritualité* (Paris: Desclée, 1987), pp. 7–13.

15. Robert P. Maloney, C.M., *The Way of Vincent de Paul*, p. 21.

16. In its twenty-fifth session, the Council of Trent issued the following Reform Decree with regard to bishops:

> It is to be desired that those who assume the episcopal office know what are their duties, and understand that they have been called not for their own convenience, not for riches or luxury, but to labors and cares for the glory of God. For it is not to be doubted that the rest of the faithful will be more easily roused to religion and innocence, if they see those who are placed over them concentrate their thoughts not on the things of this world but on the salvation of souls and on their heavenly country. Since the holy council desires these things to be of the greatest importance in the restoration of ecclesiastical discipline, it admonishes all bishops that they reflect on these things and also by the actions and behavior of their life, which is a sort of perpetual sermon, give evidence that their deportment is consistent with their office; but above all that they so regulate their whole conduct that others may derive therefrom examples of moderation, modesty, continence, and of that holy humility which recommends us so to God.

(see *The Canons and Decrees of the Council of Trent*, trans. H. J. Schroeder, O.P. [Rockford: TAN Books, 1978], pp. 232–33).

17. One of the main provisions of the 1516 Concordat of Bologna was the concession to the French monarchy by the papacy of the right to appoint all bishops and other high ecclesiastical officials in the kingdom, thousands of appointments in all.

18. See *France Religieuse*, pp. 374–84.

19. Under the influence of Pierre de Bérulle, many of the contemporary French reform spiritualities were characterized by a very "high" theology of the priesthood. See Paul Cochois, *Bérulle et l'École Française* (Paris: Éditions du Seuil, 1963), pp. 12–33.

20. We may summarize the reform decrees of the council's twenty-second session concerning the life and conduct of clerics as follows: "Nothing leads others to piety and to the service of God more than the life and example of those who have dedicated themselves to the divine ministry. For, since they are observed to have been raised from the things of the world to a higher position, others fix their eyes on them as upon a mirror and derive from them what they are to imitate."

21. For the text of this decree, see the reform decrees of the twenty-third session of Trent, chap. 18.

22. See Antoine Degert, *Histoire des séminaires français jusqu'à la Révolution*, 2 vols. (Paris: Beauchesne, 1912).

23. See *France Religieuse*, pp. 389–96.

24. Ibid., pp. 324–40.

25. As has been noted, the Edict of Nantes had been established only as a short-term solution to keep national peace until some method of establishing religious unity in the country could be developed. By the terms of the edict, the Protestants became a country within a country with the right to fortify certain towns and maintain a large army. This situation was unacceptable to Bourbon absolutism. Religious warfare broke out again in the 1620s, leading to the definitive military defeat of the Protestants at the siege of La Rochelle in 1628. The ultimate solution to the "problem" of Protestantism in France was a political and military one, leading in 1685 to Louis XIV's revoking the edict.

26. See *France Religieuse*, pp. 395–404.

27. Cited in *France Religieuse*, pp. 418.

28. Ibid., pp. 434–43.

29. Ibid., pp. 404–07.

30. See Joseph Bergin, *Cardinal de la Rochefoucauld: Leadership and*

Reform in the French Church (New Haven: Yale University Press, 1987).

31. See *France Religieuse*, pp. 407–08.

32. Their official name is the Congregation of the Mission. The popular designation "Lazarist" comes from the traditional mother-house of Saint Lazare in Paris. In English-speaking countries, they are usually called Vincentians, a name they sometimes share with the members of the Society of Saint Vincent de Paul.

33. Mezzadri, "L'Église en France," p. 371.

34. See Elizabeth Rapley, *The Dévotes: Women and Church in Seventeenth Century France* (Montreal: McGill-Queens University Press, 1992).

35. See *France Religieuse*, pp. 410–15.

36. The most significant of these groundbreaking foundations proved to be that of the Daughters of Charity, founded in 1633 by Vincent de Paul and Louise de Marillac.

37. See Edward R. Udovic, C.M., " 'Caritas Christi Urget Nos': The Urgent Challenges of Charity in Seventeenth Century France," *Vincentian Heritage* 12 (1991): 85–104.

38. See Paul Christophe, *Les Pauvres et la pauvreté. IIème partie: Du XVI siècle à nos jours* (Paris: Desclée, 1987), pp. 33–49.

39. " 'On the Eminent Dignity of the Poor in the Church': A Sermon by Jacques Benigne Bossuet," trans. with intro. Edward R. Udovic, C.M., *Vincentian Heritage* 13 (1992): 37–58.

40. For a brief history of the Jansenist controversies see Jedin, *Church*, pp. 24–56.

41. Mezzadri, *L'Église en France*, pp. 390–91.

INTRODUCTION. VINCENT DE PAUL: HIS LIFE AND WAY

1. The governor of Saint-Quentin, De la Font, wrote to Vincent thanking him for his efforts on behalf of the impoverished population of that town. The governor asked him "to continue to be the father of this country" (Coste, *CED* 5:378, letter 1871).

2. Cited in Hughes, *Frederic Ozanam*, p. 58.

3. See, for example, Vincent's remarks to Bernard Codoing: "I have a particular devotion to following the adorable Providence of

God step by step." (Coste, *CCD* 2:237.) On Canfield, see Kent Emery, Jr., *Renaissance Dialectic and Renaissance Piety. Benet of Canfield's "Rule of Perfection"* (Binghamton, NY: Medieval and Renaissance Texts and Studies, 1987).

4. The account of his vicarious suffering has been disputed, beginning with Antoine Redier (1927) and continuing to the present. The details are available in Stafford Poole and Douglas Slawson, "A New Look at an Old Temptation," *Vincentian Heritage* 11, n. 2. (1990): 125–42.

5. The principal reason lies in Louise's unexplained obscurity until practically the present day. The four-hundredth anniversary of her birth in 1991 was the occasion for bringing her definitely to greater public notice. Vincent himself is undergoing a period of reevaluation, paradoxically in the opposite direction. There is a shift from the fruitfulness and activity of his public life to a recovery of his hidden and interior life, here called Vincent I, the journey to freedom and to the poor. Whatever picture emerges, it will still most likely contrast with the friendship of Francis de Sales and Jane Frances de Chantal, which focused a great deal on the relationship itself and was characterized by expressed emotional intensity. I imagine Francis and Jane facing each other, while I think of Vincent and Louise side by side inflamed by the same love of God and sharing a common mission to the poor. See Wendy M. Wright, *Bond of Perfection: Jeanne de Chantal and François de Sales* (Mahwah, N.J.: Paulist Press, 1985).

6. Coste, *CED* 13:191.

7. Benedict XIII beatified Vincent de Paul, 21 August 1729; and Clement XII canonized him, 16 June 1737. On 22 June 1883, Leo XIII designated him heavenly patron of "all associations of charity which come from him in any way and exist in French territory."

8. These figures are the estimates made by André Dodin, *Vincent de Paul and Charity*, p. 47.

9. Ibid.

10. Conference 195; Coste, *CED* 12:93.

11. Coste, *CED* 12:132.

12. Abelly, *Life* 1:103.

13. Coste, *CED* 11:32.

14. Coste, *CED* 12:139.

15. Ibid.
16. Coste, *CED* 12:262.
17. Coste, *CCD* 1:81, letter 49, around 1630, to Louise de Marillac.
18. Abelly, *Life*, Book 3, chap. 5, section 1, p. 46.

INTRODUCTION. LOUISE DE MARILLAC: A SPIRITUAL PORTRAIT

1. Biographies and studies on Louise de Marillac are few in number. See, however, Joseph I. Dirvin, C.M., *Louise de Marillac of the Ladies and Daughters of Charity* (New York: Farrar, Straus, and Giroux, 1970); Margaret Flinton, D.C., *Louise de Marillac. Social Aspect of Her Work* (New Rochelle, N.Y.: New City Press, 1992); and Vincent Regnault, D.C., *Saint Louise de Marillac, Servant of the Poor*, trans. Louise Sullivan, D.C. (Rockford, Ill.: TAN Books, 1983).
2. *Spiritual Writings*, pp. 1–2.
3. Calvet, *Louise de Marillac*, p. 46.
4. "Fille naturelle," the expression used in the postmortem inventory of the possessions of her father. "Louis de Marillac. Inventaire après décès (24 juillet 1604)," *Annales de la Congrégation de la Mission* 125 (1960): 324.
5. Cited by Poinsenet, *De l'anxiété à la sainteté: Louise de Marillac*, p. 33.
6. *Spiritual Writings*, A. 2, pp. 1–2. Also, see below.
7. *Spiritual Writings*, A. 2, p. 1.
8. Ibid.
9. Saint Vincent, probably mistakenly, referred to the thirty-eight years of their friendship (see Conference 118; Leonard, *Conferences*, 4:315.)
10. *Spiritual Writings*, A. 91B, p. 754.
11. Coste, *CCD* 1:54.
12. *Spiritual Writings*, L. 1, p. 6.
12a. *Spiritual Writings*, A7, pp. 714–717.
13. Coste, *CCD* 1:80.
14. *Spiritual Writings*, M. 8B, p. 834.
15. *Spiritual Writings*, A. 1, pp. 689–91.

16. Coste, *CCD* 1:81.
17. Coste, *CCD* 1:158.
18. Coste, *CCD* 1:79.
19. Coste, *CCD* 1:150.
20. Coste, *CCD* 1:215–16.
21. Coste, *CCD* 1:150.
22. Coste, *CCD* 1:87.
23. Coste, *CCD* 1:110–11.
24. Coste, *CCD* 1:200.
25. Coste, *CCD* 1:217.
26. Coste, *CCD* 1:67.
27. Coste, *CCD* 2:602.
28. Coste, *CCD* 2:600.
29. Coste, *CCD* 3:212; see also *CED* 13:751, document 182, the deliberations of the Council of 25 April 1659.
30. (Request addressed to the king by the municipal magistrates of Angers, January 1639,) cited in Élisabeth Charpy, D.C., *Petite vie*, p. 63.
31. Coste, *CED* 13:539.
32. Coste, *CCD* 3:181.
33. See, for example, Coste, *CED* 10:123, 332, 679.
34. Coste, *CED* 13:798.
35. Coste, *CED* 9:129; Leonard, *Conferences* 1:117.
36. Abelly, *Life* 1:225.
37. See Six and Loose, *Saint Vincent de Paul*.
38. Thomas Dubay, *Caring: A Biblical Theology of Community* (Denville, N.J.: Dimension, 1973), pp. 7–28.
39. *Spiritual Writings*, A. 21, pp. 701–02.
40. 2 Cor 5:14: "The charity of Christ impels/urges us."
41. *Spiritual Writings*, A. 27, pp. 827–29.
42. *Rules of the Daughters of Charity*, Chap. 1, parag. 1.
43. Dodin, *Saint Vincent de Paul and Charity*, p. 56.
44. *Spiritual Writings*, L. 647, p. 666.
45. *Spiritual Writings*, p. 835.
46. *Spiritual Writings*, L. 303B, p. 140.
47. *Spiritual Writings*, L. 179, p. 203.
48. *Spiritual Writings*, p. xxix.
49. Calvet, *Louise de Marillac*, pp. 194–95.
50. *Spiritual Writings*, L. 97, pp. 107–08.

51. *Spiritual Writings*, L. 121, pp. 129–30.
52. *Spiritual Writings*, A. 100, pp. 832–33.
53. *Spiritual Writings*, A. 91B, p. 754.
54. *Spiritual Writings*, A. 7, p. 701.
55. *Spiritual Writings*, L. 121, p. 130.
56. *Spiritual Writings*, L. 11, p. 18.
57. *Spiritual Writings*, L. 566, p. 588.
58. *Spiritual Writings*, L. 32, p. 104.
59. *Spiritual Writings*, L. 557B, p. 520.
60. *Spiritual Writings*, ibid., p. 521.
61. *Spiritual Writings*, L. 344, p. 139.
62. *Spiritual Writings*, L. 429, p. 353.
63. *Spiritual Writings*, A. 25, p. 802.
64. Charpy, *La Compagnie*, p. 904, L. 787. Louise de Marillac died 15 March 1660.
65. Louise de Marillac was beatified 9 May 1920, and canonized 11 March 1934. Pope John XXIII named her, 10 February 1960, the patroness of all those who devote themselves to Christian social work.

Introduction. The Legacy Unfolds

1. "Introduction" and "Elizabeth Ann Seton" by Vie Thorgren; "Rosalie Rendu, D.C." and "Frederick Ozanam" by Sister Frances Ryan, D.C. Edited by John E. Rybolt, C.M.
2. Two major recent works on Elizabeth Seton are Joseph I. Dirvin, *Mrs. Seton: Foundress of the American Sisters of Charity.* (New York: Farrar, Straus and Giroux, 1962); "New Canonization Edition," 1975; and Ellin Kelly and Annabelle Melville, eds., *Elizabeth Seton: Selected Writings.* (New York: Paulist Press, 1987.) Both volumes have good bibliographies.
3. Dirvin, *Mrs. Seton*, p. 11. The manuscript of "Dear Remembrances" is in the archives at Saint Joseph's Provincial House, Emmitsburg, Maryland.
4. Elizabeth's other children were William, Richard, Catherine, and Rebecca.
5. Elizabeth also lost many family members to tuberculosis,

including her sister-in-law and "soul's sister," Rebecca. Elizabeth herself died of tuberculosis.

6. 12 March 1812.

7. 3 November 1816.

8. Occasionally, other names occur in early records: Sisters of Charity of Saint Joseph or, even, of Saint Joseph's (Dirvin, *Mrs. Seton*, pp. 248–49).

9. She wrote the following lines as part of an instruction probably to be given to the Sisters:

> Thus he might well say to us, "come learn of me for I am meek and lowly of heart" and at the same time know how much you ought to do so—and have I been as my blessed Lord have I learned to bear the weaknesses of others, they are obliged to bear with mine, and is it reasonable that I should require from them indulgence for the many faults that escape me and yet be unwilling to allow any of them—the bad qualities of others should perfect and purify my Charity rather than weaken it, for if I should only have charity for those who are faultless, it will be entirely without merit, or rather it would not be any at all as there are no persons without faults. And if I had to live only with angels this mild and gentle conduct would be of no use as it would not be required.

(Kelly and Melville, eds. *Elizabeth Seton:*, pp. 325–26).

10. *Ibid.*, p. 325.

11. *Ibid.*, p. 330.

12. The most comprehensive work on Rosalie Rendu is the volume prepared for the cause of her beatification: Congregatio de Causis Sanctorum, *Canonizationis Servae Dei Rosaliae Rendu . . . Positio super virtutibus et fama sanctitatis* (Rome, 1993). All direct quotations are, as much as possible, based on the original sources cited in this volume.

13. Melun, p. 6.

14. They had made their postulancy for three months at the hospital in Gex, beginning 13 February 1802.

15. Napoleon reestablished the community by the decree of 22

November 1800. The habit, set aside officially on 21 August 1792, was resumed on 25 March 1805.

16. Since the Daughters of Charity did not take first vows for five years after their seminary (novitiate), requesting the habit was the act by which the young sisters were allowed to continue their training (Melun, p. 29).

17. *Echoes of the Company* (Feb. 1926), p. 47.

18. To thank her for her work, King Louis Philippe gave her a bronze medal in 1832, the first of several official recognitions. Her renown, understandably, caused some antagonism against her within the community.

19. Danemarie, p. 163. Undoubtedly these words are reconstructed from recollections of Rosalie or others. Once again, her bravery was commemorated by a medal, this one struck by the National Guard in 1848. Although it was dedicated to all religious communities, it bore her image in the act of calming the rioters. The text on the medal quotes her: "Strike [me]. I do not fear your bayonets. I fear only God."

20. André, p. 110.

21. The most important works on Ozanam are those volumes prepared for his cause of beatification, especially Sacra Congregatio pro Causis Sanctorum, *Beatificationis et canonizationis servi Dei Friderici Ozanam . . . Disquisitio* (Rome, 1980.) This is to be supplemented by *Positio Super Virtutibus. Informatio et Summarium* (Rome, 1990.)

22. Baunard, p. 4.

23. Baunard, p. 13.

24. Vincent de Paul Bailly was an Assumptionist priest and journalist, renowned for his holiness. His cause for beatification was introduced in 1960. *New Catholic Encyclopedia*, S.V. "Bailly, Vincent de Paul."

25. Baunard, p. 68.

26. Ibid., p. 93.

27. Ibid.

28. Ibid., p. 92.

29. His dissertation, *Essai sur la philosophie de Dante* (Paris, 1838) was published in a revised form in Engish: *Dante and Catholic Philosophy in the Thirteenth Century*, trans. Lucia D. Pychowski, 2nd ed., (New York: Cathedral Library Association, 1913).

30. The first conference in the United States began in Saint

Louis, Missouri, in 1845 (Daniel T. McColgan, *A Century of Charity. The First One Hundred Years of the Society of St. Vincent de Paul in the United States*, 2 vols. [Milwaukee: Bruce, 1951], I: 53).

31. Baunard, p. 231.

32. Ibid., p. 242.

33. His complete writings appeared as *Oeuvres complètes*, 11 vols., Paris, 1855–1865. Besides a translation and commentary on the "Purgatorio" of Dante, short articles, and other studies, these eleven volumes include his major works: *La civilisation au cinquième siècle* (Vols. 1–2); *Les Germains avant le christianisme* (Vol. 3); *Civilisation chrétienne chez les Francs* (Vol. 4); *Les poètes franciscains en Italie au treizième et au quatorzième siècle* (Vol. 5); *Dante et la philosophie catholique au treizième siècle* (Vol. 6). Of these, volumes 1–2, 5, and 6 exist in English.

34. See Baunard, p. 369. Letter #95, to Dufieux, from Notre Dame de Buglose, 2 December 1852 (*Lettres de Frédéric Ozanam*, 9th ed., rev. [Paris: Gigord, 1925], p. 431).

35. Ibid. Letter #96, to Charles Ozanam, from Bayonne, 4 December 1852 (*Lettres*, p. 435).

36. Baunard, p. 370. Letter #107, to François Lallier, Easter Monday [28 March] 1853, from Pisa (*Lettres*, p. 480).

INTRODUCTION. GENERATIVITY OF THE LEGACY FOR CONTEMPORARY TIMES

1. For Louise's thoughts on the hidden life see *Spiritual Writings*, L. 303B, p. 140; L. 575, p. 659; L. 642, p. 660; A. 5, p. 715; A. 8, p. 719; and A. 100, p. 833.

2. For Louise's thoughts on thirst, see ibid., A. 21, p. 702; A. 30, pp. 733–34; and M. 8B, p. 833.

COMMON RULES OR CONSTITUTIONS OF THE CONGREGATION OF THE MISSION

1. "Codex Sarzana," trans. and ed. John E. Rybolt, C.M. *Vincentiana* 33 (1991): 303–406 (hereafter cited as Sarzana).

2. The English translation used in this edition is the official translation published in 1989 as part of *Constitutions and Statutes of the Congregation of the Mission* (Philadelphia, 1989.) It is reproduced here with permission.

3. Sarzana: "Common Rules and Constitutions of the Congregation of the Mission." The dedicatory letter from Vincent de Paul does not appear.

4. Sarzana: "Since our Lord Jesus Christ was sent into the world to do always the will of his father, to preach the Gospel to the poor, and to give the apostles and their successors saving knowledge for the remission of sin, and since the tiny Congregation of the Mission has been begun so that for its own reason it should, as best it could, follow in his footsteps, it is proper that its purpose should be: (1) to fulfill the will of God in all things, as He did, . . . (3) to help seminarians and priests to acquire the knowledge of the saints, by which to direct the people into the way of salvation."

5. Heb 5:7, 12:17.

6. Mt 6:33; Lk 12:31.

7. Jn 8:29ff. Sarzana: "Since the primary purpose of the Congregation consists in doing the will of God in all things, and doing it as well as possible, it is certain that the means by which the kingdom of God comes to the Christian people, and through us to the neighbor, [is that] each one should try to integrate this exercise into his life, as far as possible (1) by fulfilling divine and human commands, and (2) by fleeing what is forbidden; and (3) when matters are indifferent, by choosing those things which are less pleasing to the senses; (4) by tolerating calmly what is repugnant; and by following after God's will to fulfill it in all things with Christ."

8. Mt 11:29.

9. Mt 10:38, 16:24 and parallels; Rom 8:13.

10. Sarzana: "Christ said: Anyone who wants to come after me must deny himself and take up his cross each day. Each one, therefore, must be most conscientious without interruption . . . gratification of each of his senses in matters both permitted and forbidden, especially those things which run greatly contrary to the teaching of the gospels."

11. Lk 14:26.

12. Sarzana: "Christ, the Lord, . . . God the Father. All of us, then, will flee what is out of the ordinary in all those things which

can make us stand out in the sight of others, particularly regarding food and clothing, but also spiritual practices, and individual opinions. We should understand that we cannot be out of the ordinary especially in the very careful observance of our rules and constitutions. Likewise, all our striving should be for perfection; we have been called to this and we should work on it alone. Christ, too, taught us this by his own example, since he was not out of the ordinary, except that he was sent to fulfill the law, and to carry out his Father's will, which he commended to others." The English should read: "Rules or Constitutions."

13. Mt 5:44.

14. Sarzana: "If it should happen that Divine Providence should ever allow the Congregation, one of its houses, or one of its members to be subjected to, and tested by, slander or persecution, we will praise and bless God for this, and joyfully thank him for it as an excellent and perfect gift coming down from the Father of lights. We will regard it as all joy when we fall into various temptations, and each one will refrain from any complaint, curse, or revenge against those abuse us with calumny or who persecute us. Instead, we will pray for all of those and do good to them if possible. Christ taught us this by word and deed, as did the apostles, of whom it is written: They went out joyfully from the council [Sanhedrin] since they had been found worthy to suffer abuse for the name of Jesus" (Acts 5:41).

15. Sarzana: "God has told everyone . . . a serious fault, without delay and in a spirit of love and humility, he will inform the superior. He will be content that all his defects are pointed out to the superior."

16. Sarzana: The last sentence does not appear.

17. Sarzana: The paragraph concludes thus: "Therefore, no one should use anything as though it were his own personal property. Instead, each one should try always to choose whatever is poorer or more fitting for a poor person. No one should ever use anything as his own, nor lend or receive anything, nor give away something belonging to the house without the superior's permission."

18. Sarzana: "No one will keep money to himself, nor place it with others. No one will have anything else without the permission of the superior."

19. Sarzana: "No one will have any books without permission. If

he does receive use of any, he will not write anything in them nor make any notes."

20. Sarzana: "No one will take as his own what is for the use of others. Likewise, he will not accept anything from non-confreres either for himself or for others without the permission of the superior."

21. Sarzana incorporates this paragraph into paragraph one.

22. Sarzana: This paragraph does not appear.

23. Sarzana: This paragraph does not appear.

24. Sarzana: "Our rooms should never be locked; neither should there be a safe in them, or anything else locked, without the superior's permission."

25. Sarzana: "No one will aspire after any benefice, or ever solicit any dignity or office whether in or out of the Congregation."

26. With some slight verbal changes, Sarzana reads paragraphs 1, 2, and 3 together in one unit.

27. Sarzana: The final sentence reads: "For example, if it seems good in the Lord, we should withdraw not only from licit but even from pious and holy works."

28. Sarzana: This paragraph does not appear.

29. Sarzana: The following section is inserted here: "and in all our duties which deal with the neighbor, according to our rules, we will constantly show to the bishops that we are those servants in the Gospel. As a result, we will come and go according to their wishes, and whatever they command we will observe, and we will undertake nothing in their dioceses concerning the neighbor without the bishops' permission. As a result, we will never be able to dispense ourselves or be freed from this obedience under any pretext. Furthermore. . . . "

30. Sarzana has the following paragraphs of the rules in this order: 11, 12, 4, 7, 15, 16, 8, 5, 6, 9, 10, 13, 14. Further, the following appears as the last paragraph: "No one will hear the confessions of our own confreres or of others, unless he has been assigned to do so by the superior general, the visitor, or his own superior."

31. Sarzana contains only the first sentence.

32. Sarzana does not contain the first sentence.

33. Sarzana does not contain the first sentence.

34. Sarzana: "None of our lay brothers should want to study Latin. If any of them feel such an inclination, ... "

35. Phil 4:5.

36. Sarzana places the subsequent paragraphs in the following order: 6, 7, 3, 4, 5. After paragraph three, the following appears: "All who enter or leave the house should be careful not to ring the bell too much or repeatedly."

37. Sarzana: "No one will sleep at night with nothing on, with insufficient bedclothes, or with the window open."

38. Sarzana arranges the subsequent paragraphs as follows: 9, 3, 15–16, 14, 11, 13, 12, 10, 4b, 8, 5, 6.

39. Qo 3:7, Prv 10:19.

40. Sarzana begins the paragraph thus: "We should keep silent, then." It concludes thus: "But no matter when, all will strive to speak in a low voice."

41. Sarzana: This paragraph does not appear.

42. Sarzana: "In our conversations, we will invite each other to love our vocation and desire our own perfection. We will always praise virtue and mortification, and defend with humility and gentleness those who belittle them. But if we dislike any of these, we should make this fact known to the superior or director, and take care especially not ever to reveal it to the others, either publicly or privately."

43. Sarzana: "We should diligently avoid being argumentative in conversation, even if only in fun. Instead, we will declare that we understand and agree with the others, and we will prefer the opinion of others where freedom of opinion is allowed."

44. Sarzana: "Everyone . . . confidentiality about what is said at chapter with regard to faults and penances." Sarzana also has the following paragraph: "The list which contains various items for conversation and topics to be discussed in our recreations and conversations, will always be available, as much as possible."

45. Mt 22:21.

46. Sarzana joins paragraphs 15 and 16, with some small alterations.

47. Mt 5:14.

48. 2 Tm 2:4.

49. Sarzana arranges the subsequent paragraphs in the following order: 5, 6, 4, 11, 12, 13, 14, 7, 8, 15, 16.

50. Sarzana: This paragraph does not appear.

51. Sarzana: This paragraph does not appear.

52. Sarzana: "Except while traveling, no one is to eat or drink. . . . "

53. Sarzana: "If, while traveling, . . . anywhere else. He is to be subject in obedience while there to the superior. Likewise, anyone who goes there on business will do nothing without the advice and direction of the superior or of the visitor if he is there for some time. Also, the superior of the other house will retain his responsibility over the companion which the confrere has brought with him to the house in what pertains to confession and direction."

54. The English should read: "Rules or Constitutions."

55. Sarzana: "According to the Bull of our institution we are to venerate the Most Holy Trinity, the mystery of the Incarnation, and the Most Blessed Virgin Mary, Mother of God, with special worship; the Congregation will fulfill this most faithfully at least in the following three ways: first, by celebrating with special dignity and the greatest possible personal devotion the feasts of the Most Holy Trinity, the Incarnation of the Lord, and the Assumption of the Blessed Virgin Mary; second, besides the worship which each one should manifest pubicly, by assisting with special attention at the acts of adoration and praise both in Mass and the divine office, as well as in common daily prayers, which are specially directed to honor them; third, by striving with all our strength to inculcate knowledge, honor, and veneration of them in the minds of the people wherever we can by our instructions and example."

56. Sarzana: "Since the most holy sacrament of the altar contains in itself, as it were, the sum of all the mysteries of our faith, and since in some respects our salvation and the entire good of the Church depends on the worship rightly given to it, the Congregation will profess special and tireless honor to it. Nothing will be more important for us than attentively and tirelessly to see that all give due honor and reverence to this sacrament. The following are among the ways by which it is customary to render honor. First, to frequently visit it; second, wherever we are when it is carried out or back [to the sick], and we are notified by the sound of a bell, to adore it on bended knee, and if possible to accompany it; third, whenever the sacred name is pronounced, to remove our hat; fourth, when passing by churches to say these words with head uncovered: Praised be the most holy sacrament of the altar; fifth, particularly to instruct others what they are to believe of this great

mystery and how they are to worship it, and to work hard to prevent anything irreverent or disordered from happening to it."

57. Sarzana: This paragraph does not appear. The subsequent paragraphs appear in this order: 10, 9, 6, 7, 5, 8, 12, 13, 16, 14, 15, 17, 18, 19, 20. Paragraphs 10 and 11 were joined.

58. Sarzana: "All will recite the divine office in common, generally even during missions, in a middle tone of voice. Only those places are excepted where, because of foundations or other need, we are obliged to the Gregorian Chant."

59. Sarzana: The following lines do not appear: "One of the most important ministries . . . be done in an orderly way."

60. Sarzana: "All of us are to make two sorts of examination of conscience every day. One, the particular, is to be made before the midday and evening meals, focusing on some virtue to be acquired; and the other, the general, is to be made in the evening on all the actions of the day."

61. Sarzana: Paragraph 10 concludes with the following, which now appears in paragraph 11: "at which time each one will give an account of his conscience in the manner customary in the Congregation. We will also do this every three months, and as often as the superior thinks necessary."

62. Sarzana: The following does not appear: "So that we . . . ranked with sinners."

63. Sarzana: The following text does not appear: "As well as this . . . along the path to holiness." In addition, the following paragraph appears in Sarzana: "Each one will have, for the entire time of his life, the intention of applying himself to the exercises of the mission in the Congregation according to our institute. He will do this on entering and will often renew it." The term "institute" was used by the founder to refer to the Foundation Contract dated 17 April 1625 (Coste, *CED* 13:197–202).

64. Sarzana has a different formulation for the care of the poor: "in front of the door of the house, to prefer spiritual to a corporal alms, that is by catechizing the poor."

65. Sarzana: The final sentence of the paragraph does not appear.

66. Sarzana: The subsequent paragraphs appear in the following order: 10, 2, 5, 6, 7, 9, 8, 3. Paragraphs 4, 11, 12 do not appear in Sarzana.

67. Rom 10:15.

68. Sarzana: "No one is to preach on the missions or catechize without being named to it by the provincial. The director, however, when it seems necessary, can substitute others who are properly prepared, provided he tell the superior as soon as possible in writing why he made such changes."

69. Sarzana: The final sentence does not appear.

70. Sarzana: The paragraph begins thus: "According to the counsel which our Lord Jesus Christ gave to his apostles when he sent them to preach to every creature, 'As you have received freely, give freely,' and also since St. Paul. . . . "

71. Sarzana: "No one during his sick calls should work to settle quarrels and disputes unless he has the permission of the director."

72. Sarzana: The paragraph concludes thus: "To fulfill better this mystery of ours, the plan drawn up for missions will be religiously observed, in addition to those matters contained in this chapter."

73. Sarzana: A special heading for Chapter XII does not appear. Further, paragraph 1 does not appear. The subsequent paragraphs follow this order: 5, 7,4, 2, 3, 6, 9, 10, 8, 11, 12, 13, 14.

74. Mt 6:23.

75. Gal 3:3.

76. Mt 6:2, 15, 16.

77. Sarzana: "Since human recognition is often the cause of intellectual pride, no one should praise any confrere because of his preaching or catechizing, or because they carry on external works amid human applause. Yet they can be prudently commended, in their absence, for their humility, mortification and other virtues." Sarzana also has the following paragraph: "All will take diligent care not to censure or condemn the sermons of others, nor other public activities. If it is necessary to warn someone about these, it belongs to the superior to do so, or to depute someone else. He will do so in private and with due moderation."

78. Sarzana: The following text does not appear: "As simplicity. . . . "

79. Sarzana: The text "should also use this simple ordinary way of speaking. And they should . . . " does not appear.

80. 1 Cor 1:10. Sarzana: The text "Since novel . . . and their followers" does not appear.

81. From a sermon of Zeno of Verona in PL 11:398. It is not known how Vincent became acquainted with this citation, the only one in the rules not taken from the Bible.

82. Rom 12:3; 1 Cor 8:1.

83. Sarzana: The following text does not appear: "as long as our primary aim . . . and of him crucified."

84. Mt 20:26–27 and parallels.

85. Sarzana: The following text appears after "by falling over it." "Hence, when this nascent monster is encountered, each and every one will employ whatever means they can think of. The first of these is to become more humble in our own estimation by making an act of deep humility. Second, to seek the lowest place. Third, to request from God and the superior that we be removed from our superior position, even from the duty of preaching or of leading others by which we might have seemed to be someone special. Instead, the superior could assign us to some lowly position on the mission according to his pleasure."

86. Nm 11:29.

87. The English should read: "Rules or Constitutions."

88. Sarzana: After "Saul's armor" the following text appears: "that is, confidence in human means which fight directly against the teachings of the Gospel, since experience teaches us that such weaponry not only cannot be overcome, but also cannot be assailed."

89. Lk 17:10. Sarzana: The first sentence reads: "Each one is to have his own copy of these Common Rules . . . and should read them through, or hear them read, every month."

CONFERENCES OF VINCENT DE PAUL TO THE CONGREGATION OF THE MISSION

1. The following essay is based, in part, on the introduction to the conferences of Saint Vincent as compiled by Pierre Coste, C.M., the revision prepared by André Dodin, C.M., and the translation of that introduction by Joseph Leonard, C.M. See Pierre Coste, C.M., *Saint Vincent de Paul: Correspondance, Entretiens, Documents*, Part II, "Entretiens," Tome 11 (Paris: Lecoffre, 1924), pp. v–xx; André Dodin, C.M., *Saint Vincent de Paul: Entretiens spirituels*

aux missionaires (Paris: Éditions du Seuil, 1960), pp. 19–34; and
Conferences of Saint Vincent de Paul [to the Congregation of the Mission], compiled by Pierre Coste, C.M., trans. Joseph Leonard,
C.M. (Philadelphia: Congregation of the Mission, Eastern Province, U.S.A., 1963), pp. 1–13 (hereafter "Coste, *CED*"; "Dodin,
Entretiens"; and "Leonard, *Conferences CM*." The base translation is
Leonard's; this has been reviewed and corrected following Dodin.

2. Bertrand Ducournau (1614–1677) was received into the community on 28 July 1644, and became Vincent de Paul's secretary in
the following year. Remaining as secretary to Vincent's first two
successors, René Alméras and Edmond Jolly, he also served as community archivist at Saint Lazare until his death.

3. René Alméras (1613–1672) was received into the Congregation of the Mission in 1637. Following his ordination two years
later, he served Monsieur Vincent and the community in several
important positions, including that of superior in the first house in
Rome, as well as superior general following the death of the holy
founder. His father, René the elder (1575–1658), who had at first
opposed his son's decision to enter the Congregation, himself joined
the community in 1657—one year before his death.

4. In this regard, we have the personal testimony of Father
François Lefort in testimony given during the process for Vincent's
beatification; see Coste, *CED* 11:v, and Leonard, *Conferences CM*,
12.

5. Coste provides a clear insight into the level of Brother
Ducournau's achievement; see Coste, *CED* 11:xv–xvi, and Leonard, *Conferences CM*, 7–8. A brief portion sheds light on only the
beginning of the difficulties he would have had to overcome:

> How could a person write what the Saint was saying
> without arousing his attention? If one, and with still
> greater reason, if a few of his hearers, were allowed to
> write while he was speaking he could not have failed to
> observe them. Even if we suppose the reporters were well
> concealed behind pillars the noise made by writing on a
> piece of paper or turning over a leaf would have betrayed
> them some time or other. On the other hand, to reconstruct a discourse from memory after it had been delivered
> also presented certain difficulties. A long discourse cannot

be remembered word for word. There are bound to be gaps and inexact statements in the written text.

6. Coste, *CED* 11:xvii, and Leonard, *Conferences CM*, 9. The most recent imprint of this work—a one-volume facsimile of the original three-volume study—is Louis Abelly, *La Vie du Venerable Serviteur de Dieu. . . .* An English translation exists.

Louis Abelly (1604–1691), an admirer of and associate in the work of Monsieur Vincent from the earliest days of his own priestly ministry, was likewise the recipient of the saint's recognition and support. Having served as chancellor to the bishop of Bayonne, he eventually became bishop of Rodez (1662–1666). He entered retirement because of poor health, spending his last years at Saint Lazare in prayer and writing.

7. *Collection de conférences de Saint Vincent de Paul . . .* (Paris, 1844). This collection had been preceded, in 1825, by the publication of his conferences to the Daughters of Charity.

8. *Avis et conférences . . .* (Paris, 1881). Jean-Baptiste Étienne and Antoine Fiat, the thirteenth and fifteenth successors of Saint Vincent, served as the superior general from 1843 to 1874 and 1878 to 1914, respectively.

9. Dodin, *Saint Vincent de Paul.*

10. For example, see "Conference, 17 May 1658."

11. Coste, *CED* 11:v, and Leonard, *Conferences CM*, 1.

12. See "Conference, 6 December 1658."

13. See ibid. Because he was a Gascon, these gestures and facial expressions would have come naturally to Vincent, and he did not use them to ridicule others.

14. See "Conference, 6 December 1658."

15. 1 Pt 1:6–9.

16. Conference 112; Coste, *CED* 11:169–72; Dodin, *Entretiens,* #35, 123–26; and Leonard, *Conferences CM*, 168–71.

17. Étienne Charlet was the provincial superior of the Jesuits in France, 1616–1619.

18. Conference 180; Coste *CED* 12:1–14; Dodin, *Entretiens,* #103, 413–26; and Leonard, *Conferences CM*, 413–23.

19. Based on the testimony given by Brother Pierre Chollier in the process for Vincent's beatification, the persons spoken of here were Father Jacques Eveillard and the aforementioned Brother Ber-

trand Ducournau. Pierre Chollier (1646–1716), having entered the congregation in 1668, served as personal secretary to several superiors general; he also wrote the biographies of several confreres including that of Brother Ducournau. Jacques Eveillard was one of the confreres who briefly served on mission in Poland (1654–1655).

20. Lk 4:18 (citing Is 61:1): "The Spirit of the Lord is upon me, because *he has anointed me to bring glad tidings to the poor.* He has sent me to proclaim liberty to captives and recovery of sight to the blind, to let the oppressed go free, and to proclaim a year acceptable to the Lord."

21. Anne of Austria (1601–1666), wife of Louis XIII and queen regent (1643–1651) for her son, Louis XIV.

22. Acts 1:1: "In the first book, Theophilus, I dealt with all *Jesus did and taught.*"

23. Mentioned in the book of the prophet Jeremiah as models of faithfulness (Jer 35:1), the Rechabites were somewhat reactionary in holding that Israel must return to a nomadic way of life in order to be faithful to their convenant with God.

24. Ordained in 1622, Antoine Portail (1590–1660) was Vincent de Paul's first associate in the work of the Congregation, and served as his right-hand man until his death—only seven months before that of the holy founder.

25. The Collège des Bons Enfants became the first house of the Congregation of the Mission, and served as the community's center until 1632, when Saint Vincent took possession of the priory of Saint Lazare.

26. "From whom all good things come," from the collect of the Fifth Sunday of Paschaltide.

27. 2 Cor 3:5: "Not that of ourselves we are qualified to take credit for anything as coming from us; rather, our qualification comes from God."

28. As noted by the copyists, the book to which Vincent referred was *The Treatise on Spiritual Perfection* by the Jesuit Alfonso Rodríguez (1538–1616).

29. That is, novitiate, the term preferred by the founder for both the novitiate of his confreres and of the Daughters of Charity.

30. Ordained in 1616, Jean Bécu (1592–1667) was one of the founder's first companions, joining the Congregation in 1626. Jean

Gicquel (1617–1673) entered the Congregation in 1647, and was superior of Saint Lazare from 1655 to 1660.

31. May the blessing of our Lord Jesus Christ descend on you and remain forever, in the name of the Father, and of the Son, and of the Holy Spirit. Amen.

32. "Sancta Maria, succurre miseris," the prayer to the Blessed Virgin with which Monsieur Vincent commonly ended conferences and other gatherings. "Holy Mary, be thou a help to the helpless, strength to the fearful, comfort to the sorrowful, pray for the people, plead for the clergy, intercede for all holy women consecrated to God; may all who keep thy sacred commemoration feel the might of thine assistance" (*The Raccolta* [New York: Benziger, 1957], no. 349, p. 255).

33. Jn 13:34: "I give you a new commandment: love one another. As I have loved you, so you also should love one another."

34. Lk 10:23: "Turning to the disciples in private he said, 'Blessed are the eyes that see what you see.' "

35. Mt 13:16: "But blessed are your eyes, because they see, and your ears because they hear."

36. Conference 195; Coste, *CED* 12:73–94; Dodin, *Entretiens*, #118, 489–510; and Leonard, *Conferences CM*, 596–613.

37. The meaning of this phrase is "the God of hosts." Vincent understands it more literally as "the God of virtues."

38. Mt 5:48.

39. "Ever higher."

40. Mt 16:26: "What profit would there be for one to gain the whole world and forfeit his life? Or what can one give in exchange for his life?"

41. Jn 17:3.

42. "In doubts, the safer part is to be held."

43. Ps 19:5: "Their report goes forth through all the earth."

44. Jn 20:21: "As the Father has sent me, so I send you."

45. Vincent is mistaken here. While Luther was ordained, Calvin was not.

46. It may be understood that, in using the phrase "those three torrents," Monsieur Vincent had in mind Lutherans, Calvinists, and Anglicans.

47. Mt 25:34–36.

48. Mk 3:21: "When his relatives heard of this they set out to seize him, for they said, 'He is out of his mind.' " As noted by Leonard, *Conferences CM*, (n. [h], 614), Vincent does not quote this text literally.

49. Mk 10:4.

50. For example, Mt 18:3.

51. Is 49:15: "Can a mother forget her infant, be without tenderness for the child of her womb? Even should she forget, I will never forget you."

52. As noted by Coste, *CED* 12:89, this passage varies from a quotation from this conference provided by Abelly, *Life* (Book III, Chapter XI, section II, 122).

53. Lk 4:18.

54. For example, Dt 32:1–6.

55. Jn 16:16, "A little while and you will no longer see me, and again a little while later and you will see me."

56. Mt 24:11: "Many false prophets will arise and deceive many."

57. Acts 20:29.

58. Vincent makes reference here to chapter 64 of the *Rule of Saint Benedict*.

59. In Coste, *CED* 12:92, the text reads, "Ce seront des esprits libertins, libertins, libertins." Reflecting on the word *libertins*, Leonard, *Conferences CM*, (n. [o], 614) explains: "In the early part of the seventeenth century in France the word meant a free-thinker. As atheism and immorality were connected in men's minds, *libertin* gradually came to mean a man who led a loose life. The context here would seem to show how the older meaning was changing into the newer."

Letters of Vincent de Paul

1. References are to Coste, *Correspondence, Conferences, Documents*, abbreviated as *CCD*, followed by volume number and page.

2. [Vincent de Paul,] *Letters of St Vincent de Paul*, trans. and ed. Joseph Leonard, C.M. (London: Burns, Oates and Washbourne, 1937.)

3. Letter 12. Coste, *CCD* 1:23–24.

4. By her marriage, Louise de Marillac had become "Mademoiselle" Le Gras.

5. A small place in Marne.

6. At that time, Monsieur Vincent's associates in his mission work were Antoine Portail, Louis Callon, François du Coudray, and Jean de la Salle. One of these missionaries was with him in Loisy.

7. Letter 36; Coste, *CCD* 1:62. The beginning and end of the letter are missing.

8. Letter 73; Coste, *CCD* 1:112–13. François du Coudray (1586–1649) was the third member of the Congregation of the Mission, after Vincent de Paul and Antoine Portail. At the time of writing, du Coudray was living in Rome to negotiate papal approval of the new congregation.

9. André Duval (1564–1638), a priest and renowned doctor of the Sorbonne, was the author of several works, and the friend and advisor of Vincent de Paul, who never made an important decision without having recourse to Duval's learning.

10. Letter 188: Coste, *CCD* 1:263–66.

11. A Benedictine monk whose cousin, Jacques Le Bret, was an auditor of the Roman Rota and, later, bishop of Toul.

12. Alphonse de Richelieu, brother of the cardinal-minister.

13. Probably Giovanni Giglioli, an Italian, who joined the Congregation as a brother in 1629.

14. Letter 275; Coste, *CCD* 1:383.

15. Letter 383; Coste, *CCD* 1:552–57. Jane Frances de Chantal (1572–1641), the widowed foundress of the Order of the Visitation, was in Annecy.

16. By a contract dated 3 June 1639, a benefactor gave Saint Vincent 40,000 livres to be taken from the Melun taxes for the upkeep in Annecy of two priests and a brother capable of giving missions, plus 5,000 livres for the purchase of rosaries and devotional leaflets and booklets. The missionaries were to be on duty by 15 September, and were to work without charge for eight months of the year in the parishes the bishop would assign to them, and every five years from 1641 on, in Brie-Comte-Robert (Seine-et-Marne).

17. Saint Francis de Sales.

18. Urban VIII (pope 1623–1643).

19. This project never materialized.

20. "The angel of the Lord declared unto Mary. . . . "

21. Three lines were deliberately inked out on the original letter.

22. In Troyes.

23. Françoise-Madeleine Ariste, elected 20 May 1638, died in Troyes on 10 June 1667, after governing that house for twelve years.

24. The name given to the superior who leaves office. The sister concerned here is Mother Claire-Marie Amaury. In the first year of her entrance into the first monastery of Paris, Mother Amaury remained for seven months in the grips of a horrible temptation, which Saint Vincent himself related at the process of beatification of Saint Francis de Sales.

25. A word left out of the original text.

26. Letter 806, Coste, *CCD*, 2:648–49. Jules Mazarin (1602–1661), born in Italy, served in the papal diplomatic corps and was nuncio to France in 1635–1636. Cardinal Richelieu recommended Mazarin to Louis XIII, and he became the chief minister of Queen Anne of Austria during her regency, a position he held until his death.

27. The École Polytechnique now occupies the site of the Collège de Navarre.

28. Michel Le Tellier (1603–1685) was secretary of state from 1643 to 1666, Chancellor and Keeper of the Seals of France from 1677 to 1685. "As Councillor of State," he said one day, "I had a great deal to do with Monsieur Vincent. He did more good for religion and the Church in France than any man I have ever known; but I especially observed that at the Council of Conscience, where he was the most important member, never was there question of his own interest or of the ecclesiastical houses which he had established" (Testimony of Claude Le Pelletier, 121st witness at the process of beatification).

29. Letter 1512, Leonard, *Letters*, pp. 281–82. The Sisters arrived at this town in 1647.

30. The village of Valpuiseaux, near Étampes, had suffered severely from acts of brigandage and theft on the part of the troops. The inhabitants and the Sisters also had sought refuge in the towns.

31. The dangers were occasioned not only by soldiers and looters. Wild beasts were prowling about the countryside, and even in the towns, seeking for corpses. It is stated in the August number of

the *Relations*, a regular report of charitable needs and activities, that, even in Étampes, three women had been devoured by wolves.

32. A parish in Paris.

33. Louise de Marillac.

34. Letter 2824, Leonard, *Letters*, pp. 408–09. Guillaume Desdames entered the Congregation of the Mission in 1645. He went to Poland in 1651 and remained there until 1669, when he returned to France. He went again to Poland where he died, 1 June 1692.

35. Letter 3032, Leonard, *Letters*, 466–67. The missionaries were due to sail to Madagascar in December. Philippe Patte, a brother of the Congregation of the Mission, was then at Nantes. He was an accomplished surgeon, a talent he put to good use in Madagascar, where he died in 1664.

36. Letter 3089, Leonard, *Letters*, pp. 487–88. Sister Mathurine Guérin (1631–1704) entered the Daughters of Charity in 1648. She became Louise de Marillac's secretary, and was superior at La Fère at the time of this letter. She was superior general for four different periods.

RULES OF THE DAUGHTERS OF CHARITY, SERVANTS OF THE SICK POOR AND PARTICULAR RULES FOR THE SISTERS OF THE PARISHES

1. The translation used for this edition is based on *Rules of the Daughters of Charity, Servants of the Sick Poor*, 1976. It has been reproduced with permission. This text has been lightly edited for ease in comprehension. Further corrections are noted in the notes. The texts of the conferences cited in the notes were taken from Joseph Leonard, C.M., trans. *The Conferences of St. Vincent de Paul to the Sisters of Charity*, 1952. These have been checked against the original version published by Pierre Coste, *CED*, and corrected as needed. The only other edition of the original rules is a Spanish work, Miguel Pérez Flores, C.M., ed., *Reglas Comunes de las Hijas de la Caridad Siervas de los Pobres Enfermos* (1989). In that work, the editor printed side by side, with some omissions, the original 1655 rules and their revised, and official, 1672 form. In the cases where the text of the conferences does not give the full text of the rules, this

Spanish edition has been followed. The 1655 text given by Vincent de Paul is referred to in the notes as "Saint Vincent."

2. These rules were also those that many other communities adopted for their own use.

3. See John E. Rybolt, C.M., "From Life to the Rules: The Genesis of the Rules of the Daughters of Charity," *Vincentian Heritage*, 12 (1991): 173–99.

4. Saint Vincent, article 1: "They will often remember that the main purpose for which God has called and gathered them is to honor our Lord, their patron, serving him corporally and spiritually in the person of the poor, whether children, the needy, the sick, or prisoners; and to be worthy of such a holy occupation and of such a perfect patron, they should try to live a holy life, and to work carefully for their own perfection. To accomplish this, they will do whatever they can to practice well these rules, which are as so many means to arrive at it." Cited incompletely in Conference 71, 18 October 1655, Leonard, *Conferences* 3:106–19. Text from Pérez Flores, p. 62. In the following notes, where the texts of the two rules disagree only in some small details, the identical words are marked with an ellipsis [. . .].

5. Saint Vincent, article 2 concludes here.

6. Saint Vincent, article 4: "They shall hold the maxims of the world in horror and embrace those of Jesus Christ, amongst others those which recommend mortification, both exterior and interior, contempt for self and the things of this world, choosing humble and painful employments rather than those that are honourable and agreeable, always taking the last place and reserving the best for their neighbour being persuaded that with all this they are still better off than they deserve on account of their sins." Conference of 2 November 1655; cited from Leonard, *Conferences* 3:120, 131.

7. Saint Vincent, article 5: "They shall have no attachment [to creatures], especially to places, employments or persons, not even to their relations and Confessors, but shall always be prepared to abandon all [cheerfully (omitted)] when so commanded, representing to themselves that Our Lord says we are not worthy of him [nor of following after him] if we do not renounce ourselves [and our disordered actions, whatever they may be] and leave father, mother, brothers and sisters to follow him [when he calls us]." Conference

NOTES

73, 6 June 1656; Leonard *Conferences* 3:135, with sections in brackets restored from article 5.

8. Saint Vincent, article 6: The text is repeated nearly verbatim in Conference 74, 23 July 1656; Leonard, *Conferences* 3:157–72.

9. Saint Vincent, article 41: The text of this rule appears verbatim in Conference 97, 9 June 1658; Leonard, *Conferences* 4:124–39.

10. Saint Vincent, article 7: "They shall honour the poverty of Our Lord and rest content with having their little needs supplied with the usual simplicity, [considering that they are servants of the poor, and that thus they should live a life of poverty. Accordingly, none of them will keep, whether at home or outside, anything for the common use as their own. Consequently, each one will keep everything in common, as the first Christians did, such that they will not be able to dispose of anything nor give from the property of the Community, nor even from their own property, nor to receive or acquire from elsewhere without the consent of the superioress in small and ordinary matters; for those that are extraordinary and of consequence, they will also need the permission of the Superior.]" Conference 76, 20 August 1656; Leonard, *Conferences* 3:180–96. Material in brackets is from article 7.

11. Saint Vincent, article 8 ends with "given her or not." Conference 81, 17 June 1657; Leonard, *Conferences* 3:239–51. The expression "Sister Servant" was used normally, and has continued in use, to refer to the local religious superior.

12. Saint Vincent, article 9 ends: "their distant houses." Conference 82, 5 August 1657; the rule is not quoted, however. Leonard, *Conferences* 3:252–66.

13. Saint Vincent, article 10 concludes thus: " . . . any serge or linen for their clothing; but they will ask from her for habits already made. She will furnish them with them. Also, they will be held to bring or send to her every year the surplus of their money, taking out the cost of food, to pay for the habits which they have received from her. And if they need to purchase some small necessities, they will ask her permission in advance. And as to food, medicine, linen, money and other things destined for the poor, they will be careful not to touch them for the use of the Sisters, except for when they are sick. They should remember this would be to rob the property of the poor." See also Conference 115, 25 November 1659, on the rules for the Sisters in the parishes; Leonard, *Conferences* 4:282–93.

14. Saint Vincent, article 17: The passage is cited in conference 86, 15 November 1657, in its entirety, and in conference 87, 18 November 1657, in part; Leonard, *Conferences* 3:304–17, 4:1–16.

15. Saint Vincent, article 15: "The sick Sisters should not lose patience nor murmur at not always being treated according to their liking. They shall remember that they do not know as well as the doctor and the nurses what they need; and that, being poor, they should be content to suffer something for the love of God who is thus pleased to exercise their patience." This passage does not appear in the conferences.

16. Saint Vincent, article 11: see Conference 84, 8 September 1657; Leonard, *Conferences* 3:280–90.

17. Saint Vincent, article 18 concludes thus: " . . . through the streets; they will especially guard themselves from speaking, aside from necessity, with men, both priests and others, even though they hold pious conversations. The reason for this is dangerous results." Conference 87, 18 November 1657, cites the text only partially; Leonard, *Conferences* 4:1–16.

18. I.e., games.

19. Saint Vincent, article 19: "And inasmuch as holy modesty is necessary not only to edify their neighbor with its silent and continual preaching, but also to preserve purity, which is easily tarnished by immodest acts, they will be careful to observe it at all times and in all places, even in their recreations. They shall keep themselves from levities, unbecoming gestures and excessive laughter, and especially from touching one another without necessity, even through playfulness and in token of friendship; unless it be to embrace in a spirit of cordiality those who have been newly received, or who come from the country, or to become reconciled with someone to whom they have given pain; in which cases they are allowed to kiss each other on the cheek, but never on the mouth. But with regard to those of the other sex, the Daughters of Charity will never allow them to kiss them nor touch them in any way, or under any pretext." Conference 87, 18 November 1657, cites only the first few words; Leonard, *Conferences* 4:1–16.

20. Saint Vincent, article 25 (of "Employment of the Day"): "If, after having accomplished all that is prescribed by the rules, they have some free time and nothing to do, especially in the way of sewing and spinning, they shall ask permission of the superioress or

the Sister Assistant to try to earn a portion of their food. Those who live in distant houses will do the same concerning the Sister Servant, and both groups will be aware of not losing a minute of time, realizing that God will demand from them an exact accounting." Conference 110, 10 August 1659; Leonard, *Conferences* 4:257–60.

21. Saint Vincent, article 27: "They shall not leave the house without the permission of the superioress, to whom they will say where they are going and why; and on their return, they will present themselves again to her, and report on their trip. The Sisters in the parishes and other places will do practically the same with the Sister Servant, and she will likewise inform her companion before leaving." Conference 89, 9 December 1657, cites only the opening words; Leonard, *Conferences* 4:29–41.

22. Saint Vincent, article 18 (of "Employment of the Day"): "Before leaving the house, they shall take holy water and kneel down before an image of Our Lord to ask God's blessing and the grace not to offend him; on their return, they shall do the same in order to thank him for having preserved them from sin, or to ask his pardon for whatever fault they have found." Conference 108, 16 March 1659; Leonard, *Conferences* 4:232–43.

23. Saint Vincent, article 28: "They shall not pay any visits, not even to Sisters of another parish, without the permission of the superioress, except in case of necessity as, for instance, in the case of those who are ill. They shall not have others visit them, even for recreation. That which regards particularly the Sisters who do not live with the superioress is that they are not even to let anyone enter their rooms without great need, particularly men, not even if they are priests or their confessors, except when they are ill. Even less are they to go to see them in their rooms. If it is necessary to speak with them, this will happen in the church or at the door of the house, and in very few words, and not at the wrong time, no matter what good reasons and intentions they may have." Conference 94, 23 December 1657, cites only the opening words; Leonard, *Conferences* 4:100–02.

24. Saint Vincent, article 26 concludes with the words: " . . . or of the Sister Servant of the place where she resides." Conference 89, 9 December 1657, cites only the opening words; Leonard, *Conferences* 4:29–41.

25. Saint Vincent, article 24; "Although the incessant labors . . .

and with that of the reverend superior [Conference 89: "director"], in extraordinary things. However, they shall bear in mind . . . out of the case of necessity, especially to control their tongue. They should understand that they are obliged to all this inasmuch as they are Christian women." Conference 89, 9 December 1657, cites the first half of the article; Leonard, *Conferences* 4:29–41. Article 19 of "Employment of the Day": "On every Friday, and on the eves of Feasts of Our Lord and of the Blessed Virgin, they shall fast, and on every Wednesday in Advent they shall abstain, yet, however, the sick [and those who go to attend the sick,] may take in the morning . . . permission of the superior, or of him who is deputed for their direction." Conference 108, 16 March 1659; Leonard, *Conferences* 4:232–43.

26. Saint Vincent, article 20: "They shall render honor and obedience to the Bishops . . . as the Superior and Director General of their company, . . . and other places where they are established." The same article continues with the same text as in paragraph 2 of the 1672 rules. Conference 88, 2 December 1657, cites the text only in part; Leonard, *Conferences* 4:17–28.

27. Lk 10:16.

28. Saint Vincent, article 22: "When they are sent . . . they will go to receive kneeling the blessing of the pastor; . . . in the assistance of the sick." Conference 88, 2 December 1657; Leonard, *Conferences* 4:17–28. Article 23: "They shall also show great respect . . . nor against the intentions of their Superiors." Ibid.

29. Saint Vincent, article 21: "They shall also pay honor . . . and to the Ladies of Charity of the individual parishes, to the Officials, as well as to the physicians, punctually and faithfully carrying out their orders. The sick Sisters also ought to obey the infirmarian or physician in all that relates to their offices." Conference 88, 2 December 1657; Leonard, *Conferences* 4:17–28.

30. Saint Vincent, article 25: "They will not write nor receive letters without the permission of the superioress, into whose hands they will place those which they have written, for her to send them or keep them as she judges. Those who are distant from the house of the superioress will do the same as regards the Sister Servant. Yet each one should know that this rule does not oblige them to show to anyone the letters which are written to the superior, the director, or the superioress, any more than those which they may receive from

them." Conference 89, 9 December 1657, cites only the opening lines; Leonard, *Conferences* 4:29–41.

31. Saint Vincent, article 36; "They shall [often] remember the name of Daughters of Charity which they bear, and shall strive to render themselves worthy of it by the holy love which they shall ever bear toward God and their neighbour. They shall above all live in great union with their Sisters and never murmur or complain of one another, studiously driving away any thoughts of aversion from one another they may have, [and they will flee whatever can cause the disunity of the Sisters, particularly movements of envy at seeing the others better situated and more honored]. Conference 93, 4 March 1658, with material in brackets quoted from article 36; Leonard, *Conferences* 4:85–99.

32. Saint Vincent, article 38: "They shall willingly bear with their companions in their little imperfections . . . against the rules; for this holy condescension . . . union and peace in the Community." Conference 95, 30 May 1658; Leonard, *Conferences* 4:103–10.

33. Saint Vincent, article 37 concludes with ". . . and the resentment that might remain on account of the fault committed." Conference 93, 4 March 1658; Leonard, *Conferences* 4:85–99.

34. Saint Vincent, article 16: "And whereas too much tenderness for self might often lead the Sisters . . . where she resides. Those who are at a distance . . . to others in practising this Rule." Conference 85, 11 November 1657; Leonard, *Conferences* 3:291–303.

35. The Rosary.

36. Saint Vincent, article 40, Conference 96, 2 June 1658; Leonard, *Conferences* 4:111–23. Saint Vincent, article 40: "but affections of flesh and blood."

37. Saint Vincent, article 31: "They shall not from curiosity inquire into the affairs of the house in order to criticize what is being done there, and in particular they shall not murmur against the proceedings of the superior, the superioress or the Sister Servant, the rules and good customs of the Company, for this sort of murmuring is calculated to bring down the malediction of God on the person who indulges in it and on the person who listens to it with pleasure and, in fine, on the entire Community, on account of the great scandal which it causes." Conference 91, 30 December 1657; Leonard, *Conferences* 4:56–70.

38. Saint Vincent, article 32: "They shall take great care in their

conversations not to disclose the faults of others, especially to their Sisters, nor listen to those who speak uncharitably of others. They shall, on the contrary, prevent them from doing so, as far as they are able; if they cannot, they shall withdraw immediately, as if they had heard the hissing of a serpent." Conference 91, 30 December 1657; Leonard, *Conferences* 4:56–70.

39. Saint Vincent: "From the end of night prayer until after morning prayer on the following day they shall observe strict silence. [If it still be necessary to speak together, they shall do so in a low tone and in few words.]" Conference 106, 25 November 1658; Leonard, *Conferences* 4:217–27.

40. Saint Vincent, article 12: "Their chief care will be to serve the sick poor, treating them with compassion, meekness, cordiality, respect and devotion [even the most troublesome and difficult, since it is not so much to them that they render service, as to Jesus Christ]. . . . " The rest of this article repeats paragraph 2 of the Common Rules. Conference 85, 11 November 1657; Leonard, *Conferences* 3:291–303.

41. Saint Vincent, article 13: "And as ill-directed charity, especially if it is done against obedience, . . . " Conference 85, 11 November 1657; Leonard, *Conferences* 3:291–303.

42. This paragraph was omitted from the 1954 edition.

43. Saint Vincent, article 20 (of "Employment of the Day"): "On Saturdays and the eves of Feasts they shall go to Confession . . . without his permission." Conference 108, 16 March 1659. Article 21 continues in the same conference: "Every month they shall make a review to the director whom the superior will have deputed, and for the same purpose they will present themselves to the superioress, to give her . . . another day." Leonard, *Conferences* 4:232–43.

44. Saint Vincent, article 22 (of "Employment of the Day"): "Every year they shall make, if it can be done, the spiritual retreat and their general confession . . . in the house of the superioress, according to what the superior will have prescribed for them." Conference 108, 16 March 1659; Leonard, *Conferences* 4:232–43.

45. Saint Vincent, article 23 (of "Employment of the Day"): "Whenever . . . punctual in attending, provided that it not . . . stricter obligation." Conference 108, 16 March 1659; Leonard, *Conferences* 4:232–43.

46. Saint Vincent, article 24 (of "Employment of the Day"): "Those who reside in villages at a distance from the house of the superioress, and who, therefore, cannot visit it as often as those who are near, shall however go there for all the above purposes, when they can do so easily, so that those who are one or two days' journey shall endeavour . . . ask permission either by letters or otherwise. As for others who live at a much greater distance, as, for example, sixty or eighty leagues or thereabouts, they shall not leave the place, if not ordered to do so. As for their retreats, conferences, monthly confessions, communications, and other spiritual helps, they shall have recourse to their ordinary directors who will be appointed to those duties in these places. And when an extraordinary confessor shall visit them for some days, they shall have recourse to him for all the above-mentioned matters." Conference 110, 10 August 1659; Leonard, *Conferences* 4:257–60.

47. This paragraph has been often revised. This brief text has been translated from Luigi Mezzadri and Miguel Pérez Flores, *La Regola delle Figlie della Carità* (1986), p. 108. Another version, longer and probably original, appears in other sources, taken from article 20 of "Employment of the Day": "They will receive communion on Sundays and feasts, and not more often than two days in succession without the permission of the Superior, or in his absence, of his representative or of another deputy. Besides, they will not be dispensed from communion on the assigned days without that same permission. To obviate many of the abuses which could arise from this general permission to communicate on the approved days, and to have together the merit of receiving this sacrament always out of obedience, those who are in the house of the superioress will ask her permission each time to receive communion. Those who live in the parishes and other places will do the same concerning the Sister Servant, but neither they nor the others will ever receive communion if the director or confessor does not permit it." Conference 108, 16 March 168; Leonard, *Conferences* 4:232–43.

48. Saint Vincent, article 12 (of "Employment of the Day"): "On Fridays they shall assist at the little conference which is held after night prayer in presence of the superioress or her deputy, [concerning the faults committed . . . or bad example. Those who reside in the parishes . . . presence of the Sister Servant]." Conference 106, 25 November 1658; Leonard, *Conferences* 4:217–27.

49. Saint Vincent, article 33: "To prevent . . . to externs; but they shall have recourse to the superioress or to her representative, or to the superior or director appointed by him, and in case of need. . . . " Conference 92, 6 January 1658; Leonard, *Conferences* 4:71–84.

50. Saint Vincent, article 35: "They shall be particularly careful . . . and confessions, and this mainly as regards the faults which are mentioned there or are heard, and the penances which are performed or given, since, besides the offence. . . . " Conference 92, 6 January 1658; Leonard, *Conferences* 4:71–84.

51. Saint Vincent, article 29: "As neither . . . charitably the superioress or the superior of the serious faults . . . made known to the same superior and the superioress, and she will be content . . . both in public and in private." Conference 90, 23 December 1657; Leonard, *Conferences* 4:42–55.

52. Saint Vincent: "The schedule for the work of the day and of the year which the Daughters of Charity are to keep." This section, in twenty-seven articles, has its own enumeration.

53. Saint Vincent, article 1: "They will rise at four o'clock, giving their first thoughts of God. They shall dress with diligence, and each one will make her bed. After they have dressed, they shall take holy water . . . all the actions of the day." Conference 102, 21 July 1658; see also Conference 105, 17 November 1658; Leonard, *Conferences* 4:179–84, 196–216.

54. "Come, Holy Spirit."

55. Saint Vincent, article 2: "At half-past four they shall recite the customary vocal prayers in common, and afterward they shall read the points of the meditation, which shall be made for half an hour, beginning with the *Veni Sancte Spiritus* [and finishing with the *Angelus Domini*, etc., and then the Litany of the Name of Jesus, and other customary prayers. Those who live in the parishes, and who do not know how to read, will meditate on some mystery of the Passion or another which will be assigned them, whether on a certain image, or something else. And as to the vocal prayers, they will say those which they know by heart, at least the *Pater, Ave, Credo,* and *Confiteor* with some decades of their chaplet]." Conferences 102, 21 July 1658, and 103, 13 October 1658; Leonard, *Conferences* 4:179–84, 185–90.

56. Saint Vincent, article 3: "After prayer, they shall devote

themselves to whatever . . . office, [and then they will go to mass if they can at that time; if not, this will happen at some other more convenient time]. Conference 105, 17 November 1658; Leonard, *Conferences* 4:196–216.

57. Saint Vincent, article 16 (of "Employment of the Day"): "In addition to the above, they shall say the Rosary and shall do so at different times, [such as a decade after morning prayer, two in the church while waiting for Mass to begin, or if it has begun, until the Gospel, one after the noon Angelus, and one other after the evening Angelus.]" Conference 107, 8 December 1658; Leonard, *Conferences* 4:228–31.

58. Saint Vincent, article 4: "After Mass they shall go to breakfast, and afterward each one shall take up her respective duty; [but if they cannot hear Mass until later, there should be no difficulty in having breakfast before leaving]." Conference 105, 17 November 1658; Leonard, *Conferences* 4:196–216.

59. "Have mercy," the opening word of Ps 50 (51).

60. Saint Vincent, article 5: "At half-past eleven . . . for practice; and then they will dine, having said the *Benedicite* before and thanksgiving afterward; there will be reading at table, if it can be held. If not, they shall do so immediately before the meal, during which they shall occupy themselves on what has been read, or on some other edifying matter. After the thanksgiving, they will say the *Angelus*, [and if they do not know it, three Hail Marys.]" Conference 105, 17 November 1658; Leonard, *Conferences* 4:196–216.

61. Saint Vincent, article 6: "After dinner, . . . they may converse on something edifying. . . . " See Conference 105, 17 November 1658; Leonard, *Conferences* 4:196–216.

62. "God is love, and he who abides in love abides in God, and God in him." 1 Jn 4:16.

63. Saint Vincent, article 7: "From two o'clock until three, they will strictly keep silence as best they can, to honor that of our Lord. They will begin it with spiritual reading, which one sister will read aloud in order to have good thoughts while at work, concluding by these words: *Christus factus est . . . ad mortem* etc., which will be recited aloud while kneeling, to offer to God the Father the moment at which his son gave up the ghost for the salvation of our souls, and to pray for all those who are in their agony and in a state of mortal sin, as well as for all those in purgatory, to whom this divine merit

should be applied. At the conclusion, they shall kiss the ground. Those who do not know how to read will say a *Pater* and an *Ave Maria*, and once, the *Requiescant in pace, Amen* ["may they rest in peace, Amen"]. Those who, by reason of their work, will have reason to speak during that hour, will be able to do so, provided they say only what is necessary, and pay attention from time to time that this is the period of silence, even while walking on the streets at this same time. Those sisters recently arrived, who are in the house of the superioress, will be careful to attend the instruction given there to learn the duties of a good Christian and a true Daughter of Charity. The other Sisters, even the elderly, will try to attend occasionally, both to give good example, and because there is always something to help everyone." Conference 105, 17 November 1658; Leonard, *Conferences* 4:196–216. The last section of this paragraph is found in the Common Rules, paragraph 17.

64. "Christ became obedient for us, unto death, death on a cross. Because of this, God highly exalted him," a liturgical passage based on Phil 2:8–9.

65. The Our Father (*Pater noster*), and the Hail Mary (*Ave Maria*).

66. Saint Vincent, article 8: "After the hour of silence, work should be continued; it is allowable, as before, to converse on some edifying topic, [but more seriously and piously, the time of recreation being past]." Conference 106, 25 November 1658; Leonard, *Conferences* 4:217–27.

67. "Bless," the traditional term used to begin the grace before meals.

68. Saint Vincent, article 9: "At half past five . . . until six, [if they have the opportunity; then the particular examen as at dinner, then they will go to supper . . . reading at table, . . . and everything else . . . dinner]." Conference 106, 25 November 1658; Leonard, *Conferences* 4:217–27.

69. Saint Vincent, article 10, Conference 106, 25 November 1658; Leonard, *Conferences* 4:217–27.

70. Saint Vincent, article 11: "At eight o'clock they shall go to the place prescribed for holding night prayer in common [in the customary way; that is, to read the Martyrology where it can be done, and then the points of the next day's meditation, the general examen, and then to recite the litany of the Virgin, the *Pater*, the *Ave*, and the *Credo*, and other ordinary prayers. Afterward at least

the beginning of each point of the same meditation will be read again, and then they will prepare to retire]." Article 13 continues: "At nine o'clock, after taking holy water . . . they shall go to bed, trying to go to sleep . . . next day's meditation." Conference 106, 25 November 1658; Leonard, *Conferences* 4:217–27. See also Conference 105, 17 November 1658 (Leonard, *Conferences* 4:196–216), where Saint Vincent acknowledges that the time for retiring had not been mentioned explicitly.

71. Saint Vincent, article 17: "On Sundays . . . except for the time spent on working days for manual labor, . . . spiritual exercises, such as reading books of devotion, listening to the sermon or the catechism, or the divine service, or in pious conversation, by the practice . . . suitable to their state. All this should not keep them from taking their little recreation together after the meal, according to time which will remain." Conference 107, 8 December 1658; Leonard, *Conferences* 4:228–31.

72. Saint Vincent, article 15: "Those who have permission . . . in the morning, and the same after dinner. . . . " Conference 106, 25 November 1658; Leonard, *Conferences* 4:217–27.

73. I.e., games.

74. Although article 26 was omitted from the Common Rules, it is worth citing here: "Although everyone should do her best to observe all those rules exactly and even the order of day prescribed for the various duties, nevertheless, a Sister should not be scrupulous about altering the time and even of leaving some of her work undone, when extraordinary needs of the sick, or the children or any other such necessity demands it; [they should recall that their principal care is the faithful service of the poor, both spiritually and temporally, and in doing so they are leaving God for God, and thus they accomplish in this the will of God]." Conference 110, 10 August 1659; Leonard, *Conferences* 4:257–60.

75. Saint Vincent, article 27: "They shall read the rules once a month, or hear them read, and also the rules of their office, if this can be done conveniently, and shall examine and see if they have practised them well or not, in order either, in one case, to give thanks to God or, in the other, to ask His forgiveness." Conference 100, 10 August 1659; Leonard, *Conferences* 164–71.

76. Mt 11:12.

77. René Alméras (1613–1672) succeeded Vincent de Paul as the

superior general of the Congregation of the Mission. He verified the text of the rules, marking the official manuscript with his seal to guarantee uniformity amid the numerous changes that began to occur in various manuscripts.

78. Conference 111, 24 August 1659; Leonard, *Conferences* 4:261–67.

79. Conference 113, 19 October 1659; Leonard, *Conferences* 4:271–72. This was article 3 in the Saint Vincent version.

80. Saint Version, article 4: "And the better to procure this spiritual help they shall contribute to it as far as their small ability and want of it allow and according as the nature and dispositions of the sick may require. Now, the help they shall strive to give them. . . . " Conference 113, 19 October 1659; Leonard, *Conferences* 4:271–72.

81. Saint Vincent, article 6: "If the sick . . . aforesaid acts." Conference 114, 11 November 1659; Leonard, *Conferences* 4:273–81. It is possible that the conference text reports only part of the rule.

82. Article 7, Conference 114, 11 November 1659; Leonard, *Conferences* 4:273–81.

83. Saint Vincent, article 8: " . . . regulating their time and exercises according as the number and the needs of their patients are great or small. And as their evening employments are not as great and urgent as those of the morning, they shall as a rule devote this time to instructing and exhorting them in the manner already prescribed, especially when they bring them their medicines." Conference 114, 11 November 1659; Leonard, *Conferences* 4:273–81.

84. Article 9, Conference 114, 11 November 1659; Leonard, *Conferences* 4:273–81.

85. Article 10, Conference 114, 11 November 1659; Leonard, *Conferences* 4:273–81.

86. Article 11, Conference 114, 11 November 1659; Leonard, *Conferences* 4:273–81.

87. Article 12, Conference 115, 25 November 1659; Leonard, *Conferences* 4:282–93.

88. Article 13, Conference 115, 25 November 1659; Leonard, *Conferences* 4:282–93.

89. Saint Vincent, article 14: "In order to avoid the great inconveniences that might arise, they shall not undertake to nurse the sick at night, nor women in labour, nor persons who lead an evil life. And if they are asked to so do by the poor . . . tell them very

humbly that their superiors forbid them to do so. If, however, certain cases of necessity seem to oblige them to come to the assistance of any of those three classes of patients, they shall only undertake them at the express orders of the superioress of the Company of Charity and also, if there is need, they shall ask the advice of the superioress of the house, without however informing anybody that they have done so." Conference 115, 25 November 1659; Leonard, *Conferences* 4:282–93.

90. Article 15, Conference 115, 25 November 1659; Leonard, *Conferences* 4:282–93.

91. Saint Vincent, article 16: "When any Sister . . . third day of illness so that she may send someone to visit the patient and do all that may be necessary in the circumstances." Conference 115, 25 November 1659; Leonard, *Conferences* 4:282–93.

92. Saint Vincent, article 17: "They shall be careful to put to the best use, and take care of, the money of which they have the disposal. Accordingly, the Sister Servant shall keep under lock and key money intended for the poor; and her assistant shall keep the money intended for themselves under another key, which she will retain, but she shall not purchase anything without the consent of the Sister Servant except in case of urgent necessity and ordinary things of little consequence." Conference 115, 25 November 1659; Leonard, *Conferences* 4:282–93. The last half of the above article is incorporated into rule 17 following.

93. Saint Vincent, article 18, 1: "To prefer . . . which leads them to act thus." Conference 115, 25 November 1659, which treats of the rest of the sections of article 18; Leonard, *Conferences* 4:282–93.

94. Article 18, 2.

95. This article is not cited in the conference.

96. Saint Vincent, article 18, 4: "Not to undertake . . . the will of the Ladies who hold office."

97. Saint Vincent, article 18, 5: " . . . any remedies or have their blood let, nor consult . . . without the permission of the Superioress of the house."

98. Article 18, 6.

99. Saint Vincent, article 18, 7: " . . . with whatever the superioress may give. . . . "

100. Article 18, 9.

101. Article 18, 10.

102. Saint Vincent, article 18, 11: "They shall not allow externs to enter their rooms unless to bleed or dress the sores of some poor person, not to speak of allowing them to eat or sleep there,. . . ."

103. Saint Vincent, article 18, 12: "They shall not go to priests' houses, unless they are poor and sick; . . . as her companion a girl or woman belonging to the house."

104. Saint Vincent, article 18, 13: " . . . to gain an indulgence, without the permission of the superioress, or the superior, from whom they shall ask it, and not from others, and they shall do so in time."

105. Saint Vincent, article 18, 14: " . . . sewing or spin-ning. . . . "

106. Article 18, 15.

107. Saint Vincent, article 18, 16: " . . . their employments to the confessor of the Mother House, and also give an account of their employments to the superioress."

108. Saint Vincent, article 18, 17: " . . . service of the sick; and the following order of day shall be observed as a general rule: (1) Immediately after morning prayer or, in summer, after the points of the meditation have been read, they shall take care to bring the sick their medicines; on their return, they shall go to Mass, during which they may also make their prayer, if they were unable to do so in the morning at four o'clock. (2) After Mass, they shall breakfast in their room on a piece of bread. (3) They shall then proceed to the house of the Lady (of Charity) who provides the pot of soup for the sick, at the usual time, or sooner if need be, so that their dinner may be ready at the appointed time. (4) After dinner, they shall take care to collect the doctor's prescriptions and prepare remedies which they shall bring to the sick at the proper time, and shall also fetch the soup-pot for the following day to the Lady whose turn it is to take charge of it. (5) After supper, they shall prepare the medicines for the following morning and, if there is any urgent matter to be attended to, they shall do so diligently, without wasting any time, so that they may be able to retire to rest at nine o'clock. (6) When they can instruct little girls living in the parish, provided this does not interfere with their visiting the sick, one of the two shall devote herself to it, although she should be assisted by the other in case of need; and they shall do this only with the approval of the supe-

rioress. In this case they shall observe, as well as they are able, the rules drawn up for the mistresses of schools, which will be given to them for this object."

109. The published text concludes: "Reviewed by us, William M. Slattery, Superior General and the Council of the Community, 8 September 1954."

CONFERENCES OF VINCENT DE PAUL TO THE DAUGHTERS OF CHARITY

1. The translation of these conferences is that given in Joseph Leonard, C.M., trans. *Conferences of St. Vincent de Paul to the Sisters of Charity*, 4 vols. (Westminster, Md.: The Newman Press, 1952). The translation has been corrected where necessary against the text of Pierre Coste, C.M., *CED*, and lightly edited for ease of reading.

2. Conference 1, 31 July 1634. Leonard, *Conferences* 1:1–11.

3. Vincent de Paul (or his scribes) frequently does not quote verbally but gives the substance of the text, (here Mt 18:20).

4. Jn 14:23: "Anyone who loves me will be true to my word, and my Father will love him; we will come to him and make our dwelling place with him."

5. Jn 17:11.

6. Jn 14:23: "Whoever loves me will keep my word, and my Father will love him, and we will come to him and make our dwelling with him."

7. Grandchamp (Sarthe), according to a manuscript.

8. Ps 50 (51).

9. Françoise Marguerite de Silly, Madame de Gondi (1580–1625).

10. Marie Joly (d. 1675).

11. This Michelle, one of several with this name, was one of the first Daughters of Charity. She died about 1642.

12. Barbe Angiboust (1605–1658).

13. Louise de Marillac has doubtlessly misinterpreted Monsieur Vincent here, because he is most probably referring to Pope Clement VIII, who had not been canonized.

14. Based on Jn 15:17.

15. That is, the ecclesiastical superiors and the head of the La-

dies of Charity. At that time the Ladies still exercised some responsibilities over the Daughters in their apostolate in the Confraternities of Charity.

16. The manuscript reads "sixth."

17. *Introduction to the Devout Life,* by Saint Francis de Sales.

18. Saint Louis, King Louis IX, was known for his charitable activities. He founded the Hôtel Dieu of Paris.

19. Conference 12. Although this conference does not quote Vincent de Paul by name, both he and Louise de Marillac took part in it. It has been dated from a remark in Conference 11, referring to another conference to be held on the deceased Sisters in two weeks. Dated: July 1642. Leonard, *Conferences* 1:71–73.

20. A little village in the outskirts of Paris.

21. The Hospital of Saint Louis was founded in Paris in 1607 to receive plague victims.

22. Conference 118. From a report written by Sister Marguerite Chétif in the Archives of the Daughters of Charity. Dated: 3 July 1660. A second conference (119) on the virtues of Louise de Marillac was held 24 July 1660. From internal evidence, it is clear that this conference was delivered at Saint Lazare. Leonard, *Conferences* 4:309–23.

23. Louise de Marillac, Mademoiselle Le Gras, died on Passion Sunday, 15 March 1660.

24. Antoine Portail (b. 1590), one of the original companions of Vincent de Paul, died on 14 February 1660.

25. Lk 6:24.

26. Lk 9:58.

27. Mt 26:22: "Surely it is not I, Lord?"

28. Marie Louise de Gonzague, the wife of John Casimir V, king of Poland, was a member of the Ladies of Charity, and brought the Daughters of Charity to Poland.

29. Acts 1:24.

30. Mt 16:6.

31. Actually based on Is 24:16.

32. A small village just north of Paris, close to Saint Lazare. The Daughters of Charity had their motherhouse there from 1636 to 1641.

33. Vincent de Paul regularly closed with a blessing, and a

prayer to the Blessed Virgin, in this case the one beginning "We fly to your patronage, O Mother of God."

Writings of Louise de Marillac

1. *Spiritual Writings of Louise de Marillac* by Sister Louise Sullivan, D.C. (Brooklyn, NY: New City Press, 1991). See also Louise de Marillac, *Écrits spirituels* (Tours: Mame, 1983). The first published collection of her letters dates only from 1960. Her letters written to Vincent de Paul appeared in the critical edition of Pierre Coste, 1920–1925.

2. *La Compagnie des Filles de la Charité aux Origines: Documents,* ed. Elisabeth Charpy (Tours: Mame, 1989).

3. These are published in chronological order in ibid.

4. See: [Vincent de Paul,] *The Conferences of St. Vincent de Paul to the Sisters of Charity,* trans. Joseph Leonard, C.M. 4 vols. (London: Burns, Oates & Washbourne, 1938; reprinted: Westminster, Md.: The Newman Press, 1952; reprinted: London: Collins Liturgical Books, 1979 [1 vol. ed.])

5. *Spiritual Writings,* A. 2, pp. 1–2. 4 June 1623. The original document does not bear a title. The term "Light" was given to it by a nineteenth-century archivist. This document is also sometimes referred to as "Light of Pentecost."

6. Louise had wanted to be a Capuchin nun, and had undoubtedly made a promise to God to do so. However, Father Champigny, her first spiritual director, told her that her delicate health would not permit her to become a religious. Following the advice of her family, Louise married Antoine Le Gras on 5 February 1613. He was secretary to the Queen Marie de Medicis. Their son Michel was born the following October 18.

7. Pierre Camus (1583–1652), bishop of Belley, a friend of the Marillacs and of Francis de Sales, who ordained him a bishop. After six years as a bishop, Camus retired to spend the rest of his life in service of the poor.

8. Sunday, 4 June 1623.

9. The church of Saint-Nicolas-des-Champs, rue Saint-Martin, Louise's parish church.

NOTES

10. Vincent de Paul was, at the time, a tutor in the Gondi household, situated in the parish of Saint-Savior.

11. Francis de Sales, bishop of Geneva and founder of the Sisters of the Visitation, had died on 28 December 1622.

12. *Spiritual Writings*, L. 111, pp. 121–22. This document can be dated, on internal evidence, to 1644.

13. *Spiritual Writings*, A. 31B, pp. 830–31. This document is undated.

14. *Spiritual Writings*, M. 8B, pp. 833–34. Date: 1660.

15. *Spiritual Writings*, L. 557B, pp. 520–21. The letter is to be dated, on internal evidence, to about 1656. Sister Françoise, a native of Beauvais, exercised several important positions in the Company, being its assistant from 1672 to 1675.

16. Pierre de Beaumont (b. 1617), superior of the priests of the Mission at Richelieu.

17. *Spiritual Writings*, L. 651, pp. 673–74. Sister Marguerite Chétif (1621–1694) joined the Daughters of Charity in 1649. Louise recommended her to Vincent as her successor; Chétif served as superioress general from 1660 to 1667.

18. Gamboge was a resin used as a cathartic.

19. This Lady of Charity welcomed the Daughters of Charity into her home when they arrived in Arras, and she later gave them a small house and garden for their use.

20. *Spiritual Writings*, L. 655, p. 677. This letter is to be dated, on internal evidence, to January 1660. Also, this date was added to the back of the original by Brother Ducournau, Vincent's secretary.

21. That is, the Daughters of Charity.

22. Barbe Angiboust (1605–1658) entered the Company in 1634. She filled several important roles in the Company, and enjoyed Louise's confidence. Louise Ganset was sent to Richelieu in 1638, to minister to the galley convicts in 1644, and to Maule a few years later. *Spiritual Writings*, L. 11, p.18.

23. As early as 1637, Armand Duplessis, Cardinal Richelieu, asked Monsieur Vincent for missionaries for the town, south of Chinon, which he had constructed at the beginning of the seventeenth century. The Daughters of Charity were sent there at the end of the year 1638 to serve the sick and to run the school.

24. Madame Goussault, born Genevieve Fayet. In 1631, she became the widow of Antoine Goussault, advisor to the king and

president of the administration of finances. She suggested the establishment of the Confraternity of Charity of the Hôtel-Dieu to Monsieur Vincent and became its president. She favored sending the Daughters of Charity to Angers. She died like a saint on 20 September 1639.

25. *Spiritual Writings*, L. 131, p. 766. This document can be dated to 1646. These topics proposed by Louise de Marillac were treated by Vincent de Paul in a series of conferences in 1646: Conference 24, 13 February 1646: On the Love of our Vocation and on Helping the Poor; Conference 25, 1 May 1646: On Indifference; Conference 27, 19 August 1646: On Meekness and the Practice of Mutual Respect; Conference 28, 22 October 1646: On Concealing and Excusing the Faults of One's Sisters.

26. *Spiritual Writings*, A. 85, pp. 770–74. This document can be dated, on internal grounds, to 1647. The town of Montreuil, a short distance east of Paris, had a Confraternity of Charity founded in 1627.

27. The numerous letters of Anne Hardemont permit one to follow her career in the Daughters of Charity.

28. After Marie Lullen's unexpected death in 1649 or 1650, Vincent held a conference on her virtues, together with those of three other Sisters.

29. *Spiritual Writings*, L. 377, pp. 406–07. The letter can be dated, on internal evidence, to about October 1652. The recipients were Françoise Carcireux and Charlotte Royer. Sister Françoise entered the Company in 1640 or 1641. She was later one of the assistants at the motherhouse. Two of her sisters became Daughters of Charity, and one brother joined the Congregation of the Mission. Sister Charlotte came to Richelieu in 1648, and was still in the Company in 1660, at the time of the death of the foundress.

30. Pierre du Chesne (d. 1654) had been, among other things, a missionary in Ireland and Scotland. Vincent de Paul was sending him to visit the houses in Brittany.

31. Gilbert Cuissot (1607–1666) entered the Congregation of the Mission in 1637 at thirty years of age. The superior of Cahors since 1647, he came to Paris in July 1651 for the general assembly. He returned to Cahors in January 1653.

32. Laurence Dubois (1623–1685). Her great meekness toward the poor, her uprightness and simplicity were well known. *Spiritual*

Writings, L. 425, p. 463–64. This letter can be dated, on internal evidence, to 1655.

33. Barbe Angiboust (1605–1658), one of the first Daughters of Charity, was highly regarded by Louise.

34. *Spiritual Writings*, M. 69, p. 803–04. This document is undated.

35. *Spiritual Writings*, A. 60, p. 788–89. This document is undated.

36. This sentence is left incomplete in the manuscript.

37. *Spiritual Writings*, L. 4, pp. 9–11. The letter is to be dated, on internal evidence, to about 1634.

38. The duchess of Liancourt, born Jeanne de Schomberg (1600–1674), Lady of Charity. She established the Confraternity of Charity on her estates.

39. The lay president of the Confraternity of Charity.

40. A parish in Paris.

41. A suburb west of Paris, now called Colombes.

42. *Spiritual Writings*, L. 202, p. 235–36. This letter is to be dated, on internal evidence, to 17 January 1648.

43. For Bicêtre as the residence of the foundlings, see Letter 86.

44. Genevieve Poisson, see Letter 28.

45. Monsieur Vacherot was the Community's physician.

46. Julienne Loret, see Letter 220.

47. Elisabeth Hellot, see Letter 152.

48. Julienne Loret (1622–1699), an orphan, entered the Company in 1644. She was the first directress of the Seminary (novitiate), and served several times as an assistant to the superioress general. *Spiritual Writings*, L. 354, p. 375–76. This letter can be dated to 1651.

49. Philippe Bailly, see Letter 339.

50. These are ingredients for the preparation of medicines for different kinds of illnesses.

51. Marguerite of Vienne, a Sister who lived for many years at the motherhouse.

52. *Spiritual Writings*, L. 556, p. 682; no address, no date. This letter was perhaps addressed to Françoise Carcireux.

53. A sol, also spelled sou, was a unit of money, worth 1/20 of a livre (an old name for a franc).

54. *Spiritual Writings*, L. 277B, p. 76.

NOTES

55. The date was on the back of the letter with Monsieur Vincent's reply; see Coste, *CED* 8:523.

56. Madame de Traversay, see Letter 48.

57. The duchess of Aiguillon, Marie de Vignerod (1604–1678). The niece of Cardinal Richelieu, she helped Monsieur Vincent out of her immense fortune.

58. Father Jean Guérin, the younger, entered the Congregation of the Mission in February.

59. *Spiritual Writings*, unnumbered document, p. 835.

60. The sisters who attended Louise de Marillac during her final moments on earth faithfully transcribed these last words of hers, which they regarded as her spiritual testament. Gobillon, her first biographer, quotes them in *The Life of Mademoiselle LeGras, Foundress and First Superior of the Company of the Sisters of Charity, Servants of the Sick Poor* (London: Sisters of Charity, 1984), p. 61.

Bibliography: Sources, Biographies

Abelly, Louis. *La Vie du Venerable Serviteur de Dieu, Vincent de Paul, Instituteur et Premier Superieur General de la Congregation de la Mission.* Paris: Florentin Lambert, 1664; reprint edition: Paris: Archives of the Motherhouse of the Congregation of the Mission, 1986. The English translation is *The Life of the Venerable Servant of God Vincent de Paul*, ed. John E. Rybolt, C.M., trans. William Quinn, F.S.C., 3 vols. New York: New City Press, 1993.

André, Marie. *Soeur Rosalie.* Toulouse: Apostolat de la Prière, 1953.

Baunard, Louis. *Ozanam in his Correspondence.* New York: Benziger Brothers, 1925.

Calvet, Jean. *Louise de Marillac: A Portrait.* Trans. G. F. Pullen New York: P. J. Kenedy and Sons, 1959.

Charpy, Élisabeth, ed. *Petite vie de Louise de Marillac.* Paris: Desclée De Brouwer, 1991.

Charpy, Élisabeth, ed. *La Compagnie des Filles de la Charité aux Origines: Documents.* Tours: Mame, 1989.

"Codex Sarzana," transcr. and ed. John E. Rybolt, C.M. *Vincentiana* 33 (1991): 303–406.

Congregatio de Causis Sanctorum. *Canonizationis Servae Dei Rosaliae Rendu . . . Positio super virtutibus et fama sanctitatis.* Rome, 1993.

Constitutions and Statutes of the Congregation of the Mission. Philadelphia, 1989. [Includes *Common Rules of the Congregation of the Mission*.]

BIBLIOGRAPHY: SOURCES, BIOGRAPHIES

Danemarie, Jeanne [pseud; Marthe Ponet-Bordeaux]. *A travers trois Révolutions, Soeur Rosalie, Fille de la Charité*. Paris: Plon, 1947.

Dirvin, Joseph I., C.M. *Mrs. Seton: Foundress of the American Sisters of Charity*. New York: Farrar, Straus and Giroux, 1962; "New Canonization Edition," 1975.

Dodin, André, C.M. *Saint Vincent de Paul et la Charité*. Paris: Éditions du Seuil, 1st ed., 1960; 5th ed., 1983. The English translation is *Saint Vincent de Paul and Charity: A Contemporary Portrait of His Life and Apostolic Spirit*, trans. Jean Marie Smith and Dennis Saunders; ed. Hugh F. O'Donnell, C.M., and Marjorie Gale Hornstein. New Rochelle, N.Y.: New City Press, 1993.

Gobillon, Nicolas. *La Vie de Mademoiselle Le Gras, Fondatrice et Premiere Superieure de la Compagnie des Filles de la Charité, Servantes des Pauvres Malades*. Paris: André Pralard, 1676. A partial English translation is *The Life of Mademoiselle Le Gras, Foundress and First Superior of the Company of the Sisters of Charity, Servants of the Sick Poor*. London: Sisters of Charity, 1984.

Hughes, Henry L. *Frederic Ozanam*. Saint Louis: Herder, 1933.

Kelly, Ellin, and Annabelle Melville, eds. *Elizabeth Seton: Selected Writings*. New York: Paulist Press, 1987.

[Louise de Marillac.] Sainte Louise de Marillac. *Écrits spirituels*. Tours: Mame, 1983. The English translation is *Spiritual Writings of Louise de Marillac: Correspondence and Thoughts*, trans. and ed. Louise Sullivan, D.C. Brooklyn: New City Press, 1991.

Maloney, Robert P., C.M. *The Way of Vincent de Paul: A Contemporary Spirituality in the Service of the Poor*. Brooklyn: New City Press, 1992.

Melun, Armand M. de. *Life of Sister Rosalie, a Sister of Charity*. Trans. Joseph D. Fallon. Norwood: Plimpton Press, 1915.

Mezzadri, Luigi, C.M. "L'Église en France au temps de Saint Vincent." *Vincentiana* 28 (1984): 356–92.

Mezzadri, Luigi, C.M., and Miguel Pérez Flores, C.M. *La Regola delle Figlie della Carità.* Milan: Jaca Books, 1986.

Frédéric Ozanam: A Life in Letters. Trans. and ed. Joseph I. Dirvin, C.M. Saint Louis: Society of St. Vincent de Paul, 1986.

Pérez Flores, Miguel, C.M., ed. *Reglas Comunes de las Hijas de la Caridad Siervas de los Pobres Enfermos.* Salamanca: CEME, 1989.

Poinsenet, Marie-Dominique. *De l'anxiété à la sainteté: Louise de Marillac.* Paris: Fayard, 1958.

Rules of the Daughters of Charity, Servants of the Sick Poor. [Emmitsburg, Md.:] Saint Joseph's Provincial House Press, 1976.

Rybolt, John E. "From Life to the Rules: The Genesis of the Rules of the Daughters of Charity." *Vincentian Heritage,* 12 (1991): 173–99.

Sacra Congregatio pro Causis Sanctorum. *Beatificationis et canonizationis servi Dei Friderici Ozanam . . . Disquisitio.* Rome, 1980.

Sacra Congregatio pro Causis Sanctorum. *Positio Super Virtutibus. [Frederick Ozanam.] Informatio et Summarium.* Rome, 1990.

Six, Jean-François, and Helmut Nils Loose. *Saint Vincent de Paul.* Paris: Centurion, 1980.

[Vincent de Paul.] *Avis et conférences de saint Vincent de Paul aux membres de la Congrégation.* Paris, 1881.

[Vincent de Paul.] *Collection de conférences de Saint Vincent de Paul, de plusieurs de ses lettres et de quelques conférences de M. Alméras, son premier successeur.* Paris, 1844.

[Vincent de Paul.] *Conferences of Saint Vincent de Paul [to the Congregation of the Mission].* Comp. Pierre Coste, C.M., trans. Joseph Leonard, C.M. Philadelphia, Pa.: Congregation of the Mission, Eastern Province, U.S.A., 1963.

[Vincent de Paul.] *The Conferences of St. Vincent de Paul to the Sisters of Charity*. Trans. Joseph Leonard, C.M. 4 vols. London: Burns, Oates & Washbourne, 1938; reprinted: Westminster, Md.: The Newman Press, 1952; London: Collins Liturgical Books, 1979 (1 vol. ed.).

[Vincent de Paul.] Dodin, André, C.M. *Saint Vincent de Paul: Entretiens Spirituels aux missionaires*. Paris: Éditions du Seuil, 1960.

[Vincent de Paul.] *Letters of St Vincent de Paul*. Trans. and ed. Joseph Leonard, C.M. London: Burns, Oates and Washbourne, 1937.

[Vincent de Paul.] *Saint Vincent de Paul. Correspondance, Entretiens, Documents*. Ed. Pierre Coste, C.M., 14 vols. Paris: Gabalda, 1920–1925. An English translation is *Saint Vincent de Paul. Correspondence, Conferences, Documents*, ed. Jacqueline Kilar, D.C. (Vols. 1, 2) and Marie Poole, D.C. (Vols. 2, 3, 4). Brooklyn: New City Press, 1985–   ).

Index

Other Volumes in this Series

Early Dominicans • SELECTED WRITINGS
John Climacus • THE LADDER OF DIVINE ASCENT
Francis and Clare • THE COMPLETE WORKS
Gregory Palamas • THE TRIADS
Pietists • SELECTED WRITINGS
The Shakers • TWO CENTURIES OF SPIRITUAL REFLECTION
Zohar • THE BOOK OF ENLIGHTENMENT
Luis de León • THE NAMES OF CHRIST
Quaker Spirituality • SELECTED WRITINGS
Emanuel Swedenborg • THE UNIVERSAL HUMAN AND SOUL-BODY INTERACTION
Augustine of Hippo • SELECTED WRITINGS
Safed Spirituality • RULES OF MYSTICAL PIETY, THE BEGINNING OF WISDOM
Maximus Confessor • SELECTED WRITINGS
John Cassian • CONFERENCES
Johannes Tauler • SERMONS
John Ruusbroec • THE SPIRITUAL ESPOUSALS AND OTHER WORKS
Ibn 'Abbād of Ronda • LETTERS ON THE SŪFĪ PATH
Angelus Silesius • THE CHERUBINIC WANDERER
The Early Kabbalah •
Meister Eckhart • TEACHER AND PREACHER
John of the Cross • SELECTED WRITINGS
Pseudo-Dionysius • THE COMPLETE WORKS
Bernard of Clairvaux • SELECTED WORKS
Devotio Moderna • BASIC WRITINGS
The Pursuit of Wisdom • AND OTHER WORKS BY THE AUTHOR OF THE CLOUD OF
   UNKNOWING
Richard Rolle • THE ENGLISH WRITINGS
Francis de Sales, Jane de Chantal • LETTERS OF SPIRITUAL DIRECTION
Albert and Thomas • SELECTED WRITINGS
Robert Bellarmine • SPIRITUAL WRITINGS
Nicodemos of the Holy Mountain • A HANDBOOK OF SPIRITUAL COUNSEL
Henry Suso • THE EXEMPLAR, WITH TWO GERMAN SERMONS
Bérulle and the French School • SELECTED WRITINGS
The Talmud • SELECTED WRITINGS
Ephrem the Syrian • HYMNS
Hildegard of Bingen • SCIVIAS
Birgitta of Sweden • LIFE AND SELECTED REVELATIONS
John Donne • SELECTIONS FROM *DIVINE POEMS*, SERMONS, *DEVOTIONS AND
   PRAYERS*
Jeremy Taylor • SELECTED WORKS
Walter Hilton • *SCALE OF PERFECTION*
Ignatius of Loyola • *SPIRITUAL EXERCISES and SELECTED WORKS*
Anchoritic Spirituality • *ANCRENE WISSE and ASSOCIATED WORKS*
Nizam ad-din Awliya • MORALS FOR THE HEART
Pseudo-Macarius • THE FIFTY SPIRITUAL HOMILIES AND THE *GREAT LETTER*